Narrative of the North China Campaign of 1860

Containing personal experiences of
Chinese character, and of the moral and
social condition of the country; together
with a description of the interior of Pekin

Robert Swinhoe

Alpha Editions

This edition published in 2019

ISBN : 9789353807313

Design and Setting By
Alpha Editions
email - alphaedis@gmail.com

NARRATIVE

OF THE

NORTH CHINA CAMPAIGN

OF 1860;

CONTAINING PERSONAL EXPERIENCES

OF CHINESE CHARACTER, AND OF THE MORAL AND SOCIAL
CONDITION OF THE COUNTRY; TOGETHER WITH A
DESCRIPTION OF THE INTERIOR OF PEKIN.

BY

ROBERT SWINHOE,

OF H. M.'S CONSULAR SERVICE IN CHINA, STAFF INTERPRETER DURING
THE CAMPAIGN TO H. E. SIR HOPE GRANT.

WITH ILLUSTRATIONS.

LONDON:

SMITH, ELDER AND CO., 65, CORNHILL.

M.DCCC.LXI.

PREFACE.

In reading descriptive narratives and accounts of travels, I have often wished that the writers, instead of pitching upon the salient points alone for narration, had given a fuller detail of all the minor occurrences; which, though unimportant in themselves, often reflect light upon the chief events, and give a continuity to the whole. This I have tried to accomplish in the following work; and though some readers may consider such parts uninviting and of small import, there may be others who will be thankful for a full and truthful narrative.

It has been my object to write a complete account of the campaign, in conjunction with my own experiences in it, and I have thought it best to note every event in order as it occurred; for if any portion were cut out, it would spoil the free course of the narrative.

In describing the various occurrences, I have endeavoured to enliven the subject with anecdotes gathered on the spot, both from members of the expedition and in conversation with natives of the places visited.

Each chapter, as it was written, was forwarded home; and as now, with the closing chapter, I am unable to leave my duties in China to revisit England for the purpose of passing the work through the press, I must beg the indulgence of the reader for its literary defects and errors; I trust, however, that they are few and unimportant.

I ought to state that I have made free use of descriptions of scenes and places already published in periodicals, as also of printed official documents; but I have in every case acknowledged the source from which such extracts are derived.

ROBERT SWINHOE.

Amoy, 17th June, 1861.

CONTENTS.

CHAPTER I.

PAGE

Preparations for the Expedition.—Cantonese Coolies.—Strange Rumour among the Chinese.—Dress of the Coolie Corps.—Causes of the Unhealthiness of Victoria.—The Peninsula of Kowloon.—Occupation of Chusan by the Allies.—Difficulty of procuring Transport.—Accidents to British and French Transports.—Departure from Hong Kong—Lam-yit Islands.—Arrival in Talien Bay 1

CHAPTER II.

Description of Talien Bay.—Sampson's Peak.—Excursions among the Villages.—Surveying Party.—A fortified Chinese City.—The Dialect of Leautung.—Landing of the Troops.—Chinese Grief for the Dead.—Depredations of the Punjaubees and of the Coolie Corps.—Character of the Villages.—Search after missing Officers.—General Michel and his Staff—Arrival of Lord Elgin . . . 14

CHAPTER III.

Visit to Odin Bay.—Chinese Game.—Appearance of Bustard Cove.—Encampment at Odin Bay.—The Commissariat.—A sagacious Purveyor.—Chinese Cattle-Dealers.—A Day's Sale.—Visit to the City of Chin-chow.—Hostility of the Natives.—Inspection of the Cavalry at Odin Bay.—Chinese Avarice.—Re-embarkation.—Departure from Talien Bay.—Distribution of the Force.—A Canard.—Memorandum issued to the Troops 34

CHAPTER IV.

A Waterspout.—Landing of the 2nd Brigade.—The Position of Pehtang compared to Arcola.—A dreary Bivouac.—Landing of the 2nd Division.—Description of Pehtang Village.

PAGE

—Loot.—Quarters of the Troops.—An elegant Chinese
House.—Wretched Condition of the Natives.—Aspect of
the Forts.—The French Commissariat.—A Reconnaissance
in force.—Skirmish with Tartars.—Adventures of a Chinaman 53

CHAPTER V.

March from Pehtang.—Sight of the Enemy.—Order of Battle.
—Splendid Practice of the Armstrong Guns.—Charge of
Tartar Cavalry—Attack on the Entrenched Camp.—Tartar
Bravery.—The wounded.—Scene in the Enemy's Camp.—
Village of Sinho.—A Night Alarm.—A Spy.—Affair of
Tangkoo.—Flight of the Enemy.—Tartar Gunners.—
Quarters of the Troops.—The Takoo Forts.—Deputation
of Natives.—Interview with Hangfuh.—Exchange of Pri-
soners.—Chinese Views of the War . . . 84

CHAPTER VI.

Plan of Attack on the Takoo Forts.—Difference of Opinion
between the English and French Generals.—Bridge of
Boats. — Approaches to the Forts. — The Eve of the
Assault.—Advance on the Forts.—Description of the
Assault.—Unconditional Surrender.—Casualties.—Tartar
Courage.—Description of the Forts.—Chinese wounded.
—Variety of Races.—The wounded Cake-seller . . 120

CHAPTER VII.

Entrance to the Peiho.—Arrival at Tien-tsin.—Appointment of
a Commission to inspect the Captured Forts. — Head-
quarters of San-kolinsin.—A Ludicrous Scene.—Denizens
of a Chinese Swamp.—Going to Market.—A garrulous
Chinaman. — Chinese Vehicles. — Advance of the Main
Body.—Camping Grounds.—Chinese Villages . . 147

CHAPTER VIII.

San-kolinsin's Tactics.—Description of Tien-tsin.—A Scientific
Mission.—" Own Correspondents."—Chinese Duplicity.—
Advance of the Allies.—A Topographical Department.—
Russian Secretary.—Description of the Country.—Yang-
tsun Village.—Flag of Truce 184

CHAPTER IX.

PAGE

Chinese Committee of Supply.—Looting.—Encampment at Ho-
see-woo.—Negotiations.—Conference at Tung-chow.—
Baiting a Trap.—Chinese Deserters.—Mandarin Spy.—
An ominous Expedition.—A Llama's Grave.—Chinese
Fox-Hunt.—The "black Prince."—The Noise of Battle.—
Engagement near Matow.—Reconnaissance to Tung-chow.
—Gallantry of Colonel Walker.—Mr. Parkes' Account . 215

CHAPTER X.

City of Chang-chia-wan.—Wanton Destruction of Property.—
Deserted Chinese Women.—Advance from Chang-chia-
wan.—Another Encounter with the Tartars.—Dashing
Charge of the Dragoon Guards.—Various Conflicts with
the Enemy.—Yung-leang Canal.—Ruffianism of the
Coolies.—A Grandee's Monument.—Arrival of Reinforcements 243

CHAPTER XI.

A refractory Mandarin.—Punjaubee Couriers.—Letters from
Prince Kung.—Advance of the Allies.—Letter from
Mr. Parkes.—Chinese Mahommedans.—Bivouac.—Flight
of the Tartars.—Chinese Mendacity.—French Advance on
the Summer Palace.—A Celestial Funeral.—Friendly
Feeling of the Natives.—Outside the Palace.—An Im-
perial Eunuch.—Description of the Palace.—Rare Loot.
—The Summer Park 271

CHAPTER XII.

Release of Messrs. Parkes and Loch.—Looting the Summer
Palace.—British Share of the Spoil.—Discovery of Secret
Documents.—Preparations for attacking Pekin.—Sur-
render of the An-ting Gate.—Restoration of other
Prisoners.—Spirit of Retaliation.—Funeral of Murdered
Prisoners.—Lord Elgin's Reasons for the Destruction of
the Summer Palace.—Firing the Yuen-ming-yuen.—
General Description of the Palace and Grounds . . 303

CHAPTER XIII.

PAGE

Letter of Lord Elgin to Prince Kung.—Preparations for At-
tacking Pekin.—Approach of Chinese Rebels.—Recon-
naissance round the Walls.—Signing the Convention.—
Tung-chow.—Curious Mode of Fishing.—Description of
Pekin.—The "Altars of Heaven and Earth."—Llamaseries.
— "Prayer-machines." — Chinese Religions. — Pekinese
Vehicles.—Chinese Dromedaries.—Falconry.—Resources
and Produce.—Cultivation.—Poverty of the Inhabitants.—
Neglect of Education 338

CHAPTER XIV.

Declaration of Peace.—Marauding Parties.—Death of Dr.
Thompson.—Proclamations.—Canton Coolies.—The down-
ward March of the Second Division.—H.M.'s Legation.—
Disordered State of the Country.—The Cold Season.—
Departure of the remaining Force.—Embarkation of the
Troops.—Increase of Cold—Results of the Campaign.—
Overweening Confidence of the Chinese.—Rapid Commu-
nication of News.—Our future relations with China.—
The present Condition of the Country.—Conclusion . 376

ILLUSTRATIONS.

Portrait of Prince Kung (to face Title).

Tartar Soldiers at Tangkoo .   .   .   .   to face page 102

Interior of North Fort, Takoo, at the angle where the British
Troops entered .   .   .   .   .   to face page 133

Plan of the Peiho Forts .   .   .   .   „   143

An-ting Gate of Pekin, occupied by the Allied Forces „   317

Grand Entrance of the Winter Palace, Pekin   „   353

THE

NORTH CHINA CAMPAIGN OF 1860.

CHAPTER I.

Preparations for the Expedition — Cantonese Coolies — Strange
Rumour among the Chinese—Dress of the Coolie Corps—
Causes of the Unhealthiness of Victoria—The Peninsula of
Kowloon—Occupation of Chusan by the Allies—Difficulty of
procuring Transport—Accidents to British and French Transports—Departure from Hong Kong—Lam-yit Islands—Arrival
in Talien Bay.

I HAD procured three months' leave of absence from
Amoy, and was enjoying myself to the best of my
ability at Canton, in rambling through its narrow
painted and gilded streets, and inspecting its old
yamuns, temples, and pagodas, when one morning it
was announced to me that I was placed by Mr. Bruce
at the disposal of Sir Hope Grant, for the time
being, as interpreter. Accordingly, I went down by
the first boat to Hong Kong; where all was bustle
and preparation for the intended expedition to the
north. Ships were being chartered by the score;
troops were arriving by shiploads almost every day;

1

the streets swarmed with them, so that nearly every other man seemed to be a soldier. Cantonese coolies were being hired in numbers to form a corps for the transport of the munitions and stores of the army, under the auspices of Major Temple. These men were each to receive the large sum of nine dollars, or 1*l*. 17*s*. 6*d*. a month, besides two suits of clothes, and rations. Notwithstanding the high rate of wages offered, the gallant Major failed to obtain as many as he deemed necessary, or any but the very scum of the population; because a strange rumour had got afloat among the Chinese, that in all the fights they were to be thrust forward to receive the brunt of the battle, while the British, being well sheltered behind, would be able to fire away at the enemy without harm or danger to themselves. No amount of persuasion could convince the majority of the pig-headed natives that we only desired the coolies as carriers. The fact of their all being dressed uniformly, and frequently drilled, with their bamboos over their shoulders, by the sergeants appointed from various regiments to control the incoherent mass, presented to the minds of the populace positive proof that the term "coolie," or porter, was merely a blind held up to hide the real purpose for which the corps was intended, viz. to be drilled and employed as fighting men. It was a matter of little account, so far as the actual usefulness of the corps was concerned, that the refuse population did form its chief ingredient; but the actual benefit to the people of Hong Kong from such enlistment was incalculable, because they were at once and easily rid of the gangs of low thieves that infested the more secluded parts of the island, and so frequently plundered and injured the harmless inhabitants, both foreign and native. I was assured by a gentleman who had been long a resident in the colony, that after the departure of the expedition, robbery had become a thing almost unknown on the island.

The dress of the Coolie Corps, to an English eye, was somewhat grotesque. They were uniformly clothed in Chinese jacket and nether garments, while their feet were left naked. On the jacket, both before and behind, was inscribed, within a black circular line, the number of the individual, and that of his company immediately below, with a black line separating the two. Their pig-tailed heads were surmounted by bamboo caps of a somewhat flattened conical shape, with the letters C. C. C., signifying Canton Coolie Corps, painted conspicuously in front. The officers commanding this grotesque body were mostly drawn from the Royal Marines, but the regiments of the line had also contributed a few. The

1—2

British officers and soldiers so appointed were at once distinguishable by two narrow white stripes running down the sides of their trowsers. A few of the better class of coolies who could speak a little English, were promoted over their countrymen to the rank of lance-corporals, corporals, and sergeants; and in such cases one arm of their loose jackets was marked with one, two, or three angular white stripes, according to their rank.

As I belonged to Amoy, it was compulsory on me to return and take my orders thence. This proceeding did not take long, and a few more days saw me back again at Hong Kong. I reported myself to the Military Secretary, who at once ordered me a passage in the transport steamer *Lightning*, and at the same time desired me to call on the Quartermaster-general, who would supply me with a tent and give me any necessary advice. A bell tent was duly issued; and no advice being deemed necessary, I went on board the steamer, and had my luggage carefully stowed in readiness for a speedy departure.

But before following the expedition to the north, let us glance at some of the events which had taken place within the preceding few months.

Victoria, Hong Kong, has long had the reputation of being one of the most unhealthy places on the earth's surface, owing to the Settlement being completely shut in from the gentle southerly gales by the towering rocks that rise immediately behind it, and retain for hours after sunset the violent heat which had pervaded the atmosphere during the sunny hours of the summer's day. Again, when the sun suddenly appears after a heavy shower, the saturated moisture is quickly evaporated, and collects in unhealthy vapour along the hill-sides, where it hangs for days together undisturbed by the gentle influence of a cooling breeze. The opposite peninsula of Kowloon has, therefore, been for years looked to with longing eyes by the community as a spot that ought to become British property, where merchants might build their bungalows, and enjoy the cool evening breeze after sultry days spent in their counting-houses in Hong Kong. But now, when troops were fast arriving, the necessity of having some place to stow them ashore began to force itself on the authorities. There was sure to be some delay in their progress northward, and it was certainly not advisable to keep them on board ship any length of time in the harbour of Hong Kong. Kowloon is open to the southerly breezes, and has the double advantage of a large sandy plain, where the horses of the cavalry may be able to stretch their legs after the long sea-voyage from India. The French, moreover, were much in want of some such place, and began to cast wishful looks at Kowloon; and, as nothing could be more disagreeable to the interests of Great Britain than to have so dangerous a neighbour within gun-shot of a rich and flourishing colony, this fact alone tended to accelerate the movements of the British Government. Instructions were, therefore, sent up in March to Mr. Commissioner Parkes, at Canton, to arrange with the Governor-General of the Two Kwang for a lease of the peninsula of Chim-sa-tsoey, or Kowloon; and Colonel McMahon, of the 44th Regiment, was ordered to occupy it with the detachment under his command.

At this time rumours were afloat that the French were going to fall on the island of Chusan, while some averred that their views were more ambitious, and that they even coveted the island of Formosa. But all such tales were flung to the idle winds when we received the announcement that the English and French had managed to take joint possession of the island of Chusan. This was carried into effect on the 21st of April. The men-of-war and transports having moved into the harbour, at noon of the same day a deputation from General Grant and the two Admirals, accompanied by an armed guard of Marines, proceeded into the city of Tinghai, and reached, without opposition, the residence of the Chinese military commandant. The mandarins, finding opposition of little avail, gave in to the proposed terms, and the same evening they came to a conference on board the general's ship, the *Granada*. The city of Tinghai was to be held in much the same manner as Canton; that is to say, the troops were to take military possession, and commissioners were to be appointed to assist the civil mandarins in controlling the inhabitants. The island is generally considered healthy, and, from its central position, would form a good depôt for troops, and would, in case of supplies running short in the north, be of material assistance to the commissariat, as its propinquity to the mainland made it always easy to procure fresh provisions in great quantity, without the chance of creating suspicion.

The 99th Regiment, the right wing of the Royal Marines, one company of the Royal Engineers, and Major Rotton's battery of Artillery, were shortly after landed, under command of Brigadier Reeves, colonel of the 99th. The 67th were kept on board ship, until all had orders to proceed northward. Only three companies of the 99th were left to occupy the place. Sir Hope Grant and Staff then steamed to the sacred island of Pootoo, the favoured spot of Buddha's priests and votaries, as this place had the notoriety of being remarkably healthy. The General's intention was to convert the far-famed temple of Pootoo into a general hospital for soldiers, but the idea was relinquished.

Transport was still a question of difficulty. The military train, to do their work efficiently, required a multitude of baggage-animals. Accordingly, Amoy, Canton, and Manila, were ransacked for ponies, and the large prices that were paid for the most worthless creatures were quite fabulous. To do justice, however, to the British consul at Amoy, who procured and sent down 110 from that place, I must add that the Amoy animals showed the best. Commissioners were also sent to Japan to buy up all the ponies they could procure there.

Just as the army was about to start, an unfortunate disaster occurred to H.M.'s steam transport *Assistance*. She was steaming along about fifty yards from the shore, when she struck on an unknown rock. It was reported that there was at least 10,000*l*. worth of stores on board, which were destroyed or damaged. The French were still more unfortunate, in losing the fine steam transport *Isère* on a rock near Amoy; while another of their vessels, *La Reine des Clippers*, was burnt to the water's edge at Macao, with all the winter clothing for the French troops on board, besides 600 tons of coal.

" Is it to be peace or war? " was the anxious inquiry of every one; but no one knew. An ultimatum had been sent in to the Chinese authorities at Shanghai for transmission to Pekin, and the answer was something like that returned by Yeh at Canton to Admiral Seymour. It was in a somewhat insolent strain, to the effect that they wished to argue the point; at least, so it was reported. Whatever the reply was, it was considered unsatisfactory. Still war was not openly declared; everything depended upon Lord Elgin and the advices he would bring out. In this state of uncertainty and doubt orders were at last issued to proceed northward. It was with joy we received them, as we were sick of lying in Hong Kong harbour, broiling under a June sun, with nothing to do.

On the 9th of June the *Lightning* steamed round to Deep Bay, on the other side of Hong Kong, and, taking the *Sirius* in tow, proceeded up the coast. The *Sirius* had on board Brigadier Pattel and fifty-five troopers of the King's Dragoon Guards, with their horses. My fellow-passengers on board were mostly officers on the General's Staff, for whom there was not room on board the *Granada*. And a curious group we were: there was just that amount of disagreeableness that usually occurs among Englishmen who are strangers to one another, and yet are fully aware of the appointment and position that each holds; in a word, there was no conviviality.

The sea was smooth; and there was nothing to divert the attention from the usual monotony of a sea life, until the 11th of June, when the face of the water was covered with a rust-like appearance, and *schools* of small porpoises kept showing their backs, as they gambolled on their way to the south. The rust and the course of the porpoises, the sailors assured us, were signs of a northerly gale, which, in fact, met us pretty sharply on the following day. As the sea-rust floated past, we could not resist the opportunity of hauling some of it on board in a bucket. We found that its appearance was occasioned by an infinity of small animalcules, shaped like diminutive worms, with both ends pointed, but they exhibited little sign of motion. There were also among them a few tiny creatures—small balls of hair of a smoke grey colour—with tail-like appendages. These last were about the size of dust-shot.

The gale increased; and finding it difficult to proceed with the *Sirius* in tow, our captain wisely ran to shelter on the lee of the Lam-yit islands, where we found several other vessels of the northern expedition also anchored. In this delightful anchorage we were detained till the 16th; and as we frequently rambled ashore, it will not, perhaps, be considered irrelevant to make a few remarks on the place;

for it is seldom visited, and consequently little known.

Several of the ships in harbour with us contained Seikh cavalry, so that it was necessary to send the syces ashore to procure forage. These gentry, as was to be expected, had not been well drilled in the rights of *meum* and *tuum*, and therefore it did not surprise us to hear sad stories from the natives of the fresh supplies they had stolen, or of the injuries they had inflicted. But then the natives were suffering greatly from alarm at the sight of so many ships in their hitherto unfrequented harbour; and, from the position of the islands, their fears attributed to us a far different design to the one we entertained.

The island of Lam-yit, or *South Sun*, south of which we anchored, is the largest of a group of islands known as the Yits, not far from the city of Hinghwa, on the Chinese coast of the Formosan channel. It is about twelve miles in circumference, a muddy creek dividing it nearly in two; and it is bounded by a sandy beach, and rocks running into the sea. Ranges of hills occur on both sides, chiefly formed, as on the opposite coast of China, of disintegrated granite of hoary aspect, with occasional strips of clay. Natural vegetation is extremely scanty; and not a tree occurs on the island, except stunted peach or wild pear, hidden in some chasm on the hill-side. The little available portion of the flat land is worked by the natives for agricultural purposes; and the sandy soil, strengthened by rank manure, is forced to yield crops of rice, ground-nuts (*Arachis hypogæa*), &c., in an apparently thriving condition. But it does not require much knowledge of the coast of China to see that it is not upon the produce of the fields that the natives depend for maintenance. They are nominally fishermen, but actually pirates: and a filthier and more squalid race I have seldom seen. Their dialect has a few expressions in common with that of Amoy; but the greater part of it is distinct, and would probably be found nearer related to that of Hinghwa. We managed, however, to make ourselves understood.

On the 16th of June the gales abated, and we again put to sea.

Abreast of the "Saddles" the *Sirius* was cast off, and we pushed on ahead, at an accelerated speed of about ten knots. We were out of sight of land, when suddenly a small red-backed dove (*Turtur humilis*) appeared on wing alongside. It flew round the ship and then away astern over our wake until it disappeared out of sight. In a few minutes it returned, catching us up in no time, took a sweep round our bows, and again vanished in the distance. These sweeping flights were repeated upwards of twenty or thirty times before it finally disappeared. Now, if we were going ten miles an hour, what must have been the speed of the dove; and how astonishing it is that, after so many swift and apparently fatiguing flights, it still felt itself strong enough to fly to shore without taking any rest!

At sundown on the 21st of June we arrived at Talien-wan, without any further incident worth recording. A vast number of ships had already assembled there, and we soon had plenty of visitors and inquirers after news. The freshness of the air, so different from the steaming furnace we had just left, was truly delightful. But there was a great outcry for fresh water, a very few streams only having been discovered; and there was a great paucity of wells in the villages. Some troops were at once landed under the direction of the officers of the Royal Engineers to dig more wells. Ships were daily arriving by dozens, and it would be a fearful drawback to find no constant supply of water.

I felt anxious to go ashore, as I wished to obtain some knowledge of the natives; having heard that the people of these parts were Mantchoorian Tartars, and not Chinamen.

CHAPTER II.

Description of Talien Bay—Sampson's Peak—Excursions among
the Villages—Surveying Party—A fortified Chinese City—The
Dialect of Leautung—Landing of the Troops—Chinese Grief
for the Dead—Depredations of the Punjaubees and of the Coolie
Corps—Character of the Villages—Search after missing Officers
—General Michell and his Staff—Arrival of Lord Elgin.

How the name of *Talien-wan* (*wan* signifying bay)
came to be applied to this fine bay in the most
southern peninsula of Leautung, which was chosen
for the rendezvous of the British expedition previous
to the descent on the Peiho, remains a mystery, unless
it occurs in some old Jesuit map. It is at the present
day unintelligible to the natives, who repeatedly exploded with laughter when I spoke with them on the
subject. The expression is explained by some as
meaning "a series of bays united;" by others, as
"girdle-bay." What the name means, and whether
intelligible or not to the Chinese, is of less account
than the fact that Talien Bay offers good anchorage to a multitude of ships. It is open to
the south-east, and measures about nine miles from
north to south, and about thirteen from east to

west. The entrance, some twelve miles across, is
dotted with three small islands, which must somewhat check the fury of the rolling waves during
south-easterly gales. The shores of the bay are
much indented, forming a series of lesser or subor-
dinate bays, the most important of which, so far
as they answered the purpose of the expedition by
affording good anchorage and suitable landing-places
for the troops, were named Victoria Bay, on the south-
east; Hand Bay and Pearl Bay, side by side on the
north-east; Odin Bay, a few miles to the south; and
Bustard Cove, between the last named and Pearl Bay.
The land makes a gradual slope to the sea on the
west side, and in the north-east corner; the rest of
the shore is for the most part precipitous and rocky.
Talien Bay is formed by two long peninsulas that
stretch out on either side and converge towards the
entrance of the harbour. The rocks are chiefly composed of stratified limestone, with masses of quartz
occurring here and there, belonging to what geologists
term the "metamorphic formation." The hills are
covered with verdure, though no trees of any size
occur, except in and around the villages which are
scattered over the flat country. "What a delightful
spot for a botanist!" you exclaim to yourself as you
scramble up the hill-side and put your foot accidentally on a lovely pink, or scratch your fingers

in grasping at a rosebush, on which dozens of large
bright red flowers cluster, at once gladdening the
eye with their tints, and delighting the sense of
smell with their delicious fragrance. You at last
attain the summit of the hill, and look proudly
down on the fine fleet of ships sleeping lazily below
on the calm, still waters of the bay, with no per-
ceptible signs of life, save here and there small
specks of boats hastening to and fro. And in the
distant valley on the land side, from amidst a group
of bushes, you hear the soft notes of the *striated
cuckoo,* so like in tone to those of a familiar species
associated with the days of your boyhood. You
reflect on the objects of the expedition ; the insulted
honour of your fatherland, which that proud show
of masts is here to avenge ; and your heart beats
anxiously for the future. The whirr of wings, and
a dashing of something past you, recal you from
your reverie. The disturbers of your solitude are
a flight of rock pigeons returning from their feeding
ground—a sign that it is getting late. The sun has
set, and the anxious screech of the fillet swift (*Cypselus
vittatus*), uttered as the birds dart round your head,
signifies that it is time for you to withdraw your
intruding steps, and leave them to the quiet enjoy-
ment of their rocky cradles.

Rising up out of a plain in the north-east, and

surmounting all the neighbouring hills, stands a mountain, over two thousand feet in height. It forms a very prominent feature in the landscape, and has been named Sampson's Peak, but the Chinese name for it is *Ta-hih-shan*, or *Great Black Hill*.

Sir John Michell was the only one of the three generals that had as yet arrived in the bay; and as I was the first interpreter on the spot, I called on him and offered my services. Meanwhile, we amused ourselves by rambling about among the hills and the almost deserted villages. On one occasion, in company with a friend, I had toiled over a hill, and we were descending on the other side, when we saw a pig feeding below in a sequestered field. From the fact of its being alone, and at such a distance from any village, and being withal well covered with long hair, we made sure it was a juvenile wild boar. We descended quietly, but the little fellow had observed us, and making up the side of the hill stretched himself comfortably under a large projecting rock. We consulted how we should stalk him, and determined that, as I had the only gun between us, I should creep up and try to get a shot. The brute, however, was too wily, and made off before I could turn the corner. We returned through a village of dirty-looking houses, to which the scattered trees had given quite a charm when viewed from a

2

distance. A dirty-looking rustic, no Tartar, but a veritable Chinaman, was standing at the door of one of the hovels. I accosted him; and after expressing some words of astonishment at my being versed in the polished language of the Celestials, he began to make a series of complaints against the way his house had been broken into, and his valuable specimens of pottery dashed to pieces, by straggling parties of soldiers. I asked him if he could recognize the individuals that had committed the mischief; but he said he could not, for he was out when they entered his house. I then spoke to him about the wild pig we had just seen on the hills. He laughed, and said it was a tame pig belonging to himself, that had absconded on the noise of guns being fired from the ships, and had not yet returned. I scarcely credited this story, though I afterwards found that the pigs of the neighbourhood were remarkably hairy, and looked as if they were only half-domesticated animals of the wild boar tribe, which are said by our naval men to be frequently met with on the coast of Mantchooria.

On the 27th of June I was invited to go with a surveying party, under Major Greathed, to the head of the bay. We started at about 6 A.M., with a guard of fifty men of the 31st, under command of two officers, and proceeded in three boats belonging to

H. M. S. *Inflexible*. The morning was thick and hazy, but the sun, gradually rising, dispelled the mists as we neared the narrowing inlet, up which the party were bound. A large rock, flat at the top, stood off the left-hand shore; this we ascended, and while the others were engaged on the object of their mission, I strolled about the place. The side of the rock that faced the sea was steep and jagged; and a similar kind of precipitous hill stood out from the main opposite, within a stone's throw. The crannies and ledges of these rocks offered a fine home to the numerous rock-frequenting birds, and we found that a colony of jackdaws (*Monedula daurica*) had established themselves in this favoured spot. We stood at the top and viewed the interesting scene beneath us. The waves dashed, and curled away, with playful charges against the foot of the rock some sixty feet below, while the white-bellied daws rushed backward and forward in anxious haste to supply their young with food. The young birds kept up an incessant cry, and those that were nearly arrived at maturity rushed out to the end of the ledge, reckless of danger, in hot haste to anticipate the morsel. They soon observed us, and spread the alarm among the little community: out rushed the older birds, and assembling in a flock, flew round and round our heads, uttering reproachful cries. Along the dark sea-washed caves on the opposite side we saw that the rock-doves had also found a home; for in their flight from the neighbouring fields they would speed past us, and disappear in the dark depths of some limestone cavern.

We descended and resumed our course, until arriving at the head of the creek, we landed on a sandy beach close adjoining a mud-flat. A great number of natives from the adjacent villages clustered round us, and having assured them of no evil designs on our part, we marched into the country, and made for a hill. From this place we got a fair view of the walled city of Chin-chow, containing about 7,000 inhabitants; but the population had materially increased since the arrival of the ships in the bay, owing to so many villagers having taken refuge there through fear. We were told that the walls of the city mounted sixteen guns, manned by soldiers under the command of a *Foo-too-tung*, or brigadier, and that the civil authority was a *Fun-foo*, or magistrate. It was a well-wooded city, and presented rather a pretty appearance as it lay all silently on the edge of the great Gulf of Chelee. The villages are here styled *Tun*, or outposts, and the inhabitants are all supposed to be soldiers in time of need, grouping themselves under the captainship of their village head. This idea was no doubt entertained to ward off the Japanese, who for many years were the terror of the Chinese waters. But since the Japanese have returned from their former bad practices and withdrawn from their piratical inroads, the Chinese in these parts have abandoned all fear of attacks from the sea, though their " brazen arms " are not yet "hung up for monuments," for in many houses we found spears, which, though rusty, were yet not pleasant instruments to have presented at your breast. The peasants always explained, when asked what use they made of these spears, that they were used to kill the wolves, which did much injury to their flocks.

The province of Leautung is divided into three jurisdictions, under the control of the three large walled towns, Ching-chow, Kai-chow, and Chin-chow ; the port of New-chwang, to be opened by treaty, falling within the district of the first of these three. The whole of the small peninsula, in which Talien-wan is situated, is colonized by emigrants from Shantung and Shanse ; and judging from the size of the villages and the height of the trees planted about them, we came to the conclusion that the arrival of these colonists could scarce date back more than a hundred years. The nomadic tribes of Mantchoorian Tartars, who are said to inhabit this province, would probably be found further inland; but we could gain no information about them from the present inhabitants of the place. The natives of Talien-wan speak a broad patois of the mandarin dialect, and frequently use most unintelligible expressions. One of the interpreters, however, went so far as to say that the miserable lingo of the place was perfectly correct mandarin; and by way of proof to his statement, the first time he went ashore with some friends, he walked up to a native, and delivered a long oration to him in the most elegant Pekinese, of his attainments in which he was rather proud. The rustic listened with profound gravity; and, at the close, shook his hand, crying out *Puh-tung*. By this time nearly every one knew that *Puh-tung* meant, "I don't understand." The interpreter felt rather disconcerted, though he still firmly maintained his belief in the statement he had made, and vented his wrath on the unhappy rustic, whom he declared to be a blockhead.

We did our best to induce the villagers to bring fresh provisions, but they showed great timidity as to the probable result of doing so, pointing to the city and passing their fingers across their throats. But the almighty dollar was something of an inducement; so we found a decent little stock waiting for us by the time we returned to our boats.

On the 28th I was delighted to find it announced

in General Orders that I was appointed to the Staff
of Sir Robert Napier, General of the Second Division;
and on the following day, having taken up my
quarters on board the *Imperatriz*, that vessel steamed
across to Odin Bay to take on board the General, and
thence to Hand Bay, where most of the ships of the
Second Division were anchored. This latter bay
presented a fine shelving beach for landing troops,
but unfortunately little fresh water could be found.
It was therefore proposed to land one portion of the
Division here, and the rest farther down at Pearl
Bay; but this arrangement was found so awkward,
that Sir Hope Grant finally determined to land the
whole Division at Pearl Bay.

The First Division, under command of General
Michell, had meanwhile commenced disembarking in
Victoria Bay, opposite; and the cavalry and artillery,
under Brigadier Crofton, at Odin Bay, where the
hill streams provided the most plentiful supply of
water. General Napier also commenced landing his
men; and finding the need of an interpreter on
shore, he instructed me to land a few days before
himself, that I might make myself useful.

Sir Hope Grant and Staff, on the contrary, continued the whole time on board the *Granada*, in
Victoria Bay, whence a small steamboat was daily
sent to make the round of the harbours, and carry

orders to the various parts of the army. The head-
quarters of the Navy were also established in
Victoria Bay, and thus Admiral Hope had likewise
an excellent opportunity afforded him of sending
round his orders to the fleet. Admiral Jones, in
H. M. S. *Imperieuse*, kept his station off Bustard
Cove, where the Military Train with their baggage
animals found a nice woody retreat, of no extent, it
is true, but favoured by the presence of some pools
of water.

There were a few straggling houses only in the
immediate vicinity of the open plat of ground where
the Second Division encamped. I was fortunate
enough to hire one from the headman, and took
possession of it on the 7th July. The house belonged
to a dyer in blue, who had absconded through alarm,
leaving his large jars full of indigo to the mercy of
any one that might enter the premises. Several
large kitchen boilers, built in a row close to the
entrance, were also left half-full of liquid dye. The
house was of the most primitive description, consisting of two rooms, the larger only of which seemed
to have been inhabited, and must have answered
the dyer for as many purposes as the stall did the
cobbler in the old nursery rhyme. The chief use
made of the small tumble-down room adjoining was
to stow two large coffins in, one probably intended

as the depository of his own bones, and the other
for those of his wife, when nature shall have required
of them the debt that all men owe. A species of
indigo plant grows abundantly on the hills; but the
dye, nevertheless, is imported from the south.

We wanted to hire the headman's own residence
for the Coolie Corps, but he said he could not let
it just then, as his brother was dying in one of its
rooms from the effects of opium. We had better
wait until he was dead, and then he would do his
best for us. In the afternoon the brother was dead,
and already placed in his coffin. All the household were dressed in white weeds, and weeping round
the corpse as if their hearts would break. As soon
as the dealer saw us, he came out wiping his eyes,
and began bargaining for some timber; but finding
he could come to no satisfactory conclusion, he returned to his former post, and tears flowed copiously
from his eyes as he resumed his moanings for the
dead. The deceased was a literary character, and
as such he was dressed, with a mandarin hat on
his head. A cart and horses made of paper were
being burnt to convey his manes to their long home,
while crackers fizzed and banged in the air to drive
away the baneful influence of the departed spirit.

We succeeded in getting a lease of the house, and
of another for a Punjaubee hospital, close to the

camp of the 17th Punjaubees. The commissariat was already provided with storage rooms, and all was got into working order by the time the General came ashore. We had, however, great difficulties in procuring fresh supplies from the natives. Fowls came in pretty abundantly at first, but cattle and sheep straggled in very slowly: the fact was, the camp at Odin Bay paid so much higher prices than we, that the villagers actually drove them past our camp to grasp the better bargain.

The General pitched his tent on the side of a hill in a very central position, from which he could command a view of the whole of his Division.

Captain Con, of the 3rd Buffs, having been nominated provost-marshal, took up his quarters with me. The Coolie Corps and the Punjaubees were objects of the most frequent complaints. They plundered the natives right and left, but some wholesome chastisement, severely administered, soon reduced them to obedience. Though the natives were slow in bringing in fresh provisions, they soon found out the failing of the British soldier for drink; and but few days had elapsed before we found liquor in the camp. Proclamations in Chinese were, therefore, issued, to warn the people, but to no purpose: the cane of the provost-sergeant was the only effectual remedy.

The Coolie Corps were much addicted to opium, which formed another subject of complaint. The young officers commanding the corps, having heard, no doubt, that opium had a most deleterious effect upon the system and disinclined men to bodily exertion, thought it their duty to request the General to interdict the free circulation of this article among the coolies. I was desired forthwith to forbid the natives from bringing it into camp; but fortunately the prohibition was disregarded. The drug found its way somehow among the coolies, whom you might see within their tents smoking it at all hours of the day. Our people, like many other well-meaning philanthropists, had forgotten that where the practice of indulging in the drug had become a habit, it was not so easily laid aside. The privation of the drug, instead of invigorating the men and fitting them for work, would in most cases have had a contrary effect: the habitual smokers would have pined away, and eventually died.

And now that the army is landed and all things going on well, let us turn for a short while from the camp and take a survey of any of the numerous villages within an easy walk. You ascend a gentle undulation and perceive a village at a distance. How pretty and cosy it looks, with its groups of cottages all nestling among rows of willows and

elms! Around are fields of corn and maize of a
brilliant, healthy green; and as you look towards
the sea you see fine pasture grounds, on which a
herd of cattle are quietly grazing, intermingled with
a few horses and sheep. Along the broad road that
leads towards the village you perceive a cart laden
with sacks of millet drawn lazily along by a team
of fine oxen; and you can almost fancy you hear
the driver whistling in the delight of his heart as he
approaches his happy home.

Now let us draw nearer to the village. You pass
the cart, a clumsy, tumble-down affair on two heavy
wheels; the oxen are large and bony, but jaded
from hard work. The driver, with a large flat
face and *squinny* eyes, stares at you with a look
of mingled fear and surprise. You ask him, in as
good Chinese as you can muster, the name of the
village. He shakes his hand and points in the direction of the camp—as much as to say, "You have no
right to wander so far from bounds." Let us leave
him and enter the village. The roads are broad
enough, though not well kept, and the marks of cart-
ruts make them look home-like; but what hovels line
the way! Built of stone and mud, they look strong,
are well thatched with millet-stalks, and plastered
with mud and chopped straw. Each house has its
dirty yard in front, enclosed by a rude wall of stones,

piled, rather than built up. Most of these enclose noisome heaps of filth, with pigs and fowls scattered about, and having the free run of the house. A few of the natives, however, who are more imbued with a sense of refinement, have small gardens in front of their houses, in which the homely holly-hock is the most cherished flower. Look at those untidy slatterns in short blue cotton garments, with small feet and unkempt hair, toddling away yonder : —you will doubtless be surprised to hear our friends the villagers calling them "the lady-folk." Here is a burly-looking paterfamilias in a long blue gown, with a pipe in his hand, smiling at us. Let us go to him and have a peep at the interior of his esta-blishment. The doors are double, the outer one little more than a screen, and intended to let down in summer to keep out the glare ; the inner is a folding-door, each flap working on pivots instead of hinges, and shutting so badly that its real use must be more to look at than to keep out the winter's cold. The windows are of wooden framework, covered with thin paper, and divided into two horizontal halves, the upper half opening outward when desired, and kept raised by means of a pole. The floor is tiled, and the walls are papered, but well grimed with smoke. That platform of mud yonder, raised two and a half feet above the ground, and occupying

about one quarter of the room in space, is the cause
of all the dirt on the walls; for a stove which runs
under it, and serves to keep it warm, has an outlet
into the room and supplies it well with smoke. But
a little smoke, even in the most respectable Chinese
house, is of no account. A few chairs and tables,
of a most clumsy and antiquated form, and painful
to look at, embellish the room. A heap of un-
cooked rice is piled in one corner, and a bundle of
garlics in another; while bits of red paper on the
wall serve to invoke the blessings of eternal spring,
or continued joy and happiness, on the family. Our
Chinese friend lights his long pipe, and, after well
using it himself, offers it to you to smoke. You
thank him and light a cigar instead; and, as you
turn away, you can scarce refrain from thanking
Heaven that you have the privilege of claiming some
other nationality than that of a Chinaman.

On the 12th July I was called on to accompany
two of the General's staff going in search of Captains
Lumsden and Gordon (the former Quartermaster-
General of the Second Division, the latter belonging
to the Madras Engineers), who, while coming across
in a boat from Victoria Bay, had been upset, and, it
was feared, drowned. We had just started when
we heard that Captain Lumsden had saved his life
by swimming for several hours; but great fears

were still entertained for Captain Gordon. We saw
Captain Lumsden properly attended to and taken
back to camp, and then continued along the ins
and outs of the different bays, making inquiries for
the missing officer, and offering rewards for his recovery, dead or alive. It was past two o'clock when
we started to ride round to the Victoria Camp,
and had over thirty miles to travel; but, as the
horses were not long landed, it was deemed inexpe-
dient to go out of a walk, and at every village, and
almost of every native, we had to make the same
inquiries: so that we did not get to the camp of
the First Division till after midnight. Late as it
was, several of the Staff came to hear the good news
of the safety of one at least of the two officers,
and to welcome us to their camp. We were very
tired, and, therefore, glad to accept the proffered
shake-down. The whole of the next day we spent
with the First Division, and had plenty of time to
look about us. General Michell and his Staff were
all encamped in an enclosed space, under the friendly
shelter of some magnificent trees. They all messed
at one table, and, from the friendly turn of conversation and the General's bearing towards his officers, it
was very easy to see that he preferred being looked
up to by them at such times as a paterfamilias rather
than as the stern commander. The troops were quar-

tered out in the open fields, where the dust and dirt raised by the wind was anything but pleasant in their small bell tents. Beato, the professional photographer who followed the army, had made himself comfortable on a mound in a broad road running between hedges, and alongside was the tent of the provost-marshal. The interpreter, Mr. Gibson, was staying in a Chinese house, and messed with the General. The villagers appear to have been more alarmed on this side than on ours, for they could not be induced to bring in fresh supplies, so that the troops were a good deal dependent on the means of the commissariat at Odin Bay. The villagers even showed a little hostility; and on the occasion of some officers of the Rifles strolling to a rather distant hamlet, the natives turned out with spears and gongs, and drove them away. The General sent out, next day, a small force who took away their gongs, and advised them to be civil, or they would meet with worse treatment.

While at Victoria Bay, a marine who had attempted the lives of Lieutenant Hudson and the Second Master of the gun-boat *Leven* met his sad fate at the yard-arm of that vessel.

After a day's rest we rode back to our own camp in Pearl Bay.

General Napier sent for me and said that he was

sorry to hear that the commissariat could not provide
vegetables for the troops, and that he thought the
best thing to be done was to have a market beyond
the limits of the camp, and he would be obliged to
me if I would go out there and see that all went
smooth.   I at once started to the spot, where an out-
picquet had some time been established, and set the
thing agoing.   A market-sergeant and a provost-
sergeant were sent out to assist me.   We soon got
an influx of vegetables—much more, in fact, than
the commissariat could find any use for.   The market
was some two miles from the camp, but it answered
my purposes very well, as I was thus enabled in spare
moments to run out with a gun after birds, or to
search the neighbourhood for plants.   There were
always fowls, eggs, cattle, and sometimes sheep, to
be purchased, so there was no lack of bargaining
going on all day.

Lord Elgin arrived at Shanghai on the 29th June,
and after there receiving, and replying to, an address
from the merchants, he left in the *Feroze* for the
bay, where he arrived on the 9th July, the breath of
Mars issuing from his nostrils, much to the delight
of the whole army.   The next day the Commander-
in-Chief, Sir Hope Grant, went over in the *Granada*
to the French rendezvous at Chefoo, to see General
Montauban, and deliberate on the coming war.

3

CHAPTER III.

Visit to Odin Bay.—Chinese Game.—Appearance of Bustard Cove.
—Encampment at Odin Bay.—The Commissariat.—A sagacious
Purveyor.—Chinese Cattle-Dealers.—A Day's Sale.—Visit to
the City of Chin-chow.—Hostility of the Natives.—Inspection
of the Cavalry at Odin Bay.—Chinese Avarice.—Re-embarkation.—Departure from Talien Bay.—Distribution of the Force.
—A Canard.—Memorandum issued to the Troops.

ODIN BAY and Bustard Cove were two places I had
not yet visited; and as the army was soon to embark,
there was not much time to lose. So shouldering my
gun one fine afternoon, and leaving the market to the
kind attention of the two sergeants, off I started, by
a path winding over the hills, in preference to the
beaten track through the villages of the plain. The
hills were treeless, much as I have described, and
contained little or no game: at least I saw none. A
few hares had been shot in the neighbourhood, one of
which was shown to me. This specimen exhibited no
marked difference from the ordinary Chinese hare,
except perhaps in the ears being somewhat larger and
longer. As I pursued my solitary march up hill and
down dale, I suddenly, in turning a corner, startled a
large eagle owl, which flapped up hastily, and slowly

sailed over the valley. I at last descended into a long vale winding between hills, and noticing the footsteps of hares, followed the track till Bustard Cove suddenly burst upon my view. I must confess this was a fine sight. The space between the hills was narrow, and well stocked with stunted willows or pollards; beyond these the cone-shaped tops of the tents appeared, with the blue-grey smoke from the various camp fires curling in fantastic spirals up the hill-sides; and farther on the deep blue bay, with men-of-war and transports floating on its surface. There was nought to disturb the magic influence of the scene, save the distant murmur of the thousand tongues wafted to one's ear by the gentle breeze. The effect produced was more that of a stereoscopic picture than of a living reality.

Leaving this attractive spot, I continued my journey over hills and valleys again, until I reached the plain that faces Odin Bay, whereon the encampment was. I accosted a bold dragoon, and asked him where the commissariat might be? He repeated the word to himself, as if not quite comprehending its meaning, and then pointed to a spot which I found, on reaching, was a market. I looked about me, and seeing a dragoon officer reading before his tent, with white kid gloves on, applied to him, and was directed to a row of houses, on the backs of which the word commissariat appeared conspicuously written in large white letters. The courtyard in front and the houses themselves were well stocked with the necessaries for supporting a large army. The Commissary, Mr. Servantes, lived in one, in company with the interpreter, Mr. Adkins, of the Ningpo Consulate; and these two officers, by their united exertions, had managed to supply the whole army with fresh provisions. This success was, no doubt, mainly attributable to the sagacity of Mr. Servantes in always managing to be provided with ready money, and thus able to show the natives that he was as good as his word. The rates he fixed were rather high, if compared with the ruling prices among the natives, but they were lower than those on the coast; and by thus paying well he managed to draw the market to his own camp, and supply the troops with fresh food. The other commissaries, by refusing to pay what they considered exorbitant prices on the spot, thought to economize, but actually involved the Government in much greater expense by compelling it to send to Chusan and Shanghai for cattle, many of which either died on the passage, or arrived so lean that they produced at the best but tough beef. Mr. Adkins had exerted himself in sending men about the country to purchase stock, and his pains were well rewarded. It was a fine sight to see the heads of cattle, often

190 in number, driven up before the door for sale. The work then devolved upon the interpreter and butcher; the latter would estimate the amount of meat each animal was likely to produce, and then the former had to haggle for the price, which was generally a little below 5*d*. a pound. Sheep and goats were purchased at 2.50 dols., or 12*s*. 6*d*. a-piece for the former, and 1 dol., or 5*s*. a-piece for the latter. It was no easy matter bargaining for all the animals that were brought in, and used generally to occupy the whole day. The cattle were of a much finer breed than the small yellow cow of South China; some of the larger ones producing as much as from 500 to 600 pounds of beef. The sheep were the same as those purchasable at Shanghai, with high noses, coarse wool, and broad tails. The goats were of a middling size, and ornamented with long hair, that sprung from the back and hung down on either side. As soon as the price was arranged, it was written on a slip of paper, and handed to the owner of the bullock, who would then pass on one side and make way for the next bargainer. When the animals were all purchased, the slips of paper were handed in, and the Commissary honoured them with immediate payment. Fowls and vegetables were sent to the market, where they found a ready sale among the caterers for the different messes and the ship-stewards.

Brigadier Crofton's head-quarters were established at a joss-house; and it was curious to see papers and portfolios lying about on top of incense-burners and at the feet of ugly josses. These last were rudely made of wood and mud, and daubed with paint, and were much inferior in execution to those in the south of China.

A few officers of the Odin camp, together with the interpreter, paid a visit to the city of Chin-chow. They found the gates shut, and observed men armed with matchlocks running on the top of the wall; they asked admittance, but the mandarins refused it, and an officer of low rank was sent out to see what they wanted. They told him that they merely came on a visit, and were conducted by him into a house outside the wall, and regaled with tea and cakes. A few days after the mandarin returned the visit. He travelled in a country covered cart, with but few retainers, and came unarmed. It would have much facilitated our dealings with the natives if the General had insisted on the right of entry into the city, as the people used often to allude with alarm at what they might expect when we withdrew. An interview with the mandarins and a few threats might have led to a different state of things. The Commander-in-Chief, however, thought differently.

Though we treated the natives with marked

leniency on every occasion, and I may say in many instances with even courtesy, yet if any one wandered far from the camp it was not improbable that he would be hailed with a shower of stones, or threatened by a show of arms.   It was very certain that these unpolished rustics did not appreciate our declaration of good intentions.   The Chinese are so used to harsh treatment from their own mandarins, that a little obduracy has a far greater effect with them than leniency, which they take as a sign of weakness.

The dealers that came to Odin Bay were often from long distances inland, and in most cases they were marked men.   Not only did the prospect of a *squeeze* from the mandarins impend over them, but as they passed through the villages *en route*, the more influential of the headmen levied a kind of black-mail on them, and the vagabond classes dodged their way to fall on them unawares, and rob them.   In returning home, therefore, they used often to choose long and circuitous routes, in order to avoid these birds of prey.

On the 13th July, the *Forbin* arrived at Talien-wan with the French Military and Naval Commanders-in-Chief, who inspected the cavalry in Odin Bay the same day, in company with Lord Elgin and Sir Hope Grant. The French officers acknowledged themselves much pleased at the gallant display of the King's

Dragoon Guards and Fane's and Probyn's Troopers.
The *Forbin* left the same night for Chefoo, accompanied by the *Feroze*, with Lord Elgin on board.

Earthworks were being thrown up at the Odin
camp, as the Commander-in-Chief proposed making
it a depôt for provisions; and the following force was
detailed to be left there as a reserve: the 99th, consisting of 19 officers and 579 men; the 19th Punjaubees, of 8 English and 10 native officers and 453
men; and six guns, with 100 artillerymen.

I spent one night at Odin Bay, and returned to the
camp of the 2nd division on the day following. Short
as my absence had been, I found that the interpreter
had been missed, the General requiring some affairs
attended to, and the provost-marshal had his guard-
room full of Chinese prisoners.

And now the time of our embarkation drew near.
The Commander-in-Chief had reviewed all the troops
in the different camps, and found them in first-rate
health and spirits.   The cavalry and officers' horses
had gained their legs during their sojourn on this
pleasant shore; and the French, who were backward
in their preparations, had fixed the day for the entry
into the Gulf.   The chief men of the villages were
to be summoned and informed of our intended departure, that they might send in their claims for compensation.   General Napier, of our Division, placed

this duty in my hands ; so having collected a group of villagers round me, I accompanied them to their several lots, and told them to estimate the damage done. Each man was only too eager to make his demand, and when the whole was set on paper I found it amounted to 700 dols. This I handed to the General, remarking that as the natives were so absurdly exorbitant in their estimates, the shortest and best plan would be to give them nothing at all. For, on the one hand, we had behaved so leniently to them, and paid them so largely for everything they supplied, that they could not expect any further compensation ; and on the other, whatever sums of money we paid for damage to crops the mandarins would soon be informed of through their numerous spies and through malcontents, and the greater part would be wrested away. But no ! the policy of the British Government was to be lenient and to avoid oppression to the weak ; so the poor injured natives would have their rights attended to. Accordingly, the Quartermaster-general was ordered to give each man his just due. The claims being considered, 207 dols. were to be disbursed among the landholders. How each rascal's eyes glistened when his apportioned sum was counted into his hands ! and one old weather-beaten greybeard could scarcely stand from the agitation that shook his frame when he was told that 70 dols.

were allotted to him. In Victoria Bay I heard the natives were modest enough to ask only for 180 dols. This was indeed wonderful, as far more damage was committed to crops and houses there than in our quiet neighbourhood.

Before dawn on the 24th July the embarkation of our Division began, and continued steadily all day. The horses were taken off in grand style, in proper horse-boats with drop-boards; but the baggage-ponies and donkeys were shipped in any kind of boat at hand. It was a funny sight to watch the way the sailors managed to introduce these animals over the boats' gunwales. The animal would first be handed up to the side of the boat by means of a rope round his neck; he would then be jerked up by the ears until he sprawled his legs over the side, and then some would haul in front and others twist his tail until he tumbled into the boat. As it was feared conveyance would run short at the Peiho, orders were issued for officers to provide themselves with beasts of burden at their own cost. This accounted for the number of animals to be shipped. I purchased a strong pony to carry my traps, and another to ride on, when to my surprise I heard that, though on the Staff, the interpreter was not a *mounted* officer; or rather, as there were no regulations regarding civilian interpreters attached to the army, the matter could not at present be considered. When, of course, they found the need of his services on horseback, then they would mount him. However, after a great deal of trouble I managed to get both my animals on board H. M. S. *Adventure* all safe and sound. The animated scene of embarkation continued till nearly sunset. All hands were shipped off in the most satisfactory manner. The Adjutant-General, the Provost-marshal, and myself, remained alone. We took a stroll round to see that all was clear, and that no stragglers lingered, and then bade a long farewell to the Talien shore.

The *Imperatriz* was very crowded, and my cabin told off to some other. I found myself the only officer without a cabin or portion of one. I expostulated with the Quartermaster-General, and his answer was, that he had accidentally forgotten me. But what mattered? The discomfort would only be for a few days, and then—but I anticipate.

Sir Hope Grant and Admiral Hope had returned to Talien-wan on the 20th, and in a few hours after they arrived, H. M. S. *Actæon* and *Cruizer* and two gunboats put out to sea, *destination unknown;* but every one guessed that they were our precursors to the Gulf of Pecheli, for Major Fisher, R.E., who surveyed the coast last year, accompanied the expedition.

On the 25th the ships all formed into line according to their divisions, and made ready for starting. On the day following all were in motion, and proceeded slowly for the gulf ; and by the afternoon we could plainly discern the French fleet on the horizon, moving slowly along to the same rendezvous. Our ships had to anchor in form about twenty miles off the shore, according to a lithographed plan which was handed to each ship. Several men-of-war were already anchored on the spot to act as " pointers," and in rear of them the ships had to form in so many lines.

And now, as it may interest many of my readers to see how the force was distributed, and the names and numbers of ships employed, I will here introduce a list given me by the Adjutant-general of our Division.

DISTRIBUTION OF THE EXPEDITIONARY FORCE.

CORPS.	DETAIL.				VESSELS.
	Offi-cers.	Men.	Horses.	Fol-lowers.	
1ST DIVISION—1st *Brigade.*					
1st Royal Regiment	29	541	4	27	Macduff.
H.M.'s 31st ,, ...	12	380	2	30	Hugomont.
,, ,, ...	8	300	3	12	Australian.
,, ,, ...	10	293	3	10	Armenian.
Loodianah ,, ...	6	300	1	33	Zenobia.
,, ,, ...	4	330	1	30	Iskender Shah.

CORPS.	DETAIL.				VESSELS.
	Offi-cers.	Men.	Horses.	Fol-lowers.	
1st Division.—*2nd Brigade.*					
H.M.'s 2nd Regiment (Queen's)	23	475	...	...	H.M.'s Vulcan.
,, ,,	4	150	...	...	Assistance, Urgent, and Sydney.
H.M.'s 60th ,, ...	15	409	2	...	Alfred.
,, ,, ...	14	364	2	...	Indomitable.
15th Punjaub Infantry ...	7	619	2	79	Bentinck.
,, ,, ...	6	210	1	27	Viscount Canning.
,, ,, ...	2	100	1	...	Imperatriz.
Lt.-Col. Barry's Battery R. A.	7	220	195	100	Pioneer.
Capt. Desborough's ,,	4	100	70	47	Rajah of Cochin.
,, ,,	4	97	65	50	Euxine.
Major Fisher's Company R.E.	2	94	...	...	Adventure.
Half of No. 8 Company R.E.	2	46	...	...	H.M.S. Vulcan.
2nd Division.—*3rd Brigade.*					
H.M.'s 3rd Regiment (Buffs)	11	390	3	...	Miles Barton.
,, ,, ,,	9	376	2	...	Earl of Clare.
,, ,, ,,	7	50	1	...	Arracan.
H.M.'s 44th ,, ...	10	344	2	38	Athlete.
,, ,, ...	7	318	2	39	York.
,, ,, ...	8	218	1	20	Forerunner.
8th Punjaub Infantry... ...	6	266	2	21	Dalhousie.
,, ,, ...	8	267	...	21	Minden.
,, ,, ...	6	250	...	21	Punjaub.
4th Brigade.					
H.M.'s 99th Regiment ...	12	314	3	...	Walmer Castle.
,, ,, ...	9	325	2	...	Octavia.
,, ,, ...	9	260	2	...	Mars.
H.M.'s 67th ,, ...	17	448	2	...	Tasmania.
,, ,, ...	10	242	3	...	Cressy.
,, ,, ...	2	62	...	...	Pearl and Scout.
19th Punjaub Infantry ...	9	464	3	78	Bosphorus.
,, ,, ...	5	197	...	30	Burlington.
Capt. Mowbray's Battery R.A.	2	79	50	30	Zuleika.
,, ,,	2	74	50	30	City of Poonah.
,, ,,	2	71	50	32	Elizabeth.
Capt. Govan's Battery R.A. ...	3	85	49	94	British Flag.
,, ,,	3	86	51	50	Maldon.
,, ,,	3	71	50	26	Mary Shephard.
Major Graham's Company R.E.	4	90	2	2	Arracan.
Cavalry Brigade.					
1st Dragoon Guards (King's)	4	55	64	66	Sirius.
,, ,, ,,	4	71	82	116	Frank Flint.
,, ,, ,,	4	63	61	...	Trimountain.

Corps.	Detail.				Vessels.
	Officers.	Men.	Horses.	Followers.	
Cavalry Brigade—continued.					
Probyn's Sikh Cavalry	3	63	52	68	Lady Ann.
„ „	1	53	51	50	Traine.
„ „	1	50	54	53	Brandon.
„ „	1	52	52	54	Matilda Atheling.
„ „	3	66	70	71	Ocean Home.
„ „	5	63	78	86	Queen of England.
„ „	2	53	55	64	Nimrod.
„ „	2	54	54	80	Cambodia.
Fane's Cavalry	3	62	69	78	Vortigern.
„ „	3	92	95	123	Edith Moore.
„ „	2	69	67	74	Dartmouth.
„ „	1	69	69	93	Clarendon.
„ „	5	60	72	108	Daniel Rankin.
Lieut.-Col. Milward's Battery	7	220	145	34	Queen of the East.
Reserve.					
Guns of Position	9	280	4	...	Merchantman.
Madras Sappers	8	236	2	38	Statesman.
Mountain Guns	7	168	39	46	Michigan.
	3	51	...	21	Burlington.
Rotton's Battery	6	130	...	...	Adventure.

Soon after anchoring, General Napier was sent for to a conference on board the *Granada*, but what passed was not divulged.

Anchored near to us was the United States ship *Hartford*, with the American Minister, Mr. Ward, on board, and also a few Russian ships of war.

On the 30th the vessels were moved nearer to land, within five miles distance; but as the country was very flat, we could see nothing but a few mounds that seemed to fleck the dim distance, which we were told were the much-vaunted Takoo forts. The troops

were to be in immediate readiness to land the next
day, and we were given to understand that a landing
was to be effected somewhere in the neighbourhood
of Pehtang, the forts carried by storm, and a depôt
to be formed in the village. The morning of the
31st was cloudy and drizzling with rain, and the
sea much troubled; the attack, therefore, was postponed. Great excitement ensued, and numerous
reasons were afloat to account for the delay. One
was, that the Emperor had sent his compliments to
the General, to inform him that a *piquet* of 40,000
Tartars were lying in wait at the Pehtang forts,
and a force of 200,000 between that and Tientsin;
he therefore recommended the General to go away,
if he valued the lives of himself and people. The
Generals were rather startled at the intelligence, and
this made them hesitate. This story was, of course,
all nonsense, and I only give it here as a specimen
of the *shaves*, as they are called, that gain circulation in the camp.

A party under command of Major Fisher, R.E.,
had entered the Peiho river in one of H. M.'s boats,
under protection of the American flag, and brought
back the report that the forts were in much the same
condition as last year, and as their boat approached,
some soldiers behind the embrasures moved the guns
to bear on them, but did not fire. H.M.'s *Cruizer*

pushed up the Pehtang river past the forts on its
banks, without a single shot being fired at her;
and on her return, reported that this river was
unstaked at the mouth and the forts open from
behind, and that a large encampment of Chinese
soldiers were quartered in the plain beyond the
village. About a mile to seaward of the south fort
a place was discovered where the army might land
through the mud.

A Memorandum for the order of landing was drawn
up, and issued in General Orders; and as the reader
may learn how this difficult operation was conducted,
and gain at a glance the number and strength of
each brigade, I will give the whole Order as it
appeared.

Head-quarters, S.S. " Granada,"
Gulf of Pecheli, July 29, 1860.

GENERAL MEMORANDUM.

THE disembarkation of the troops will commence
on Tuesday next the 31st instant, according to the
following arrangements.

Every man will land with three days' cooked provisions, fifty-six rounds of ammunition, great coats,
canteens, water-bottles *full*, and haversacks. They

will wear cloth trowsers, summer frocks, worsted socks, and wicker helmets.

The men who proceed in gunboats to the shore, will have on their great-coats folded, with canteens attached.

Those in regular troop boats, great-coats folded, with canteens attached, not on their backs.

It must be borne in mind, that under whatever circumstances the troops land, it is necessary that they form quickly and regularly at once. Officers will, therefore, caution their men (and set the example themselves,) that there must be no rushing from the boats, which always causes hurry and confusion, and risks the ammunition becoming wet; the soldiers should be distinctly told that their ammunition and firelocks must be kept dry.

Every boat will have the proportion of officers belonging to the men in it, and if possible the commanding officer and adjutant should be the first to land.

The force will land in the following order; and it must be clearly understood that soldiers receive orders, and obey them, from military officers only.

1st.—The 2nd Brigade 1st Division, with artillery as detailed, will disembark at a place to be hereafter pointed out, to be ready to leave the vessels at daylight on the 31st instant:—

4

Corps.	Men.	Horses.	Guns.	Ships.
2nd Regiment ...	400	2	...	Bosphorus.
„ „ ...	220	1	...	Burlington.
60th Rifles	424	2	...	Alfred.
„ „	378	2	...	Indomitable.
15th Punjaub Infantry .	626	3	...	Bentinck.
„ „ .	216	1	...	Viscount Canning.
„ „ .	102	1	...	Forerunner.
Desborough's Battery ...	55	40	8	Rajah of Cochin.
„ „ ...	55	40	3	Euxine.
Rotton's Battery ...	50	...	Rockets	Merchantman.
Fisher's Co., R. E. ...	94	...	...	Arracan.
Pontoons.				

2nd.—The 1st Brigade 1st Division will disembark next.

Corps.	Men.	Horses.	Guns.	Ships.
1st Regiment	569	4	...	Macduff.
31st Regiment ...	392	3	...	Hugomont.
„ „ ...	308	4	...	Australian.
„ „ ...	303	3	...	Mars.
Barry's Battery ...	110	80	6	Pioneer.
Half Co. R. E. ...	50	...	...	Arracan.

Further orders will be given as to remainder of men and horses of Desborough's and Barry's batteries.

Neither baggage nor tents will be landed with the 2nd Brigade.

Immediately after the 2nd Brigade 1st Division leaves its vessels, dhoolies, with their bearers, spare ammunition, and coolies will be landed.

CAVALRY BRIGADE.

Corps.	Men.	Horses.	Guns.	Ships.
King's Dragoon Guards	59	66	...	Sirius.
,, ,,	77	82	...	Frank Flint.
,, ,,	66	64	...	Trimountain.
,, ,,	62	65	...	Eastern Empire.
,, ,,	68	68	...	Harry Moore.
Probyn's Seikh Cavalry	51	55	...	Lady Ann.
,, ,,	51	58	...	France.
,, ,,	51	53	...	Brandon.
,, ,,	50	52	...	Matilda Atheling.
,, ,,	74	77	...	Ocean Home.
,, ,,	76	90	...	Queen of England.
,, ,,	49	52	...	Nimrod.
,, ,,	54	58	...	Cambodia.
Fane's Horse	67	71	...	Voltigeur.
,, ,, ...	101	104	...	Edith Moore.
,, ,, ...	60	63	...	Dartmouth.
,, ,, ...	58	60	...	Clarendon.
,, ,, ...	77	85	...	Daniel Rankin.
Captain Milward's Battery, R. A.	201	118	6	Queen of the East.

2ND DIVISION.

Corps.	Men.	Horses.	Guns.	Ships.
3rd Buffs	408	2	...	Miles Barton.
,, ...	405	3	...	Earl of Clare.
44th Regiment ...	353	2	...	Athlete.
,, ,, ...	316	1	...	York.
,, ,, ...	286	1	...	Imperatriz.
8th Punjaub Infantry...	270	1	...	Dalhousie.
,, ,, ...	262	2	...	Minden.
,, ,, ...	268	1	...	Punjaub.
67th Regiment ...	538	4	...	Tasmania.
,, ,, ...	272	...	...	Cressy.
Captain Mowbray's Battery, R. A.	60	56	2	Zuleika.
,, ,,	67	54	2	City of Poonah.
,, ,,	68	57	2	Elizabeth.

Corps.	Men.	Horses.	Guns.	Ships.
Captain Govan's Battery, R. A.	97	73	2	British Flag.
„ „	80	74	2	Maldon.
„ „	66	40	2	Mary Sheppard.
Major Graham's Company, R. E. ...	88	5	...	Imperatriz.
Royal Marines ...	246	2	...	Adventure.
Madras Sappers ...	251	1	...	Statesman.
Mountain Guns ...	219	38	20	Michigan.

The coolies for head-quarters are on board the *Winifred* (100).

Those for the 1st Division on board the *Macduff* (50), *Hugomont* (100), *Australian* (100), *Mars* (100), *Bosphorus* (100), *Indomitable* (100), and *Malabar* (50).

Those for the 2nd Division on board the *York* (100), *Athlete* (100), *Earl of Clare* (100), *Tasmania* (100), *Cressy* (100), and *Malabar* (90).

It is essential that everything belonging to the soldiers should be placed in a safe place on board the vessels previous to landing, and the masters of transports instructed to have all articles carefully placed in the boats when sent for. One non-commissioned officer and a few men to remain in each vessel for this purpose.

By order,

(Signed)   KENNETH MACKENZIE,

Deputy Quartermaster-General.

CHAPTER IV.

A Waterspout.—Landing of the 2nd Brigade.—The Position of
Pehtang compared to Arcola.—A dreary Bivouac. — Landing
of the 2nd Division.—Description of Pehtang Village.—Loot.
—Quarters of the Troops.—An elegant Chinese House.—
Wretched Condition of the Natives.—Aspect of the Forts.—
The French Commissariat.— A Reconnaissance in force. —
Skirmish with Tartars.—Adventures of a Chinaman.

THE landing of the 2nd Brigade was positively fixed
on for the 1st August. Dark clouds hung about the
sky on the evening previous, bursting occasionally
over the ships with a deluge of rain, and threatening
by their appearance a similar treat on the morrow.
While we were lazily lounging about the deck,
grumbling at the unsettled state of the weather, we
suddenly observed a vapoury pillar lowering itself
from an ink-black cloud, and connecting with the
sea beneath, about two miles off, and thus forming
what seamen call a waterspout. At first a tail, as
it were, dropped from the dark mist above, gradually
lengthening until it touched the water, which appeared
in much commotion, and seemed to spring up towards
the cloud, whirling and tossing about the spray.
Then we observed a white hollow run up the centre

of the column, up which the water seemed to be
rushing. The spout continued for some time swaying
to and fro, and bending in curve, now becoming
nearly invisible, and now almost darkening into
opacity, till at last unlinking from the vapour above,
the mass gushed downwards, and found its level with
the waves below. A few birds (*Emberiza aureola*)
settled on the rigging, and a noisy *cicada* made its
way on board, apparently blown away from the shore.

The morning of the 1st of August at last dawned.
The sea was calm and settled, though torrents of
rain poured from heaven, accompanied by occasional
puffs of wind. We were all up, and on the anxious
look-out to see the landing party start. As I have
before stated, the expedition consisted of the 2nd
Brigade. His Excellency Sir Hope Grant and
General Michell, with their respective Staffs, headed
the party. The French had the 101st and 102nd
Regiments, the Chasseurs, a few troopers mounted on
miserable Japanese ponies, and some rifled cannon.
At 9 A.M. the signal was made for the boats to pull
off to the different transports, and about noon each
boat was loaded with its allotted number of troops,
and all ready for the start. The *Coromandel*, with
Sir Hope Grant and Admiral Hope on board, led
the way, and the gunboats, with their decks crowded
with red-jackets and military gear, and towing each

six launches full of troops, followed in order; then the *Leven, Janus, Clown, Woodcock, Drake, Watchful, Havock, Forester, Opossum, Firm, Staunch, Banterer, Bustard, Flamer, Bouncer,* and *Snap.* Admiral Jones brought up the rear; and as they crossed the bar, they were joined by the *Renard, Beagle,* and *Ringdove.*

The French flotilla did not show nearly so well as ours. Their gunboats towed a greater number of boats, and even small Chinese junks, all densely crowded with men; and one small white steam-boat well down astern, presented a very farcical appearance.

As I myself was attached to the 2nd Division, and not among the favoured few who accompanied the 2nd Brigade, I think I cannot do better than quote the able description of the landing given by *The Times'* correspondent, adding thereto a few remarks taken from the accounts of other eye-witnesses.

" The Takoo forts lay within three miles on the port quarter, looking sullen and threatening, but giving no other signs of life than a Tartar flag, which waved from the largest battery. In our rear were the combined fleets of England and France, while far ahead the blue flag of Admiral Hope streamed from the *Coromandel,* as she led up to Pehtang. Soon after two o'clock the gunboats anchored about 2,000 yards from the forts. All the embrasures were masked, and no troops visible. These forts are about three miles from the mouth of the river, the passage of which they command, the town standing immediately in their rear. On a causeway running towards Takoo, a piquet of Tartar cavalry was visible, but no communication whatever was made from their commander. Some of the inhabitants were also seen hurrying along the causeway from the town, including two men of rank in sedan chairs, protected by a mounted escort. At 3 P.M. the Generals determined on landing 400 men, half English, half French, and on making a reconnaissance towards this road. The 2nd (Queen's) supplied the English portion of the advanced party, and the boats at once pulled off to the mud-bank. They were very soon aground, and the men jumped out up to their middles in mud and water. On reaching the shore a flat of soft, sticky, slippery mud extended across on every side. Through this we waded, sinking ankle-deep at each step. For fully three quarters of a mile did we flounder and struggle before reaching a hard patch of similar mud, evidently covered by the sea during very high tides. Nearly every man was disembarrassed of his lower integuments, and one gallant brigadier led on his men with no other garment than his shirt. Immediately after the reconnoitring party had effected a landing, the Tartars retreated along the causeway, and the order was given to disembark the rest of the force at once. This was effected, without accident, by 5 o'clock, not a single shot having been fired by the enemy.

" Never did more hopeless prospect greet an army. Mud and water everywhere, and ' not a drop to drink.' Pools of brackish water were scattered about here and there, but perfectly undrinkable, and not a well or spring could be found. The ground was dotted with salt hills and groves, affording excellent cover for riflemen, but there was neither tree nor building of any sort or description.

" It had been arranged between the Commanders-in-Chief, that our troops should take up position on the right—the side nearest the town—and that the French should be formed on the left flank of the English. Immediately on landing, however, a French Colonel, whose zeal outran his discretion, rushed forward with the Chasseurs, and occupied the causeway close to the gate, on the very spot which had been allotted to the English forces. Sir Hope Grant at once halted his troops, and spoke to General Montauban. In the promptest manner, and without a moment's hesitation, the French General despatched Colonel Schmidtz, his *Chef d'Etat Major*, to recal this regiment, which was soon marched along the

causeway to its proper position. The English army
then advanced, the Rifles to the right, the 15th
Punjaubees in the centre, and the Queen's on the
left. They were on an island cut off from the causeway by a deep ditch forty feet wide, through which
the tide flowed. In plunged the brigade, and sank
middle deep in the vilest and most stinking slush;
but the men struggled gallantly on, and in a few
seconds the whole force was on the road. The sun
was sinking fast, as from the causeway, raised some
six feet from the marsh, we surveyed the position.
To the right was the town, with a wooden gate at
the end of the road. A few feet in advance of the
gate, the causeway had been cut for a breadth of
twenty or thirty feet, so as to admit the flow of the
tide to the other side; over this ditch there was a
wooden bridge. The bridge and gate were occupied,
without delay, by 100 Rifles and 100 French, without
a shot being fired. The ground in front was precisely
similar to that in our rear—mud and brackish pools—
while about six miles to the left a row of trees and
a few houses were visible. It was the position of
Arcola, an enormous marsh, with one causeway
running across it; and a resolute enemy would have
held the place against any odds. Sir Hope Grant
was strongly pressed to occupy the town at once, but
he steadily and most properly refused. Evening was

rapidly closing into night, and *consiliis nox apta ducum, lux aptior armis.* He was perfectly ignorant as to the force in the forts, and it would have been most imprudent to engage his army after nightfall in the narrow streets of a Chinese town, while during the dark it would have been utterly impossible to preserve discipline, and save the inhabitants from the horrors of a sack. So it was arranged that the gunboats should attack at four next morning, and the whole army lay down in the mud on the causeway, and waited the approach of day."

Meanwhile, Mr. Gibson, interpreter to the 1st Division, approached the village, and seeing the natives friendly disposed, allowed himself to be conducted by them to where he could have a good view of the forts. There appeared to be no life in them; and the villagers assured him they were deserted. He at once reported the circumstance, and then Mr. Parkes and Captain Williams, Deputy-Assistant Quartermaster-General, with some riflemen, came forward, and seizing a few of the natives as hostages, left them in charge of the army, while they accompanied Mr. Gibson and the Chinamen who had given him the information through the villages to the south fort. The people seemed alarmed, and anxious to know their fate, but did not offer to molest them. They entered the fort, and found four men sleeping on mats, evi-

dently left there as watchmen, as they bore no marks
of the soldier about them. The embrasures mounted
a few guns, which were found to be wooden dummies
bound with hide. The villagers warned the party
that the ground inside was mined, and showed them
the spots where the infernal machines were buried.
The party then returned with the intelligence to the
Generals. All wet and dirty, the troops had lain
down to sleep on the muddy causeway. The sky was
serenely clear, and the moon beamed placidly upon
them in their wretched and uncomfortable state.
During the night a few Tartars approached the outposts of the Rifles to within a few yards, and were
hailed by a salute of bullets that deprived one of their
number of his mount. At daybreak the Generals
passed through the village, and visited the south fort.
The sappers were set to work to dig out the mines, of
which there were four. The earth had been carefully
moved round a circle of thirty feet at intervals of six
or seven feet; eight-inch shells filled with powder and
slugs were placed in tin cases; these were connected
by fuses with traps into which flint and steel locks
were set, and they again were attached to small strong
cords. The whole were covered with matting and a
thin layer of earth carefully flattened down so as to
resemble the adjacent ground. The weight of a man
placed on these pitfalls would at once throw him upon

the traps, which might or might not have exploded, for opinions are divided upon the point.

After the Generals had taken a look round at the place, they gave orders to have the troops quartered in the town.

We must now return to the *Imperatriz*, which vessel the General of the 2nd Division and Staff had not left. On the day after the 2nd Brigade started, a Chinese junk was observed making for the shipping, through which she steered close past our ship. General Napier despatched me after her, to ascertain her object and her destination. As my boat approached, I hailed the junk in Chinese, when a man on board stood up, and, waving his hand, cried out, " No, no!" in English. On boarding her, she proved to be the bearer of a letter from the Governor-General of Cheli to the American Minister. The men on board declared that they had just come from Pehtang, that they had seen nothing of the allied troops landing, and that they knew nothing about the forts; in fact, they preferred telling innumerable lies to giving a flat refusal to communicate intelligence which might be harmful to their employers.

On the 4th, General Napier received directions to land with his Staff; so getting together a few necessaries, he transhipped into the small Calcutta steamer *Mohur*, and made for the mouth of the Pehtang

River. The tide was about half ebb as we hurried across the shallow bar without touching bottom. For more than three miles in front of the forts there was nothing visible but a large flat on either side of soft mud and ooze, in which numbers of gulls, curlews, and small terns were feeding. The largest part of the village of Pehtang rests on the south bank close in rear of the fort, but there is also a gathering of houses on the opposite side in rear of the north fort. There was only one native landing-place, which was relinquished to the French; and the Engineers and sailors were set to work to throw up four wooden piers, which were numbered from 1 to 4, and placed under the surveillance of Captain Borlase, of H.M.S. *Pearl*. A temple was reserved for General Napier and Staff, and to this place we made our way through the filth and dirt that lay ankle-deep in the narrow lanes.

Pehtang is by no means a village of the first class. The houses were strongly built, with walls of mud and chopped straw, resting on layers of reeds introduced about one foot from the ground between the upper part of the wall and the foundation, and intended probably to preserve the house from the deleterious effect of the saline quality of the earth. The roofs were thatched with rushes, covered with a thick coating of mud mixed with bits of straw. The temples and some of the better houses had tiled roofs. The streets were narrow, with offensive gutters on each side; and it was only here and there in some yard that a sickly-looking tree appeared to struggle for existence. But with all its faults, on a clear sunshiny day, Pehtang bore the aspect of a sober, well-to-do village. Alas! what a change befel the place after a shower of rain! Liquid mud streamed in torrents from the roof-tops, and its firm streets were quickly converted into positive gutters of mud knee-deep. Nearly the whole period of our stay in this wretched village did the heavens favour us with rain, hence the filthy state of the place so much complained of by our people. The country round, as far as the eye could ken, presented nothing but one vast plain of mud, unrelieved by tree or blade of grass. Salt pools occurred abundantly, and sometimes tinged with algare, or the green stems of the salt-weed. On the land side a muddy ditch partly encircled the village; and crossing this by a bridge, the one road out of Pehtang led by a causeway through a gate in a southerly direction towards the Peiho; it was on this causeway that the troops passed the first night.

The village was now in the joint possession of the English and French; the latter occupying that portion nearest the fort, on the left of the main street that leads out to the causeway; the former the rest of the village. General Michell had one temple, General Napier another, and Sir Hope Grant and Staff were quartered in the fort. Though the place had been occupied for the previous three days, many of the houses were still uninhabited; and idlers, mostly Frenchmen or coolies, were constantly to be met with, big sticks in hand, rushing into the houses and ransacking right and left. What articles they did not want to carry away they ruthlessly destroyed. The few natives that still lingered by their unusurped domiciles quietly watched with the eye of despair the destruction of all the property they possessed in the world, and the ruin of their hopes perhaps for ever. A few, both men and women, committed suicide, but the majority quietly escaped to the neighbouring villages, and many others were still to be seen retiring from the scene of destruction with their packs of worldly goods on their backs; but I grieve to say that even these poor wretches did not pass away scathless. As soon as they reached the open beyond the village, they were met by prowling soldiers, who had watched for them, and made to exhibit the contents of their packs before they were allowed to depart in peace. Sir Hope Grant had given strong injunctions against looting, and many a poor fellow was flogged unmercifully for picking up a trifle. Two of the Rifles were flogged for taking a pig, when

the French were passing all day long driving these
'unclean' animals home for their messes.   The men
were quartered in the various houses, and who could
prevent their appropriating what those houses contained?   Besides, the very provost-sergeants, whose
duty it was to suppress looting, I was confidently
assured, were greater plunderers themselves than
most others.   And if you wanted to purchase any
curiosities of the place, you were pretty sure to
succeed by having a private and confidential interview with these gentlemen.   It certainly seemed hard
against the poor villagers to be thus dispossessed of
their houses and property, when they had shown us
no resistance or hostility, but it was evidently a
matter of pure necessity.   The army must have
shelter in such a climate and such a country, and a
depôt must be formed.   They had, therefore, no one
actually to blame but their rulers, in not having
given them timely warning to clear out in the unprotected state they were left; and if they had been
warned and did not accept the warning, they had
none to blame but their own pig-headed obstinacy in
not having removed, at the first arrival of the ships,
which they could plainly see from the land, all the
goods and chattels that they cared to preserve.   Of
course, one cannot help commiserating the woful
plight in which they were situated, and lamenting

5

the stern necessity that actuated the General's occupation of the village. But does not war in all countries involve the guilty and innocent alike in ruin?—and how can a timid and mandarin-trodden race like the Chinese expect to be exempted from the usual rule? Fortunately, most of the women had been carried away, and so few cases of violence occurred.

The houses occupied by the first landing party were mostly intact, as they were taken possession of before looters had time to destroy them; but the uninhabited houses showed the fearful results of spoliation and confusion. Boxes were broken open, and with their contents lay about the floor amidst a wreck of pottery, torn books, pictures, &c. The troops that landed next were consequently quartered in houses in this condition; and the first thing they did was to gather all the broken stuff, and throw it from the houses into the street, adding thereby dangerous adjuncts to the already filthy streets, which, besides the mire and muck, teemed with the carcases of dogs and cats.

The house occupied by the Provost-marshal was as neat a habitation as any that I saw. The front rooms were shops or warehouses, opening behind on a court-yard, with a house on each side and one at the back. This last was the residence of the owner, and really very elegantly furnished, though, of course, in true Chinese fashion. The sides of the rooms had large cupboards, reaching nearly to the ceiling, made of wood neatly polished, and fitted with brass locks and hinges. The large "kangs," or store-beds, which occupied nearly one-half of each apartment, were spread with mats and pillows, and had on one side large wooden chests for clothes. The walls and ceiling were covered with elegantly-designed paper; the former being decorated with pictures, Canton-made mirrors, and Chinese mottoes on red and flowered paper. Ningpo jars and other ornaments were arranged in different parts of the rooms; and the narrow window-frames, covered with paper as usual, had gauze curtains stretched across, and a pane of glass in the centre of each window. As you passed through the residence, you came upon another courtyard with houses distributed as before. These were evidently, from the style of articles they contained, the dwellings of the female portion of the family. A larger establishment, also belonging to a merchant, on the same principle of courtyards and houses, was occupied by some of the 60th Rifles; who, on first taking possession, discovered two nicely-dressed and pretty damsels weeping disconsolately in one of the rooms. Their relatives had fled without them, and left them to the mercy of the new occupants.

5—2

They were, of course, well treated, and conveyed beyond the limits of the village out of harm's way.

Beyond Pehtang, in a northerly direction across the ditch, there was a dry flat of hard ground, sprinkled with a few houses, which was again separated from the soft mud beyond by another ditch. On the farther end of this mud flat the wretched and half-starved natives used to assemble and beg for food. With these poor houseless beings we used occasionally to go and converse, and give them any assistance in our power; and in return they would sometimes bring apples and peaches by way of thanksgiving for our attentions.

The Generals were anxious to get information about the roads and the usual state of the weather at this season of the year; and after showing them a few civilities, we used to put questions to them on these subjects; but through fear of ulterior consequences they rarely gave us satisfactory answers. They begged urgently to be allowed to go into the village for the purpose of taking a little of the superfluous provisions the houses contained, and which our troops had no occasion to touch, such as preserved vegetables and salted fish; and if they went without permission, they were sure to be turned back, as the officers naturally feared they were not the class of people to be trusted where thieving might so

easily be practised without detection. So gathering
a number of them together, I bade them follow me.
I led them to a house where I knew numbers of jars
of salt fish were stowed in the courtyard. As I
passed down a narrow street with all this tagrag and
bobtail at my heels, a soldier appeared on a house-top
with a spear in his hand. " Stand clear, sir," he
cried out to me, "until I dig this into the black-
guards." I cautioned him not to be so mad; and
taking these men into a house, made each fill his bag
with salt fish. It was stinking stuff, and the sight
of it was enough to make one feel sick; but with
what avidity these poor wretches dived into the jars
with their naked arms, and threw the mess into their
bags! I was then obliged to walk with them till
they got clear of the village again. On another
occasion, while another officer and myself were
standing near this rendezvous of beggars, we observed
two men loaded with packs, struggling across the
mud, and helping two old females along. While we
were watching them, two Frenchmen armed with
sticks rushed at them, and made them lay open the
contents of their bundles. We went up and insisted
on the release of the poor creatures, whom we assisted
to cross the ditch to the other side. One of the old
women was eighty, and the other ninety years of age,
and blind to boot, and they could hardly totter along.

They muttered thanks to us, and, being assisted on the backs of their male relatives, we saw them safely across the ditch, and then turned away to take a circuit of the village. Near another part of the ditch we observed a commotion amongst some soldiers on its bank, and saw an object floating under the surface of the mud and filth that the ditch contained. Some Frenchmen standing by were very much excited, and seizing hold of some natives who loitered about grinning at what they thought good fun, forced them down the bank and made them carry up the creature from the ditch. It turned out to be a native female who had jumped into the filth with the intention of committing suicide, and an awful figure she presented. She was still alive, and soon sat up and began to talk of " the devil's having frightened her." We procured some water, had her washed, gave her some rags from a neighbouring house, and then made two of her fellow-countrymen carry her over the mud ; but I fear before they had got very far they deposited her in the marsh and left her to her sad fate.

On the 4th, Captain Govan, of the Royal Artillery, discovered a crock of powder with a lighted slow match in it. The discovery was circulated in General Orders, with a warning to the army to be on their guard against acts of treachery. The French, more-

over, fancied the water was poisoned, as one of their
soldiers had died foaming at the mouth; so that all
the few Chinese that were found still remaining in
the village were seized by the French, and enclosed
within a paddock. Two days before this occurrence
I had met an intelligent native, carrying a French
pass, who had given me some good information and
drawn maps of the road leading to the Tartar camp.
He was still permitted to occupy a small corner in
his own house in the French quarter. Wishing to
see him again, I applied at the house where he dwelt,
and was told he had passed the whole of the previous
night in weeping, and had left early that morning.
I at once thought that he was one of the unfortunates
seized by the French. I went, therefore, to visit the
captives. They were all seated in the yard, looking
the picture of misery, but my friend was not there.
One man was pointed out to me as the person who
had been charged with poisoning the water, and that
he was to be hanged; but as, on the case being
examined, no decisive evidence was forthcoming, the
man was acquitted, and they were all brought forward
at the *Bureau de la Place*, before *le Capitaine*, and
after receiving a suit of Chinese garments apiece,
were conveyed across the river and liberated.

We have been some days ashore, and have not yet
visited the forts; so, if our readers please, we will now

go and take a look at the defences of these fortresses.
After wading through the mud of the streets, jostling
soldiers, French, English, and darkies, who are hastening in different directions on their errands, and passing
by files of coolies with bamboos over their shoulders,
laden with various military articles, we arrive at the
fosse that encircles the south fort. The road leads
over a bridge to the gate of the fort, by which we
enter. What a scene presents itself! The floor of
the fort is entirely under water. On the right are
encamped Probyn's Seikh Troopers, with their fine
Arab horses, picketed in rows, hoof-deep in slush,
notwithstanding the straw that is spread under each;
the gay pendant-topped spears belonging to each
Seikh standing fixed in the ground by the side
of his horse. The men themselves are arranged in
various groups, talking or carrying on their different
avocations. Indian water-carriers and grooms are
running to and fro, interspersed with here and there
a British soldier or Frenchman in the uniform of his
regiment, making a most curious and motley spectacle.
On the left are the tents of the Head-quarters and
Staff, and from the left cavalier the jack floats proudly
over the tents of the Commander-in-Chief, while the
right cavalier carries the tricolour.

Still farther to the right are a few French troops,
with some wretchedly lean horses in front of their

tents, and on the extreme left are a few dilapidated houses. The fort consists of two cavaliers connected by a curtain with a waving trace. Each of the cavaliers has embrasures for three guns, and the connecting curtain for four. There is one embrasure beyond the northern cavalier, a gun in which would have commanded the bend of the river; and beyond the southern cavalier are other embrasures for two guns, which might be made to bear on the spot where the Allies first landed, and to form an unpleasant obstacle to troops only armed with firelocks and floundering in the mud. The parapet wall is about sixteen feet high and eleven feet thick, and the cavaliers thirty feet high. The fort is girt in rear by a crenellated wall, which would afford but poor protection against an assailing force. The fort is built internally of thick logs of timber plastered with a mixture of mud and flax or chopped straw, of much the same material as that used for the roofs of the village, and the embrasures have mantlets to let down in front of the guns by means of ropes and pulleys. The fort on the north bank is similarly constructed, but can only mount eleven guns. Papers were found stating the total garrison of the forts to be 327 men; but these were removed, we were told, to strengthen the position at Takoo. Various were the rumours we heard of the strength of San-Kolinsin's forces.

The country people always declared their ignorance on the subject, but stated that on his arrival it was given out that Prince "Sang" (so called by the Chinese) had arrived with 20,000 troops, made up of recruits from various provinces, in addition to 40,000 Mantchoorian bannermen and retainers of the forty-eight Tartar Princes.

Fane's Seikh Cavalry were quartered in and before the house where Mr. Ward signed the American Treaty. This house was nearly as respectable as any other in the place, and was tenanted by the son of some literary magnate who held a high position in the Government. He was well disposed, we were told, to foreigners, and voluntarily offered his establishment to the commissioners for the entertainment of the American "barbarians," for which piece of generosity the Government showed their high displeasure by mulcting the son, and by degrading the father to the bottom of the list of his compeers.

One of the most thriving establishments in the village was a pawnshop, with a large carved wooden dragon, painted green, hanging before the door. In this place were quartered the 15th Punjaubees, who, I fancy, made good pickings out of it, as it was found to contain large quantities of silks and valuable fur coats. The rooms were shelved with bamboo trays, whereon were piled tier above tier of articles, all numbered and ticketed in perfect order. Our commissariat, from first landing, was excellently managed, and the troops were consequently in thriving condition, and defied the filth and baneful exhalations of the village. The same eulogy, I fear, cannot be given of the French commissariat. Their poor soldiers were compelled to search the streets and ditches for pigs, which not lasting many days, they were obliged to have recourse to the dogs and cats of the village. And it was a common sight to see several Frenchmen at a time chasing the dogs on the mud beyond the forts, whither the poor animals had sought their last refuge. A Frenchman who was observed dragging a dead dog through the streets, was asked what he was going to do with it. "To eat it, to be sure," was his reply. "What, do you eat dogs?" asked his interrogator. "I should think so," was the rejoinder; "and I only wish I could get as good food every day." A Frenchman could sit down to his *bouillon* of dog or cat, and repeat with as earnest zeal *Vive l'Empereur!* as if the Emperor himself had been accessory to the production of the flavoured dish.

Sir Hope Grant took a trip up the river in the *Coromandel*, to ascertain if there were any other roads by which the Peiho Forts might be reached, and finding that nothing but mud greeted his vision

on all sides, he returned, and, on the 3rd, sent out a
reconnaissance along the causeway. At 4 A.M., the
French, who were to take the lead, advanced, 1,000
in number, under the command of General Collineau,
supported by two rifled 3-pounder mountain guns and
a party of Engineers, and followed by the English
force, consisting of 1,000 men, drawn from the 2nd
and 60th Regiments, and the 15th Punjaubees, commanded by Brigadier Sutton. The causeway ran out
for three miles with naught but mud and water on
either side. A small roadside temple was then
reached, which formed the enemy's extreme outpost
in our direction. The Tartar videttes galloped away
over a bridge about half a mile farther along the
causeway, and joined the main body of Tartars, some
300 in number, who occupied their deserted houses
about half a mile again beyond the bridge. The
enemy waited till the French had passed the bridge,
and then opened fire with their gingals and matchlocks. The French General gave orders for his men
to deploy; whereupon the French ran through the
ditch, and, forming on either side, advanced in shelter
of the conical grave mounds that speckle this part of
the country. The Tartars retired behind the houses.
Some 2,000 of the enemy's cavalry then appeared,
and, extending right and left, threatened the flanks of
the advancing column. The French General ordered

two guns to the front and opened fire on the houses, which made the enemy again retire, and the advance was continued. The French formed on the right of the road and the English on the left, in columns in echelon of regiments, the road here being on a level with the hard, muddy ground through which it lay, which was covered with patches of the green salt-plant and pools of water. A large entrenched camp was now seen to present itself across the road, defended by a crenellated wall. The English, who were threatened by a large body of Tartar cavalry on the left flank, changed front to the left, and the 2nd Regiment sent forward two bodies of skirmishers, who advanced until drawn up by a pool of water, whence they fired at the enemy and forced them to retire. The skirmishers were then recalled. The enemy all this time were far from idle; they kept up a sharp fire, though, from the distance the missiles came, those that reached the allies were spent and almost harmless. The Brigade then pushed forward to within 1,200 yards, and halted. Skirmishers were thrown forward again by the 2nd Regiment, but were shortly after withdrawn, the enemy's fire still continuing heavy. The commanders ordered the men to lie down, and sent to Pehtang for further orders, whether to advance or retire. Sir Hope Grant and General Montauban themselves answered in person to see how matters stood, and resolved to retire, as they had no cavalry. Just as the troops were returning, two guns of Desborough's Battery came rushing up at a gallop, splashing through the mud. They had only landed the evening before; and though they had come at such speed through the mire and filth of Pehtang, yet they looked in fine condition. Each gun was dragged by six horses, who thought little of the weight, notwithstanding the muddy state of the roads, in which the wheels were half buried. The enemy must have fired their gingals at a very high elevation, as the three men who were wounded on our side, and the six men and an officer on the side of the French, were bruised more from the weight of the metal falling through the air than by any force imparted by the explosive impetus from the gun. The Tartars did not follow up the retreat, which they took to be a signal victory on their part, and, as we have since heard, sent glowing reports of to Pekin. They became much bolder afterwards, and approached our outposts with wonderful courage, a few even advancing within a few hundred yards, brandishing their swords and making grotesque gesticulations; so that, independent of the good results arising from a reconnaissance so far as an acquaintance with the country was concerned, it had its beneficial results in making the enemy more fearless of

our strength, and thus an easier prey to our Armstrongs.

Each house in Pehtang keeps its own supply of
water in jars, as none can be obtained in the immediate neighbourhood. This water, so preserved, is in
reality melted ice, which the natives procure in
winter, stowing it in jars with covered mouths for
the use of the following summer. Of course all the
water that Pehtang contained was not sufficient for
the use of the allied forces; a gun-boat used, therefore, to be sent up the river for the article, and being
several times harassed by small bodies of Tartars,
Admiral Hope at last sent up Mr. Morrison, his
interpreter, in the *Beagle*, to communicate with the
Tartar camp, and inform the officer in command that
if they would not fire at us, we would refrain from
saluting them in the same way. Mr. Morrison
walked boldly into their camp, and asked an interview
with their chief, when he gave his message, and an
understanding was at once come to on the matter.
The interpreter then gave the Tartars some white
flags of truce with Chinese characters on them,
explaining their meaning, and told them it was our
custom to respect the flag of truce, and we expected
that they would do the same. They thanked him
for his civility, and he returned. *Hang-fut*, governor
of the province, probably thinking, from this show

of friendly feeling that we had been alarmed by the valour of the Tartars on the day of the reconnaissance, at once sent letters to the Plenipotentiaries; but Lord Elgin and Baron Gros very wisely declined to treat, until our injured honour had been redeemed, and the allied colours floated proudly in the breeze on the heights of Takoo.

Dr. Lamprey, of the 67th, who had made some progress in the Chinese colloquial at Canton, brought a man to me who had been caught prowling about the outskirts of the village. His history, which he told me with tears in his eyes, is affecting and interesting, as it gives one an idea of the thousand other histories and tales of woe caused by the sudden occupation of so large a village. He was a native of Cheun-leang-ching, a village above Sinho on the left bank of the Peiho, and the first village through which the Americans passed on their road from Pehtang to Pekin. He was brought up as a boy in the study of the classics and Chinese literature, and on the death of his father married and set up a small school for beginners. His wife presented him with so many olive-branches, that he found it hard, with the pittance he made from his labours, to earn an existence for himself and family. Therefore, leaving her and the children at his native village in charge of his father-in-law, he removed his fortunes to

Pehtang, where he set up as a druggist and dealer in marine stores. By some lucky prescriptions to patients who came to him for timely aid, he earned a repute, and in two years found himself in good enough circumstances to send for his family. He continued in connubial bliss at Pehtang for nearly a year, when our ships arrived, and the cruelty of our arms wrung the village from its unoffending inhabitants.

As soon as our ships began to muster in the gulf, the rumour was rife that the barbarians would probably land at Pehtang; but he foolishly delayed his departure in the hopes that such might not be the case; for he reasoned to himself that, if he removed his goods and chattels, as many of the wiser people were doing, and we did not land there at all, all the expense so incurred would be so much unnecessary loss; so he thought he would leave it to fate. But we shall see how fate served him. The night the troops landed, he was standing at his door, when a foreign soldier asked him for water; he went into his house to get some, when the stranger seized him by the scruff of the neck and kicked him out of the house, and, before his prostrate wife and trembling mother, all the silver he had in the world, the result of his economy and hard saving for years, was robbed from the till. The plunderer went off with the

6

money, and shortly afterwards others came to tell him
that his house was wanted. He was almost driven
to despair, but, recovering himself, he tried to comfort his wife and mother, and started with them and
the little ones for the village of Ning-chay-koo, some
five miles farther up the river. His wife and mother
wept all the way, and the old lady talked of making
away with herself by jumping into the river; but, as a
dutiful son, he kept firm hold of her. When arrived
at Ning-chay-koo, he hired a country cart to take
him and his family to his native village. The driver
wanted 28 cash; he succeeded in bating him down
to 25 cash, about $2\frac{1}{2}d.$ sterling; but where was he to
get even that amount from? He was cashless, and
had no friend to supply him with the needful. While
resolving what he should do, he recollected that his
wife carried a jade-stone bracelet; this he at once went
and pawned for 1,000 cash, and, having paid the fare
for his journey, he left the remainder with his family,
and himself returned to Pehtang to see if he could
not recover some clothing and other comforts from
his old house. The sentry would not allow him to
pass, and, while he was still loitering about, he fell
into Dr. Lamprey's hands. The poor man, at the
close of his story, fairly gave way to his grief and lay
down on the ground. He was rather an intelligent
individual, and drew maps of the country for us.

General Napier, therefore, determined to attach him to his division as guide. At first, he entreated to be allowed to return to his people again, but afterwards somewhat gladly submitted to his fate, and appeared proud of the distinction of being what he considered a mandarin in the British army.

The following day (12th of August) the troops were to leave Pehtang, to try of what metal the Tartars were made and what stand their cavalry could make against the King's Dragoon Guards and the swarthy followers of Fane and Probyn.

CHAPTER V.

March from Pehtang.—Sight of the Enemy.—Order of Battle.—
Splendid Practice of the Armstrong Guns.—Charge of Tartar
Cavalry—Attack on the Entrenched Camp.—Tartar Bravery.—
The wounded.—Scene in the Enemy's Camp.—Village of
Sinho.—A Night Alarm.—A Spy.—Affair of Tangkoo.—Flight
of the Enemy.—Tartar Gunners.—Quarters of the Troops.—
The Takoo Forts.—Deputation of Natives.—Interview with
Hangfuh.—Exchange of Prisoners.—Chinese Views of the War.

LONG before light on the 12th August, a loud hum
of voices prevailed throughout Pehtang, bespeaking
that the troops were astir, and ere " the early village
cock had twice done salutation to the morn," Ratcliff,
in the person of the Deputy-Assistant Adjutant-
General, presented himself to Sir Robert Napier,
and intimated to the gallant General of the Second
Division that his " friends were up and buckling on
their armour." The First Division and the French
were to proceed along the causeway and take the
entrenched camp in the front, while to the Second
Division were allotted the duties of diverging a few
hundred yards to the right in company with the
Cavalry, and after marching across the muddy morass,
to attempt to cut off the Tartars from retreating
along the Tien-sin Road, and so force them to seek

refuge in the Takoo Forts. The 99th, who had arrived from Talien-wan since our landing, were left behind to keep possession of the village and protect the stores, besides forty men and one officer from each regiment to look after the baggage, all of which was left behind. It was a fearful trudge for the unfortunate troops across that mud, numbers kept dropping out in the line of march and rested for awhile on the side of some grave-mound; others, especially the Punjaubees, finding their boots an impediment, preferred throwing them away, and tucking up their trowsers, pushed boldly on. The appearance of languor throughout the line was distressing. The gun-carriages sank so deeply in the slush, that great fears began to be entertained of their ever getting on; but the artillerymen exerted themselves with such zest and zeal, that in spite of all hardships, they kept their position in the order of march. It was likewise painful to see the cavalry horses struggling on knee-deep with their heavily accoutred burdens. The morass seemed interminable; but a travel of some four miles brought us to harder ground, and in sight of a long line of Tartar cavalry drawn up to oppose our advance. The appearance of the enemy ahead soon inspirited the well-fagged troops and quickly made each man recover his alacrity. The head of the column had left Pehtang at 4 A.M., and though two days' hard work had been devoted to repairing the roads, the deep, tenacious mud rendered them so difficult that it was not till half-past seven o'clock that the rear of the column cleared the gate of Pehtang. It cost the troops two hours' hard labour to traverse the first two miles; and then a considerable halt was necessary to enable the rear to struggle through the heavy ground and close up, for the General was aware that he was liable to attack from the north as well as from the enemy in front; and observing the approach of the allied column to the direct attack of the entrenchment upon the causeway, and perceiving the enemy in great force both in that entrenchment and in front of the village of Sinho, he marched his troops directly towards them, taking their position in flank, and threatening their line of retreat. Three Armstrongs, the half of Milward's battery, were ordered to the front, covered by one company of the Buffs on each flank, and one in rear of the guns. The rest of the infantry were disposed in contiguous columns, with three other Armstrongs and Rotton's rocket battery to protect their left flank, and Stirling's battery on the right, while a troop of our cavalry was halted to guard the right rear, and watch their opportunity. The Coolie Corps, with reserve ammunition, hospital stretchers, &c., under protection of the left wing of the 67th Regiment, brought up the rear. The Tartar horsemen showed in great force; and as they stood in unbroken line before us, some 2,000 yards distant, were magnified by the mirage into giant warriors on giant steeds. The Armstrongs in front were ordered to advance and open fire at a range of 1,500 yards; and shell after shell burst over the devoted heads of the enemy, but the line remained unflinching for some minutes, closing up instantaneously the gaps that were made in their order by the murderous shells. Numbers of amateurs and idlers from the rear had advanced to see the effective play of the Armstrongs, and the delight was general to see how repeatedly it reached the wall of mounted men, who stood so long and so bravely discharging their wretched gingals at us without the slightest effect. At last a general move was observed among the enemy, a part edged off to the right and another to the left, their intention evidently being to surround us. Our cavalry on the right waited anxiously for a trial of strength with the Tartars, who were advancing in their direction; but they were disappointed, as the latter, after hesitating some minutes before approaching, finally retired in disorder under the sharp fire of Stirling's Battery, which began to play on them. Those that had diverted to the left steadily approached " the Buffs on the left front, apparently regardless of the fire of two of Milward's guns, of the rifles of the advanced guard, and of Rotton's rockets. They advanced to within 450 yards, and bore unflinchingly for a considerable time such a fire as would have tried any troops in the world;"* and a party of them galloping in a direction parallel to our columns, suddenly changed front, and charged the 4th Brigade. I was at this crisis dismounted from my pony, and, in company with the principal medical officer of our Division, perched on the top of a mound, watching proceedings, when we observed the enemy's cavalry charging in our direction. Great consternation took place among the Coolie Corps. The coolies were all hastily huddled together in rear of the 67th and Marines, who were at once ordered to form a square by Brigadier Reeves. The doctor, who was rather a corpulent man, sprang like a lark from the mound, let free the bridle of his pony which he held in his hand, and rushed frantically into the square formed by the Marines, shouting out to me to follow if I would save my life. Quite verdant in the usages of war, and seeing an old campaigner so alarmed, I naturally shared the contagion; but being loth to part so easily with my valuable steed, I dragged him by the bridle, and attempted to introduce myself and beast into the square. The untamed Talien-wan

* Extract from General Napier's Despatches.

animal, however, objected to be forced against his will into a dense mass of armed men, and the more I hauled the more he struggled. By this time the enemy were fast approaching, and orders were given to fire. The cracks of the rifles drove my beast nearly distracted, and he began to throw his heels about right and left to the complete disorder of our side of the square; while some of the Marines gave him a few friendly digs with their bayonets, preferring his room to his company. Seeing no help for it, I let loose the bridle, and off he scampered, neighing in great glee, accompanied by the doctor's pony, in the direction of the enemy, who no doubt secured the pair, and carried them off as trophies of their day's success to Tien-sin. The shots of the Tartars pitted about the ground, and some whizzed over our heads, but no one was hurt; whereas the firing on our side drew them up sharp before they came too near to be disagreeable to us, and after a brief space of indecision they retreated. The First Division and the French had now commenced storming the entrenched camp on our left, as the sound of heavy guns reached our ears from that quarter; and swarms of Tartar cavalry were observed rushing about ahead in all directions.*

That Division had left Pehtang in command of Sir

* Taken from Sir John Michel's Despatch.

John Michel, at about 10.30 A.M., and marched in direct line along the causeway towards the entrenched camp at Sinho. The advance of this Division was led by Brigadier Stavely, with the 1st Infantry Brigade under his command, and, in addition, a company of Royal Engineers, an Armstrong battery, 1,000 French Infantry, and a French battery; the Second Brigade followed with two 9-pounder batteries and a rocket battery, succeeded by the main column of the French. On reaching the enemy's second piquet-house, which is about 900 yards from their entrenched position, skirmishers of the 1st Royals were sent to the left, and some of the 31st to the right; and shortly afterwards, Colonel Barry's battery of Armstrong guns and Captain Martin's battery of 9-pounders (the whole under the command of Captain Desborough) opened fire on the enemy's entrenchment at a distance of about 800 yards; a French battery being on the left, together with a French and English rocket battery.

After a cannonade of twenty-five minutes, the enemy's cavalry were seen moving to their left from the entrenchments. The guns then advanced to within 500 yards, and played on the enemy's position, as also on the cavalry, who were moving to the right. The fire of two Armstrong guns quickly dispersed their cavalry, and in a few minutes the advance was

sounded and the enemy's position found to be abandoned. Stirling's half-battery attached to the Cavalry
Brigade being unable to follow the movements of
cavalry on such heavy ground, had been left with an
escort of thirty of Fane's Horse under Lieutenant
Mac Gregor. A party of 100 Tartars suddenly charged
the guns, and came on with such briskness that the
Lieutenant had hardly time to prepare his men to
receive the shock; but the little band of Seikhs under
their gallant leader was too smart for their assailants,
and they retired discomfited. Poor Mac Gregor, however, was severely wounded in the cheek and shoulder,
and his face quite blackened by the discharge of a
matchlock within a few yards of him. During the
engagement our cavalry were not idle, but their horses
were much too tired to overtake the Tartar gallo-
ways. Notwithstanding, several skirmishes occurred,
which always terminated with severe loss on the
enemy's side. The First Division and the French
were now in possession of the entrenched camp that
commands the road from Pehtang to Sinho, and the
skirmishers in our Division were taking farewell shots
at the retiring Tartars, who streamed away in the
direction of the Takoo Forts. We pushed on into
the enclosed plain in front of Sinho, passing here and
there a prostrate Tartar with lacerated body or limb
in the agonies of death.

It was curious to observe the different effect such sights produced on the different individuals of the army as they passed along. The Coolie would run forward, and, turning over his dead or dying fellow-countryman, point at his face and laugh, or rifle his pockets. The British soldier would remark— "Poor heathens! they little know our strength, though they have shown themselves brave fellows." The officer would point to the brawny carcase before him, and remark, "Egad! what fine soldiers they would make, if properly drilled and led by plucky spirits;" and the surgeon, stooping down, would thrust his finger into the wound, and, extracting a piece of shell, observe, "Wonderful instrument that Armstrong!" To one, however, unaccustomed to the "cannon's wild roar" and "the groans of the dying," these scenes struck a kind of shuddering disgust; but the excitement on the occasion, which is truly contagious, soon obliterates all the finer feelings of humanity, and makes you exclaim with the rest, "The brutes, they deserve it all; they have brought it all on themselves, by their treachery last year at the Forts, and their subsequent duplicity."

One veritable Mongolian was lying in our road with his leg broken in two places, evidently by the same shell. An angular piece of metal (of which each shell contains forty-two) had snapped his thigh in two; another had mangled the same leg below the knee; and a third had struck on the thick sole of his shoe. He was at once placed in a dhoolie, and supplied with brandy and water. The poor fellow was in great pain, and rolled about from side to side. He wore a blue button, a sign of the fifth rank, and appeared very reluctant to speak or to have anything to do with us. As he lay there in the midst of his agonies, the guide we had picked up at Pehtang went up to him with a jeer, and asked him if he did not think that the Tartars would be now convinced that our field-guns were very formidable. In the course of an hour or so, some good-natured doctor amputated the limb for him, but the operation soon resulted in his death.

The victory that the Tartars imagined they had gained on the day of the reconnaissance had made them wondrous brave; and considering that the fight on our side had been almost entirely sustained by artillery, their 6,000 or 7,000 cavalry, armed, for the most part, with bows and arrows, and spears, and only a small proportion with matchlocks, had behaved, as General Napier justly observed, " with courageous endurance." They appeared very sanguine at first; but what could such a wretched crew do against 10,000 well-armed and disciplined English troops, supported by 5,000 French? Our loss was, conse-

quently, trifling—two Seikhs killed and some dozen
wounded; while the neighbouring plain for miles
speckled with native corpses, showed that the day
had fared ill with them. The loss of the enemy
was variously estimated at from 100 to 500; but, as
numbers of their wounded were carried off the field
by their retreating comrades, and many others sent
across the river in junks, it is impossible to make
anything like an approximate guess. The Second
Division was halted for some two hours in the enclosed plain in front of Sinho; and then orders were
issued that the men might dispose themselves for the
night. So, without tent or covering, and with only
the amount of provisions our wallets contained, we
endeavoured to make ourselves as jolly as the circumstances and the marshy ground would admit of. On
our right was a small circular entrenched camp,
protected by a mud wall that encircled it. A row of
mud huts was disposed inside this wall, leaving an
open space in the centre, which was now under water.
The huts contained rags, strings of copper cash, rusty
spears and swords, bows and arrows, and other implements of Chinese warfare, and a few Chinese delica-
cies in the way of food. But every structure bore
more the appearance of a kennel than the habitation
of a human being. Some of the soldiers must, however, have had a literary turn of mind, as scraps of

writing in Chinese, Mongolian, and Mantchoorian were occasionally picked up, which showed at the same time the mixture of the races that must have wallowed together in these hovels. Another walled enclosure, hard by, was found to contain upwards of 200 shaggy Tartar ponies, apparently half-starved, and wretchedly thin; and an uncouth-looking beast, in the shape of a dromedary, fastened by a string through his nostrils to a post, stood towering above his equine brethren, denuded of hair and all bedaubed with mud, the very picture of misery. If these poor beasts were not well fed, it was through the carelessness of their masters, for close to the village stood an immense stack of fine hay, which came in handy to supply the famished chargers of the conquerors.

While endeavouring to show some little attention to the wounded victims of our Artillery, Major Probyn asked me to accompany him to an unhorsed Tartar a short distance off. I went, and found a wretched object indeed. The poor creature was kneeling in the mud, all dirty and stained with blood and gore: one hand was hanging to the wrist by a shred, his legs were broken, and the back of his head, gashed by a sabre cut, revealed the brain pulsating; and yet the poor wretch was in his senses and able to speak. I was asked to put some questions to him about the strength of the enemy's force engaged that day, and on a variety of other subjects. The sufferer answered by beseeching us to kill him outright, and put him out of his misery. I declined tormenting him with any more questions, and seeing that death must soon relieve him, we left him. A few hours more and his spirit was gathered to his fathers.

The Generals, meanwhile, were surveying their position from the wall of the entrenched camp that the First Division held. About three miles in the direction of Takoo, another entrenched camp appeared to encircle the village of Tangkoo. The road thither led by a raised causeway, with a ditch on either side. On the left was marshy ground, such as we had passed already; and on the right, the plain was intersected by numerous ditches and creeks. The country was impracticable for artillery, and the men, too, were tired after their hard morning's march. Sir Hope Grant, therefore, determined on deferring the attack; but General Montauban, not being content with the child's play of the morning, was too eager to commence operations at once on Tangkoo, and, if possible, to push on to the forts. The latter, therefore, sallied out with the French troops, supported by the 60th Rifles and 15th Punjaubees, and opened fire with the rifled cannon at the range of 1,800 yards. The Chinese answered the fire very sharply; so the

French General, after about an hour's amusement, returned, and made up his mind also to pass the night in the neighbourhood of Sinho.

A mild evening soon gave place to a damp, dewy night; but as Dr. Thompson, the principal medical officer of our Division, was kind enough to lend me a blanket, I rolled myself up in it, and, in defiance of the moist atmosphere above and the humid earth beneath, enjoyed a good rest. Next morning, the sun rose in all his splendour and soon warmed the chill from our bones as we sat sipping our cocoa on a grave mound, the sides of which had afforded us a raised pillow during the night. We strolled in the direction of Sinho. This village is situated on the side of a narrow canal, or, more properly, a ditch, which flows from the Peiho, some half-mile distant, through an orchard. Several small junks were high and dry in the mud of this creek, and crowded with men, women, and children from the village. A broad road led from Sinho in the direction of Tien-sin, with a wet trench on either side. But how different the scenery on the right to that on the left! On the latter side, an interminable flat marsh stretched towards Pehtang and along the river that flows past that village, as far as the eye could see, dotted here and there with conical grave mounds; while on the Peiho side, orchards, girt with hedges of a most

7

refreshing green, lined both banks of the river. How delightful the change from the never-ending sterile mud of Pehtang to the leafy view before us! We entered the orchards, and for a while revelled among their pleasant mazes. Water-melons, peaches, Cape-gooseberries, and a variety of vegetables were growing in abundance. We then walked through the village, which consisted chiefly of one long winding street of shops. Every house had been broken into, and its contents tumbled about. Only a few of the poorest inhabitants remained, and these were in great consternation, though the General had purposely avoided quartering his men in the town.

We also visited the defences on the road towards Pehtang, which the First Division and French had stormed. They merely consisted of a long arc-shaped, crenellated wall stretching on either side of the road, which passed right through it. Several of the arch-roofed mud huts were disposed about for the accommodation of the Tartar troops, and a very large blue awning set up on poles stood in the centre for the use of the mandarin in command of the cavalry, or for San-kolinsin himself. The mud huts were constructed by a series of bundles of long reeds curved into a semicircle with either end fixed into the ground, and so forming a roof, which was then thatched over with a coating of mud and chopped

straw. The front and rear were fixed up with mud
and reeds, leaving a square hole behind for a window,
and a larger oblong one in front for a door, in which
wooden frames were fitted; the one serving for a
window being papered, and the one that answered for
a door covered, as the rest of the building, with mud
and rushes. The enemy had no large guns in this
position, and appear to have had no infantry at all
within its walls. So that both the entrenched camps
captured at Sinho were merely strong cavalry outposts.

Orders had been sent to Pehtang for the baggage
to be conveyed to the front, and before evening all
the troops were under canvas. During the night of
the 13th, as we lay encamped in that dreary-looking
plain, two alarms occurred. The first was occasioned
by our out-piquet on the right opening fire at what
they took to be a party of mounted Tartars. Every
one in the Division was at once up; orders were given
to the men to fall in, and we fully expected that the
enemy were upon us, and that a *mélée* in the dark
would occur. The Brigade-Major rode out and found
that the piquet had formed a square and was in a
great state of alarm. The enemy, if enemy they
were, thought better of the matter and retired. After
shivering in the night air for the space of half an
hour, the alarm subsided and all hands turned in

again. But our nocturnal slumbers were doomed again to be broken, for scarce an hour had elapsed when a wretched mule got loose, and, galloping about the camp, gave utterance to its small neigh, which in the most tranquil times is apt to startle a person unaccustomed to the musical performances of this hybrid quadruped, and consequently such sounds in the dark dead of night were more apt to strike the already slackened nerves of the men with terror. A cry was raised that the Tartars were yelling and galloping about the camp. Great consternation prevailed; the men once more fell in, and the officers stood ready for an engagement, pistol in hand. The Brigade-Major was again about, and, finding the alarm to be a false one, the men were cautioned not to give way to such childish fears; and all retired, as before, with the determination not to stir again unless there was actual need. A Tartar spy had ridden up to a sentry the day previous and been taken prisoner, and this fact may have wrought upon the men's minds the suspicion that a night attack was intended. The prisoner referred to was an elderly man with perfect Chinese visage, very dirtily clad in ordinary native jacket and long frock. On his head he wore a cap, shaped like the mandarin winter cap, but without the loose red silk on the crown, and adorned instead with two cats' tails attached to the top and pointing backwards, the usual badge of the Tartar cavalry. He was armed with a rusty sword and spear, and mounted on a wooden saddle, with large circular-soled iron stirrups attached by leathern thongs. The saddle was kept on the pony's back by means of two narrow leathern girths, one round the animal's belly and the other close behind the fore-legs. The pony's headgear was of leather, roughly put together with hobnails, supporting a rough iron bit, and commanded by a single rein of rope covered with cloth. The pony was a strong little filly, of a breed closely allied to the Shetland. The rider, so far as I could understand from the frequent use of the canine letter in his speech (for he could not speak a word of Chinese), was a Mongolian. We could consequently make nothing of him, and he was handed over to the guard as a prisoner of war. The corporal, as he gave the pony's bridle to one of his men, and marched the Tartar off between the other two, apostrophized with a sneer and a grunt, " Sure, and are these our inimies ? "

Soon after daybreak, the Adjutant-General gave us notice to march at 5.30 A.M., as Tangkoo was to be stormed that morning by the First Division, and the Second Division was to halt between that village and Sinho, to be held in reserve in case of need. I had no particular duty to perform, so I hastened on,

passed the troops as they marched through Sinho,
and endeavoured to get as good a view of the affair
as circumstances would admit.   A causeway, as I
before remarked, ran from Sinho to Tangkoo, some
three miles in length, on the left of which the ground
presented a vast muddy flat, while the right offered a
low, moist plain, intersected by ditches which had
now been bridged over by our engineers, and was
separated from the river by a line of orchards extending close to Tangkoo itself; the fortifications of
which place consisted of a long, semicircular crenellated wall, three miles in length, terminating both
ends on the banks of the river.   The attack was
made from the right of the causeway; the English
on the right, near the river; the French along the
road.   Barry's battery of Armstrongs, and Desborough's 9-pounders, took the extreme right, while
Milward's Armstrongs and Govan's battery the
centre.   Trenches had been dug on the night previous, within 700 yards of the wall, to give cover to
the riflemen.   The guns in front were supported by
200 Rifles, in skirmishing order, under the command
of Major Rigaud.   The Royals and 31st followed,
and then the Queen's, 60th Rifles, and 15th Punjaubees.   About a mile below Sinho, the river takes
a bend to the south, and then trending round to the
north again, washes close to Tangkoo.   At the first

Published by Geo.e Klerr & C.o as they appear in London 185.

bend, the Tartars had constructed a battery, which
kept annoying the flank of the advancing column.
Two of Barry's Armstrongs were sent to silence this
battery; but the range being only 250 yards, our
firing was somewhat ineffective; and so three of Desborough's 24-pounders were detailed to take the place
of the Armstrongs, and they soon effectually put a
stop to its annoyance. Another battery, lower down
the reach, opened fire, and some junks moored in the
river also kept taking "pot" shots at the troops. The
task of silencing these was committed to the hands
of some of the gallant Navy, and soon the work was
completed. Some officers of the *Chesapeake*, with
twenty men, crossed the river in a junk, and having
spiked the guns in the battery, set the obtrusive
junks on fire. The battery was found to contain two
12-pounder and five 6-pounder iron guns. Some
Tartars appeared round the corner on horseback;
these the brave tars peppered well with their pistols
before they recrossed to the other bank. In the
affray, one of the sailors was wounded by a bullet
through the arm. Meanwhile the column advanced
and the guns opened fire, at about 800 yards distance,
on the entrenched camp. The Chinese replied with
spirit with their gingals and some heavy guns, and
the contest lasted hot and angry for some time; but
they had forty-two guns, French and English, to

contend with, and it soon became apparent to which
side the victory inclined. A lull ensued, which our
people took advantage of to approach nearer and
then repeat their deadly fire. At last the Chinese
guns were silenced, and Sir John Michel ordered up
the Infantry, who poured into the fortress across a
dam that stopped the flow of the ditch. The Rifles
were first in, and bowled over the Tartars as they
scampered with precipitancy from the wall, across
the open, into the village, while rockets, whizzing
through the air over their heads, in graceful curve,
spread dismay among their retiring numbers and
accelerated their speed. The fugitives escaped,
along a causeway, to a village farther down the river,
whence they crossed, by means of a floating bridge,
to the village of Takoo. The French, as usual,
claimed the merit of having first entered the fortifi-
cation, and General Montauban promoted the first
Frenchman in; but it is very certain that our troops
were within the walls while the French guns were
still bombarding the place. I hurried past the troops
as they crowded over the dam. A large space of
ground was enclosed by the crenellated wall between
it and the village, consisting of mud and pools of
salt water, as at Pehtang. Numerous mud-built
huts lined the foot of the wall, and between the gate
and the village stood a larger, square-shaped cabin,

the residence, evidently, of the mandarin in command. Numbers of dead Chinese lay about the guns, some most fearfully lacerated. The wall afforded very little protection to the Tartar gunners, and it was astonishing how they managed to stand so long against the destructive fire that our Armstrongs poured upon them; but I observed, in more instances than one, that the unfortunate creatures had been tied to the guns by the legs. This seems almost incredible; but several officers and myself saw the poor victims lying dead or dying thus tied to the weapons they were employed to use against us. All the dead had the white circular badge of the Chinese soldier on the breast and back of their coats, with characters signifying that they belonged to the camp of the General of Chihlee, and wooden tickets, marked with the same characters and the number of their position in the army, dangling from their girdles. Large baskets of powder, and shot of various sizes, lay near the guns, ready for use, with small flasks of finer powder, gun-pricks, and long coils of lighted fusee.

The whole length of wall mounted forty-five pieces of artillery, of which sixteen were brass guns and the remainder iron; the brass guns were of various calibre, from 4 and 6 to 24-pounders, and generally well made; the iron guns were mostly small.

The Chinese force within these works was variously
estimated by the Generals at from 2,000 to 6,000,
but their loss on the occasion it is difficult to set down
with anything like accuracy. Dozens of bodies lay
about the guns, dozens of others were found in the
ditch that encircled the entrenchment, while numbers
had crawled into the village to die, to say nothing of
the scores that were carried down the river in junks,
or conveyed away by the retreating force. No
cavalry was observed, though one enclosed series of
huts was found to contain a host of wooden saddles
and native horse-gear, sufficient to equip a large number of troopers. It was wonderful, notwithstanding
the hot fire of the enemy, how little injury had been
inflicted on our side. Not a single man was killed,
only three English gunners wounded and about a
dozen French. General Michel had his horse killed
under him. I hastened into the village. The looting had commenced; numbers of Frenchmen were
rushing about the streets with bayonets fixed, breaking into doors right and left, and ransacking houses.
After about an hour's delay the First Division and
French were withdrawn to their old encampment in
the plain between Sinho and Tangkoo, and General
Napier's Division were ordered to instal themselves
in the houses of the village just captured. The
Deputy-Assistant Quartermaster-General at once set

to work, and marked off the different houses to the different regiments and individuals, and the baggage coming up shortly after, each person was enabled to make himself at home in his new quarters. Most of the houses contained provisions and water, and many even warm tea, an evidence of the procrastinated departure of their occupants, and the streets swarmed with pigs. Parties were told off to capture the pigs, which soon ended in every poor swine being slaughtered; for the soldiers, glad of a spree, showed no mercy to the victims of their sport, and consequently much more meat was killed than could be consumed by the force in a week. The superfluous animals were left where they were slaughtered in the roads and highways, and, as the weather was hot, their carcases soon became offensive. General Napier and Staff were quartered in the chief temple of the village, the " San-kwan-miaou," or temple of the three mandarins, facing the river; thence, crossing a ditch by means of a wooden bridge, a road followed the bend of the river (which here turned sharp away from the village in a south-easterly direction), and led to the gate of the works some 600 yards off. From the top of the wall at this gate you observed the raised road leading through a large mud flat to a small fortified group of houses, about two miles distant, opposite the long straggling village of Takoo, in the centre of which

was a large two-storied pagoda, the head-quarters of
San-kolinsin and Staff; and still farther on, the
forts themselves, gloomy and threatening, flaunting
numerous flags in defiance. Sir Hope Grant was
in no hurry to push on his victorious arms, and
attempt to carry these formidable fortresses at once,
at the sacrifice of a great many men; but, like a
prudent Scotchman, he preferred abiding his time,
and waiting till proper reconnaissances had been
made, heavy guns well set, and other preparations
completed, before he showed the natives the metal we
were made of. The work before him was one that
required good engineering, and who better for this
work than his trusty colleague General Napier, who
had distinguished himself as a skilful officer in the
Bengal Engineers? On this account, to the Second
Division was specially assigned the making of the
necessary preparations for the capture of Takoo.
This we all felt would involve a lapse of several days
and a long stay at Tangkoo, so we endeavoured to
make ourselves comfortable. Two companies of the
Buffs were posted at the gates leading to Takoo,
under the gallant Colonel Sargent, whose experience in
the China war of 1842 made him the better able to
fulfil the duties of so important a station.

Soon after our capture of Tangkoo, the enemy
deserted the small entrenched camp we spoke of on

the road to the northern forts, and betaking themselves across the water by means of the floating
bridge, broke up the apparatus, and withdrew the
boats that formed it into the docks at the Takoo
village. A large gun, mounted on the fortress, at
the corner of Takoo village, at the end of the reach
of the river, kept plumping an occasional shot into the
streets. No damage was done, and after a few repeti-
tions, the Chinese got tired of the fun, and desisting,
suffered us to make the best of our new possession.

The first thought of General Napier's after the
immediate arrangements for the comfort of the troops
were attended to, was for the suffering natives of
the village. One series of huts was specially set
apart for the reception of these people, and a
medical officer appointed to attend them. Parties
were then sent throughout the village to search for
the wounded natives, and for all that still lingered
through age, imbecility, or other cause; and thus,
in a short time, all the helpless and destitute were
taken under our charge, and a dirtier and more motley
group eye never beheld :—women, old and young,
ugly and pretty, children and men of all shapes, sizes,
and ages, some with horrible wounds and the ghastly
agony of death on their faces, but all on their knees
weeping and trembling with fear. In the afternoon, some mounted men were seen issuing from the

entrenched camp beyond, who were at once hailed by
a shower of bullets, until they produced a white flag.
The party turned out to be the escort of a small
mandarin of the sixth rank, with white button and
peacock's feather, who was the bearer of two letters
from the governor of the province to Lord Elgin and
Baron Gros. The mounted guard halted some 300
yards off, and dismounted, while the mandarin and
some magnates of the village of Takoo that accompanied him, dressed respectably in white grass cloth
frocks, came forward and met myself and some others
inside the gate. Colonel Sargent, who went out with
me, took the letters, but refused to grant a receipt for
them, for which the mandarin so urgently entreated.

The village chiefs advanced and took up their
parable, lamenting the misunderstandings that existed
between us and their Government, and that they
should be innocent sufferers. They asked me if
there was no hope of an amicable settlement before
our wrath was wreaked on the Takoo natives. I told
them that I was sure no harm would happen to the
villagers if they remained neutral, that our quarrel
was purely with the governing party and not with the
governed, and our object to lower the pride of those
menacing batteries yonder. But as they trembled
at the prospect of their own miseries, they would
surely commiserate the sufferings of their wretched

fellow-countrymen at present in our hands, houseless and homeless. They would at once show their good feeling by taking charge of them. They replied that if there were any villagers remaining in our hands they would, of course, be only too glad to see them cared for. Accordingly, I returned, and with the General's permission, escorted out of the gates all that were not wounded. Those of the natives who were able to walk were only too glad to go, and hurried off. Among them was one stout old lady, who had a grown-up daughter lying prostrate on a stretcher with a sprained thigh. The mother hurried off without even bidding adieu to her daughter. The poor girl (rather a pretty face by the way) cried after her, " Oh, mother! mother! don't leave me here to die;" but the relentless mother turned a deaf ear to the cry. I tried to comfort the poor girl, but she was inconsolable, and finding no hope for it, I had her carried out by two of her stout countrymen, as she lay on the stretcher. Another case was that of an emaciated old woman with one foot in the grave, who in helpless second childhood lay there perfectly unconscious of all that was going on around her. And another of a plump little infant, just able to walk, whom nobody would own. We had both these carried out and delivered over with the rest of the party, some thirty in number, to the mandarin. This functionary questioned each one, whether he or she had friends in Takoo to whom they could go. They all answered in the affirmative, except the old woman and the little boy, both of whom were children, so to speak, and unable to articulate. He shook the old creature, and being able to make nothing of her, turned round to me with an affected laugh,—"What would you have me do with this insensible old block?" said he. "See her taken care of," I replied; "she is one of your countrywomen." He rejoined with a shrug of his shoulders, "I cannot afford to feed her, and I am sure no one else will. You must look after her yourselves." With that he turned on his heel, followed by the swells in the long frocks, and in their wake the ragged crowd. The old woman and the boy alone remained. I rushed after them, and cried out, "If you will not take the old woman, you must take the infant here. He is probably the child of one of your soldiers." The mandarin stopped and gave orders to have the child carried after him, but they had not proceeded far before we observed them set down the little creature in the mud and leave him. Colonel Sargent gave utterance, in a smothered voice, to something that sounded like "brutes," and sent a soldier to bring back the boy, who was crying piteously, and the infant and the old lady were restored to their former asylum.

Our plenipotentiaries returned no answer to the letters of the Governor, and on the day following another flag of truce appeared with more letters. But no answer again. On the third day another flag of truce, and still more letters, with an intimation that they had some prisoners of ours, which they would return to us forthwith. They were as good as their word, and soon restored to us a sergeant of the Buffs and a Madras Sapper. Both had suffered much from bad treatment, and could not stand, their wrists and ankles being fearfully lacerated from the effects of the tight cords that bound them. The sergeant for some time talked wildly, and was evidently out of his senses.

The next day Lord Elgin sent a letter in the hands of Mr. Parkes and some others to the entrenched camp opposite Takoo with a flag of truce. They stood on the bank of the river and waved the flag, and soon a boat was sent across for them. On landing on the other side they were shown into the presence of Hang-fuh, the Governor of Cheli, and held a conversation with him; in the course of which arrangements were made for the return of certain Cantonese of the Coolie Corps that they held prisoners, in exchange for the wounded and others of their people in our hands. The Governor declared that commissioners were on their way down to treat

8

for peace, and tried hard to procure a promise that hostilities should be deferred until Lord Elgin should meet with them. The Chinese were on this account anxious to propitiate us by the exchange of prisoners. On the afternoon of the same day the thirteen coolies were returned to us, and the wounded natives in our hands consigned to the tender mercies of the White Button. It was a sorry sight to see the emaciated appearance of these poor Cantonmen, and the frightful festering wounds on their bodies. One unfortunate man who was at once brought in on the shoulders of a red jacket had his head split open. The gashed skull laid bare the brain beneath, about the surface of which huge maggots were crawling. It was a sickening sight, and loud were the objurgations of the troops, as these wounded, limping wretches passed through them, against the cruelty of the enemy. But it was a wonder to all that they had not fared worse, when we considered how savagely cruel the Chinese usually are to their rebel countrymen, and in no other light could they have looked upon the Cantonese, whom they firmly believed to form no insignificant ingredient in our army. The only way to account for their deviation in this instance from their usual system of murdering outright was that they entertained hopes by a show of mildness to allay our dreaded wrath.

The capture of the foreigners and Cantonese by the Tartars, so far as we could gather from the incoherent statements of the different parties, happened in this wise. A sergeant of the 44th, and a private of the Buffs, with two Madras Sappers, on the day of the first fight, had left Pehtang in charge of the grog for the troops, which was carried by sixteen Cantonese coolies. They started somewhat after the troops, and being either foot-sore or the worse for liquor, sat down to rest themselves, and fell asleep. On rousing, they missed their way, and marched in the direction of some cavalry they observed at a distance, whom they took to be Seikhs. As it turned out, they were Tartars, two of whom came galloping up, and being fired at by the foreigners, returned to the main body, and brought several more with them. On seeing the large number of horsemen coming against them, the Buffs' man exclaimed to his comrade, "Ah! my boy, we shall *larn* the grand *sacret* soon;" and assisted by the two Madrassees they fired at the advancing enemy. In the affray that ensued the private was killed, and two of the coolies mortally wounded; a third escaped. The rest were all taken prisoners and carried to Tien-tsin, and on the road the Tartars murdered one of the Madrassees, and sacrificed him before a temple, or "two poles," as the coolies expressed it (each temple of any size

8—2

having two high poles erected in front). The sergeant and remaining Sapper were carried in the same cart, the coolies in two or three others. They were exhibited as captives of war in Tien-tsin and badly beaten; the coolies had their tails cut off, and then all were brought back to Takoo, whence they were restored to us.

In the different mandarin residences of Sinho and Tangkoo, Chinese letters and other documents were discovered, which laid open to us the train of Chinese ideas on our relations with them. One of these was a decree, dated the 27th March, 1860, from the "Great Council of Pekin" to San-kolinsin, generalissimo of the Forces, and to Hang-fuh, governor of Cheli, enclosing the ultimatum handed to the Chinese Government by Mr. Bruce at Shanghai, with some extracts from the newspapers. It comments on the rebellious language of the "Barbarians," and goes on to say that *Ho* has been directed to answer them. The fact is then mentioned that "Barbarian" ships are surveying the coast in the neighbourhood of Takoo to find a landing-place, and then quotes the news from the newspapers, as stated in Commissioner Ho's letter, that an invasion of 30,000 men is projected with a view to capturing the forts, and alludes to a debate in the "Barbarian" House of Commons on the subject of the war, also mentioned in Ho's letter. The translation of the decree then runs thus: " Considering that Messrs. Bruce and Bourbillon are inseparables in dishonesty, by nature sanguinary and treacherous, and seeing the ferocity and trickiness of their dispositions, when mention is made of their forces being increased with a view of taking the forts, it would be wrong not to stand on our guard. Let Prince San-kolinsin, therefore, look to it, and let the extracts from the newspapers be given to him to read. With regard to the Russian Barbarians, who come to the coast in vessels of war, they must be warned to go away, as the coast is put on the defensive." The reply of San-kolinsin and Hang-fuh to the above is to the effect that the Barbarians will not venture again to attack the forts in front; they will in all probability land at Pehtang, which is unprotected ; but in crossing the plains towards Sinho, the invincible Tartar cavalry are so disposed that they would find no difficulty in cutting up 30,000 such troops as the Barbarians possess; but if by any extraordinary good luck they should succeed in passing Sinho, then they would most certainly run their heads against the forts as they did last year. They go on to say that they put little faith in the bragging reports of the Barbarians' forces as set forth in their papers, or of their intention to try the fortune of war again at the forts ;

that their boasted announcement of preparations on a grand scale is made with the hope of alarming the Emperor and his mandarins, and to mask the cowardly fear under which the English and French were suffering since the defeat of 1859; for if they were really increasing their force this year to avenge themselves, they would never have allowed the slightest rumour of their intentions to get abroad at Shanghai.

One naturally wonders how a people, so indifferent to the topic of foreign politics as the Chinese officials, should have managed to acquaint themselves with the speeches relating to them delivered in the House of Commons and published in the newspapers; but the mandarins immediately connected with our people at the Northern ports must naturally have felt alarmed at the fact of our not having sued for peace after the defeat at Takoo; and knowing that the foreigner was a very porcupine when his blood was up, and observing that no immediate preparations were being made in any of the Five Ports, they turned for information on the subject to shroffs and teachers employed in different foreign establishments, who, doubtless, questioned their masters, and were supplied with the necessary details. These, again, were transmitted to Pekin on inquiries being made how the Barbarians behaved at their trading marts, and so reached the Grand Council; hence the issue of the decree to Hang-fuh and San-kolinsin above referred to.

Many of the Chinese clerks in European offices are capable of reading and writing English, though seldom with much proficiency; and these men are frequently employed by the mandarins for culling information which may throw light on their foreign relations. These men are accessible to bribes from all quarters, and there is consequently a difficulty to preserve reticence, even on mercantile matters.

In another letter the General of the Province acquaints the Governor of his successful sally against the Barbarians on the day of the reconnaissance, and of his forbearance to inflict too severe a defeat for fear of interfering with Hang-fuh's diplomatic plans for soothing their Barbarian anger. Hang-fuh replies that he does not wish diplomacy to interfere with the General's measures, and that he trusts that the General will do his utmost to maintain his positions at Sinho and Tangkoo, as they form the key to the forts. Before closing his letter, he offers large rewards for the capture of the Barbarian chiefs and soldiers, that he might traffic with them in the hopes of bringing the enemy to terms.

The capture of Lord Elgin is especially enjoined, as on the success of such an attempt depended the immediate termination of the war.

CHAPTER VI.

Οἱ μὲν ἐφ' ἵππων,
Οἱ δ' ἐπὶ ναῶν, πεζοὶ τε βάδην
Πολέμου στῖφος παρέχοντες·
*   *   *
Φοβέροι μεν ἰδεῖν, δεινοὶ δε μάχην
Ψυχῆς εὐτλήμονι δόξῃ.

Persæ of Æschylus.

Plan of Attack on the Takoo Forts.—Difference of Opinion between the English and French Generals.—Bridge of Boats.—Approaches to the Forts.—The Eve of the Assault.—Advance on the Forts.—Description of the Assault.—Unconditional Surrender.—Casualties.—Tartar Courage.—Description of the Forts.—Chinese wounded.—Variety of Races.—The wounded Cake-seller.

THE indulgent reader has so far accompanied us to the pleasant shores of Talien-wan, with the short though invigorating camp-life spent there; to the interminable mud-flats of Pehtang, with its scenes of misery and devastation; and thence through the two victorious skirmishes at Sinho and Tangkoo; but the greatest scene of all remains for this chapter to depict—the battle of Takoo, where Britain's noble sons, supported by their gallant allies, subdued their insolent and overbearing enemy, so overwhelming in numbers, and bravely redeemed their country's glory, which had been dimmed, but only for a while, by last year's unhappy disaster.

Tangkoo fell to our hands on the 14th August, and Sir Robert Napier's Division were housed within its walls for the purpose of making the necessary preparations for capturing the forts. Then came the question of the line of attack. Reconnaissances were made, Chinese prisoners were questioned as to the practicability of the roads, and the Commanders-in-Chief held consultation together. But behold! the allied camp was divided. Sir Hope Grant viewed the matter in one light, the French General in another. The question was, What object did we require to gain by the achievement in view? Did we wish merely to get possession of the forts and the right of entry into the river with as little loss as possible? or did we wish to surprise and capture San-kolinsin with all his Tartar hordes, and thus put an end to the possible recurrence of opposition from that quarter, regardless of life on our part, and by the stroke hold the Chinese Government helpless and sub-missive at our feet? Sir Hope Grant's policy pointed to the former, General Montauban's to the latter result. By crossing the river and attacking *en masse* the south fort, we should have cut off all possibility of retreat along the broad road leading to Tien-tsin. With the sea beyond and the river on the left flank,

the Tartars must have succumbed or perished.
Should they have crossed the river and attempted to
escape on the north side, our cavalry would have
taught them a lesson. This would indeed have
humbled the arrogant and vain-glorious pride of San-
kolinsin and his Chinese dependants; but the loss on
our side would most assuredly have been severe. For
the southern fort, with its casemated batteries and
three high cavaliers, was far more formidable than
the other forts, and had the advantage of having its
approach in rear through the long village of Takoo,
which faced the river on the one length, and was girt
with a long crenellated wall five miles long on the
land side right up to the wall of the fort itself. The
experienced military eye of our Commander-in-Chief
saw at a glance that the upper north fort commanded
all the others, and would hence afford a key to the
reduction of the whole. Furthermore, it was within
easy reach, and by no means so strong as most of the
others; and its capture would entail not nearly so
great a loss on our side as that under the French
project. The chief object to be secured was the
possession of the forts and the command of the river;
and if San-kolinsin escaped with the greater part of
his army, which he was almost sure to do, he would
have learnt a lesson not easily forgotten, and would
scarce have spirit enough to meet us again, especially

in the open field. Our object was not to subdue the country, but merely to open a way for negotiations with its Government, and at the less cost of life this was achieved the better for our country. Such were the thoughts and expressions current at the time throughout the army. Sir Hope Grant saw his way clear, and resolved to act upon his original plan, to which General Montauban at last reluctantly lent his support; not, however, without a protest that he would wash his hands of the responsibility, should the attack prove a failure. And during the heat of the fight on the day of the capture, when the incessant booming of cannon reverberated through the air and shook the earth for miles around, a French staff officer was met on a pleasure ride. He was asked why he was not in the thick of the fun? "Ah! monsieur," he replied, "c'est aujourdhui une bagatelle; demain vous verrez la grande chose." But, as we shall see, that *demain* never came.

It was found necessary to have some means of crossing the river other than that of boats, which was a long and tedious process; and the only floating bridge that had existed between the two banks was at Yuchia-poo, and, as before mentioned, was destroyed on the day of the fall of Tangkoo. It was, therefore, necessary to span the river again by a similar means; so it was proposed that a point near Sinho should

form the place of projection. Ropes, anchors, and
other materials, were brought up from Pehtang, and
Sinho and Tangkoo were searched for logs and planking. A number of large, flat, barge-like boats were
found in the dammed up ditches of Tangkoo, and
these came in handy. In passing these boats up the
river, the sailors employed for the purpose were fired
upon by the battery, now repaired and replanted with
guns, which they had so successfully silenced on the
morning of the 14th. A couple of Barry's Armstrongs
were, therefore, at once brought down to the corner of
Tangkoo, and soon put an end to the obstruction.
The boats were all passed up safely, and the bridge
commenced. It was now incumbent to select a spot
on the bank opposite for the termination of the
bridge; and on the 18th, Colonel Lévy, of the French
Engineers, crossed with 300 men to the south side
for that purpose. The river here was scarce more
than 200 yards wide, and on the bank opposite were
a few houses embosomed in orchards, with a good
hedge-flanked road leading circuitously to the highway between Takoo and Tien-tsin. As the party
advanced along this road they were fired upon by the
Tartars ensconced in the orchards on either side.
The French at once threw in skirmishers, and drove
the enemy from their skulking-places. The party
then advanced, until, opening the bushes, they came

in view of a Tartar entrenchment, defended by some two to three hundred Tartars; this they at once carried in a most gallant manner, and finding that they had got into a hive of the enemy's, and that mounted men were swarming from all directions, they sent to General Montauban for reinforcements, who speedily responded to their appeal by a supply of men and guns, and strengthened their force to about 1,400 men; and thus the French succeeded in establishing a position on the opposite side. The footing gained on the south bank before their English allies, may have been one reason which led the French to use such strenuous arguments in favour of the attack on Takoo from that side, as in such case they would have taken the initiative.

On the 19th, the French General also sent a flag of truce to visit the Governor at Takoo, but what transpired at the interview we did not hear.

The few days that had elapsed after the capture of Tangkoo had been occupied by General Napier, amongst other duties, in the planning of roads for the march on Takoo. Instead of using the already constructed causeway, which led on through the gate of our village fortress along the banks of the river to the next village, and so on, a more direct road was projected, farther away from the river, through a gap cut for the purpose in our crenellated mud-wall.

The few ditches between our village and this wall were bridged over, and the mud strengthened with a layer of rushes; then the ditch that encircled the wall had also to be bridged over, and so on, towards the object of attack. On the 19th, the Royal Engineers and Madras Sappers pushed on with their work on the road, and towards evening General Napier asked me to accompany him out to the working party to gather information from the natives as to the best approach to the forts, where the fewest ditches occurred, depth of such ditches, and usual rise and fall of tide in them, &c. Three natives, with two fine mules, had already been captured in a hut not far from the forts. These men were connected with the saltpans in their neighbourhood, which they had continued to work, notwithstanding their propinquity to a hostile force. They were filthily clad, and bore the appearance of poverty and starvation. They were quaking with alarm, yet persisted in telling direct falsehoods. In answer to our questions, they stated that the ditches were intended exclusively for the supply of the saltpans, and had nothing to do with the defences of the fort; that they were poor men, belonging to Tangkoo village, who earned their livelihood by the manufacture of salt, and rarely left the precincts of their works, so that they could give no information as to

the state of the ditches between us and the north
fort ; that the Tartars from that fort, previous to
our capture of Tangkoo, used to issue out and
traverse the country ; but since that event, none had
shown themselves outside the fort. The General
desired me to threaten them with incarceration, if
they would not speak out all they knew ; but still
we gained nothing satisfactory out of them. So
they were quietly handed over to a guard to be
marched away to our village. Fatigue parties of the
67th, under the direction of the Royal Engineers,
worked all night ; and as the remaining preparations
could easily be made on the succeeding night, the
morning of the 21st, at 6 A.M., was fixed on for the
grand *tamásha*.

Betimes on the 20th, Major Graham, of the Royal
Engineers, and Mr. Parkes, advanced towards the
forts, with a guard of the 67th. The guard halted
at about 1,000 yards from the north fort, while the
two former went close up to its walls with a flag of
truce, and asked to have a few words with the officer
in command. That worthy showed his head through
an embrasure, and demanded their business. They
replied that they came to offer terms of capitulation ;
whereat the mandarin became insolent, and said that
he would accept no such terms ; that if the allied
forces wanted the forts, they had better come and

take them. During this short exchange of words, Major Graham had time to look about him and note the strength and form of the fortress. The party returned, and soon after the enemy opened fire from both the northern forts, on the working party. Milward's battery of Armstrongs, which was stationed there in support, returned the salute, and after nearly an hour's exchange of shot, the firing ceased, and the workers continued as before. The enemy's shot had whizzed and plumped about disagreeably near, but no damage was done, save to some campkettles of the 67th.

At last the eve of the battle came, and we felt that the work would be done on the morrow, but not without a struggle; and that many a poor fellow who now laughed, and talked, and made light of the matter, would never see the sun of the 22nd. Every one looked excited, but you could see that there was an uneasiness in their minds. All tried to laugh the matter off, and to appear cheerful, lest they might betray their feelings, for, as Addison teaches us,—

> " Death, in approaching terrible, imparts
> An anxious horror to the bravest hearts;
> Yet do their beating breasts demand the strife,
> And thirst of glory quells the love of life.
> No vulgar fears can British minds control;
> Heat of revenge and noble pride of soul

O'erlook the foe, advantaged by his post,
Lessen his numbers, and contract his host ;
Though fens and floods possest the middle space,
That, unprovoked, they would have feared to pass,
Nor fens nor floods can stop Britannia's bands."

The first part of the night was calm and undisturbed,
save by an occasional hum of voices ; but before midnight the booming of a gun at intervals would startle
the restless slumberers of the camp and bring prematurely to their minds the struggle of the forthcoming
day. But these guns bespoke a still greater uneasiness in the minds of the enemy, who instinctively
felt, notwithstanding the darkness, that our fatigue
parties were advancing with their work. They occasionally shot out a light-ball to discover our position,
at which the men would lie down, and in the case
of the young recruits of the 67th, were hard to
stimulate to work again. It was indeed a night of
endurance for the Engineer officers, but they kept up
their own spirits remarkably well, and exerted their
utmost to inspire confidence into the troops that
assisted them. Their exertions were crowned with
success ; for ere the gray light on the eastern horizon
betold the approaching day, their work was completed.

The artillery was disposed as follows :—A French
24-pounder battery of six pieces, one English 8-inch
gun, and two Armstrongs, were so planted as to play
on the inner south fort, to keep down the fire they

might otherwise pour on our right flank. Two Armstrong guns and two 9-pounders were to fire from Tangkoo across the river at an entrenchment which flanked the French right; three 8-inch mortars were placed in the centre, at 600 yards range, and to the left rear an Armstrong battery, two 32-pounder guns, and two 8-inch howitzers, all of which had orders to play on the fort we were attacking. In addition to this, two 9-pounder guns, four 24-pounder howitzers, the remaining two Armstrong guns, and a rocket battery, were placed in the open ground about 800 yards in front of the fort. On the evening previous, the eight spirals of smoke blackening the seaward horizon intimated that the four English and four French gunboats were arriving at the bar ready to enter the river with the following morning's tide, and shell the lower south fort. The British gunboats appointed to this work were the *Janus, Drake, Clown,* and *Woodcock.*

At daybreak on the morning of the 21st the British force detailed for the attack left their place of encampment, which was on the muddy flat about midway between Tangkoo and the north fort (the whole distance being rather short of four miles), and advanced towards the object of assault. The force mustered 2,500 fighting men, consisting of a wing of the 44th under Lieut.-Colonel McMahon, a wing

of the 67th under Lieut.-Colonel Thomas, supported
by the other wings of those two regiments; the Royal
Marines, under Lieut.-Colonel Gascoigne; a detachment of the Royal Marines, under Lieut.-Colonel
Travers, carrying a pontoon bridge for crossing the
wet ditches; and Ensign Graham, with his company
of Royal Engineers, to conduct the assault. The
whole were commanded by Brigadier Reeves.

The French force were marched through Tangkoo
some time after the British had started. It consisted
of 1,000 infantry, and six 12-pounder rifled cannon,
under the command of General Collineau.

As soon as the daylight admitted of the enemy's
observing the advance of the attacking column, they
opened fire from all the different forts, and the storm
commenced. At half-past six a magazine in the upper
north fort blew up with a terrific roar and explosion,
shaking the ground for miles around as by an earth-
quake, and giving to the idlers at Tangkoo the
impression of a display of fireworks on a grand scale.
Some few minutes afterwards a similar explosion in
the lower north fort occurred, effected by a shell from
the little cluster of gunboats at the river's mouth.

"The field guns were all advanced to within
500 yards of the forts, and redoubled their efforts.
The fire of the forts having almost entirely ceased,
a breach was commenced near the gate, and a portion

of the storming party were advanced to within thirty yards to open a musketry fire ; the French infantry being on the right, the English on the left.

" The fire of our artillery being thus partially compelled to slacken, the enemy emerged from their cover and opened a heavy fire of musketry on our troops.

" The French under General Collineau immediately pushed on to the salient next the river, crossed the wet ditches in the most gallant manner, and established themselves on the berme, whence they endeavoured to escalade the walls ; this, however, they were unable to effect, from the vigorous resistance of the Chinese.

" The efforts of the Sappers to lay down the pontoon bridge were unavailing ; no less than fifteen of the men carrying it being knocked over in one instant, and one of the pontoons destroyed.

" At this juncture Sir R. Napier caused the two howitzers of Captain Govan's battery to be brought up to within fifty yards of the gate, in order more speedily to create a breach, and a space sufficient to admit one man had just been made when our storming party, now joined by the head-quarters wing of the 67th under Colonel Knox, who had partly crossed by the French bridge and partly swam over, forced their way in by single file in the most gallant manner;

Lieutenant Rogers, 44th Regiment, and Lieutenant Burslem, 67th Regiment, being the first to enter, when they assisted in the regimental colours of the 67th, carried by Ensign Chaplain, who first planted them on the breach, assisted by Private Lane, 67th Regiment, and subsequently on the cavalier, which he was the first to mount. At the same moment the French effected their entrance, and the garrison was driven back step by step, and hurled pellmell through the embrasures on the opposite side.

" Here the same obstacles which had impeded our advance obstructed their retreat; in addition to two wet ditches and two belts of pointed bamboo stakes, there was swampy ground and a third ditch and bank.

" The storming parties opened a destructive fire on them from the cavalier, and this was enhanced by the canister fire of Captain Govan's guns, which had been moved to the left of the fort for this purpose.

" The ground outside the fort was literally strewn with the enemy's dead and wounded. Three of the Chinese were impaled on the stakes. A few fugitives reached the outer north fort, which opened fire to cover their retreat, and was answered by the Armstrong guns with good effect."

The above is extracted from Sir Hope Grant's Report to the War Office; but if our readers would like a more particular account of the individual gallantry displayed in the affair by Britain's noble sons, I must refer them to the admirable account of the fight given by *The Times'* special correspondent, and published in *The Times* of 3rd November, 1860.

A short time after the affray, the defiant flags on the walls of the southern forts were hauled down and white flags substituted. It was thought, therefore, that the enemy desired to sue for peace, and accordingly the English and French Generals sent each an officer with Mr. Parkes to inquire what terms they prayed for. The officers were met by the interpreter of English on San-kolinsin's Staff (an impudent native of Shanghai, who had formerly acted as linguist in an American firm at that place). This man produced a letter in which it was written to the effect that, as the allied forces had taken possession of one fort, the Chinese would have the booms removed from the mouth of the river, and grant them the right of entrance up to Tien-tsin, there to make terms of peace. The letter was crumpled up and thrown in the bearer's face, with a threat that if the remaining forts did not unconditionally surrender before 2 P.M., at that hour the advance would be sounded and the next fort stormed.

The sky, which had been clouded over the whole of the morning, now began to look murky and lowering, and before the appointed hour poured down a deluge of rain, converting the hard dried mud of the flat into a slushy swamp; yet, notwithstanding, the 3rd Buffs and the 8th Punjaub Infantry had received orders to march from Tangkoo, and were advanced at 2 P. M. precisely against the lower northern fort. Two 8-inch guns were placed in position against it, but as the other siege guns could not be brought up, owing to the frightful state of the roads, the guns of the cavalier of the captured fort were manned and turned upon it.

The lower north fort had two cavaliers, and mounted many more guns than the upper. With eagerness the English and French troops marched towards it, prepared for the struggle all thought about to ensue; but what was our surprise when not a gun was fired, and the enemy of their own accord threw open the gates!

The garrison, upwards of 2,000 men, passively yielded, like so many sheep, and were sent across to the other side.

Again the southern forts lowered their flags of defiance and substituted the flags of truce, and again Mr. Parkes and others crossed over to the other side. Before evening the enemy were observed evacuating their position on the south side, and 300 English and French were crossed over to take possession of the southern forts. At dark Mr. Parkes returned with

an unconditional surrender of the whole country on
the banks of the Peiho as far as Tien-tsin; and
thus ended the first stage of the North China War,
resulting in the capture of the treacherous batteries
at Takoo, and the cleansing of the foul stain that
tarnished the glory of the allied arms in the far
East.

During the heat of the action all the houses at
Tangkoo had their roofs crowded with lookers on of
the non-combatants, and the ridge of General Napier's
temple had the honour of bearing Lord Elgin and
Staff, *The Times'* correspondent, and many other distinguished personages. While all were engaged
watching with their glasses and a variety of other
optics, the play of the shot on the walls of the north
fort, and the daring advance of the small band of
heroes, the wretched battery at the bottom of the
Tangkoo reach opened fire on our village, and the
shots repeatedly whizzed and whirred over our heads.
The two Armstrongs and the two 9-pounders planted
at the gate of the crenellated wall at length succeeded
in shutting them up, but not till the gunners had
been well soused with mud by the plumping of the
shot close by them. The enemy's range was fortunately too high.

It was a sorrowful sight to pass the litters bringing
back the wounded, each carried by two coolies. Every

one felt anxious as they passed to know what friend
or comrade was inside them. The medical department certainly deserves much credit for the expe-
ditious manner in which the wounded were carried
off the field, and especial praise is due to Staff
Assistant-Surgeon Grey for the active part he took
in this duty, constantly running up to the front with
his assistants and coolies as soon as he spied a wounded
man, and having him carefully conveyed at once to
the rear. Our poor fellows, though often in great
pain, were cheerful when they witnessed the prompt
manner with which their comforts were attended to,
and they all seemed to feel a secret joy in the result
of the day's proceedings, and to forget their pangs in
the consciousness that every man had done the
duty expected of him by his country. A large number
of the casualties were among the officers, twenty-two
of whom were more or less severely wounded. Of
the men, seventeen were killed outright, and 161
wounded. The French had about 130 casualties,
and some of their officers were killed. The loss of
the enemy was large; their dead lay everywhere,
both inside and outside of the fort. Their list of
casualties could not have been less than 2,000, and
probably more. Among the rest, they lost the general
in command of the fort, who fell by the revolver of
Captain Prynne, of the Royal Marines; and his cap

decorated with red button and peacock's feather, was
secured by that gallant officer as a trophy. The
second in command was also missing, and, it was
rumoured among the Chinese, had committed suicide.
The Tartars undoubtedly fought like brave men,
hurling down all kind of uncouth missiles at the
storming party; and when our troops had effected
an entrance, every inch of the ground inside the fort
was disputed. But I cannot help thinking that the
bravery of the enemy was a good deal due to the
peculiarity of their circumstances. By blocking us
out, they had blocked themselves in, and so fell into
a complete trap, from which there was no hope of
escape. They therefore exerted their utmost to keep
out their assailants; but when once in, they could
hardly expect quarter from the excited state of the
men's blood. There was, therefore, no alternative
but to fight hard for their lives. Thus, *magnis com-
ponere parva*, that domestic nuisance the house-rat,
if allowed a chance of escape, is only too glad to
avail itself of it; but if boxed up with a terrier
in a pit, tries hard to bite the jaws that are about
to inflict his death-wound.

The true native cowardice of the race evinced
itself in the submissive conduct of the second north
fort garrison and subsequent unconditional surrender
of the southern forts, notwithstanding the strength

of their position and the heavy armament they contained.

The fearless conduct, however, of the Cantonese coolies in our lines excited considerable admiration. They seemed to enjoy the fun, and shouted with glee at every good shot that carried a murderous mission, no matter whether it committed havoc among the enemy, or bowled over our unfortunate fellows; and those in French employ were conspicuous in the front assisting the troops and standing up to their necks in the ditches holding ladders over their heads to enable the men to cross. All this, it will be argued, shows no lack of pluck in the Chinese character when opportunity is given for its demonstration; but we must not forget that the people from whom these corps were taken were mostly thieves or pirates hardened to deeds of blood, and depending largely upon such acts for their maintenance. They witnessed on every occasion the superiority of our arms and the determined courage of our men, which tended somewhat to dispel their prior alarm, and they were full sure that on their good behaviour depended the earning of that "almighty" dollar for which every Chinaman's soul yearns, and they felt further sure that a backwardness or want of alacrity would have led to their disgrace and perhaps death. Their case was also somewhat hopeless, and, like wise men, they did their utmost to win the good graces of their employers; and so far they succeeded, for the General rewarded each man employed in the front that day with an extra month's wages. Many of the officers maintained that if the Chinese were drilled and led they would make excellent soldiers. This I do not attempt to gainsay, knowing, as all must know, how many of the Asiatics and instinctively-cowardly races, as the Bengalees and Turks, have turned out under such treatment. But I should be inclined to maintain that the habit, so characteristic of the Chinese, of sacrificing every principle of honour and justice to the accumulation of wealth in spite of the doctrines of Confucius, would be found an insuperable barrier to their ever being made good soldiers, unless a lively idea were always kept up in their minds of enriching themselves by the gutting of every captured town. The stupid indifference to death on the part of condemned Chinese culprits, too often produced by the starvation system practised in gaols, or by the individual himself having deadened his own senses by the excessive use of opium, can hardly be quoted as an argument in favour of their bravery. On the other hand, the fear of future retribution among a Christian people may too often tend to cow the bravest spirit; but to one who expects no future, the blank presented to the mind has almost invariably a worse effect. The majority of Chinese, however, have a belief that departed spirits exist independent of the body, and that these spirits enjoy no rest if the bodies meet a violent death or death by decapitation, as relatives are thus prevented from paying the proper attention to the interment of the corpse and its attendant ceremonies. A violent death, therefore, is just as much an object of dread to them as to us, and they have not the advantage we possess of believing in the justice of our cause or in the goodness of God. Moreover, they have not the inherent pluck and love of danger with which the European races are endowed.

Let us now take a glance at those Takoo fortresses which our allied commanders agreed in pronouncing impregnable from the sea, and which were almost unapproachable by land, except during dry weather. The forts were built in the alluvial mud deposit which flanks the river on each side for six or seven miles from its mouth upwards. The course of this stream is very tortuous. Flowing nearly due south from Tangkoo for about a mile, it tends along to the eastward for another mile, skirting the long village of Takoo, situated on the opposite bank; thence turning sharply to the north, it continues on the same course for a mile and a half farther, and finally bending towards the south-east, debouches into the sea. The lower north fort stands on the bank of this last reach, about a mile from the sea, and the upper north fort, which was carried by assault, about half a mile higher up on the same side. Nearly opposite to this fort, and almost in the current of the river, stands the uppermost south fort, commanding the whole reach; and somewhat lower on the south bank, is situated the largest and most formidable of them all—the great south fort,—which witnessed last year the murder of so many of our gallant tars, opposed by Admiral Hope, at such fearful odds, against its gigantic resources. Below this again, and not far from the beach, lies the fifth and last fort. The forts were all built on the same principle, being strong redoubts with thick, heavily-armed ramparts on the sea front; containing casemated batteries, with a mantlet in front of each gun. The upper north fort and the fifth fort had each one cavalier; the second north fort, two; and the large southern fort, three, mounting guns of a large calibre, many of which were taken from the gunboats that were sunk in the treacherous attack of 1859. All these guns were turned inland on the troops. The rear of the forts was protected by a crenellated wall, defended by guns and wall-pieces. The cavaliers were about thirty feet above the level of the ground, reached by a sloping ramp. The walls of the forts

PLAN OF THE
PEIHO FORTS.

NOVEMBER 1860.

IRON STAKE.

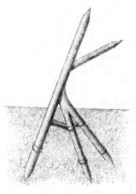

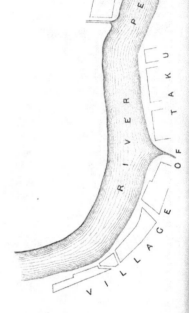

RIVER PEIHO

VILLAGE OF TAKU

SECTION OF FORTS

WET DITCH   BAMBOO STAKES   WET DITCH

Published by Smith Elder

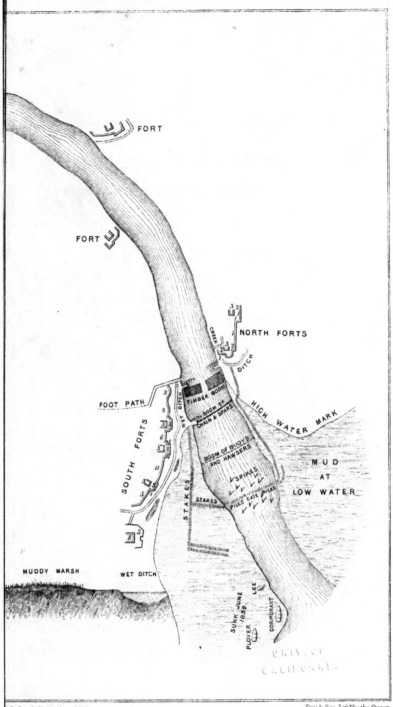

FORT

FORT

NORTH FORTS

CREEK

DITCH

FOOT PATH

WET DITCH

TIMBER BOOM

BOOM OF CHAIN & SPARS

HIGH WATER MARK

SOUTH FORTS

BOOM OF BUOYS AND HAWSERS

SPIKES

STAKES

STAKES

PILES GATE PILES

MUD AT LOW WATER

MUDDY MARSH

WET DITCH

SUNK JUNE 1859

PLOVER

LEE

CORMORANT

65, Cornhill, London, 1861.

Day & Son, Lith\(^{rs}\) to the Queen.

were built of thick logs of timber, cased in with a
coating of mud and flax, or, sometimes, chopped
straw. Besides the barracks afforded by this case-
mating of the rampart batteries, semicircular-roofed
huts of mud and straw, or logs of wood, were distributed about in somewhat neater order, but on
much the same principle as in the fortresses of
Pehtang, Sinho, and Tangkoo. Piles of shot, of
various sizes, lay about near the guns, with baskets
of powder and matchlock bullets. There was also a
number of a species of shell, filled with powder and
connected by a curiously contrived fuse. Gingalls,
matchlocks, bows and arrows, self-loading crossbows,
spears, and pikes, were also strewn about in endless
confusion; and, amongst other hand-missiles, there
were several wooden rollers, one foot in length and
six inches in diameter, stuck all over with long
spikes, and intended, no doubt, for hurling at the
storming party. The approach to each fort was
defended by from two to three encircling ditches and
belts of wooden spikes, while the berme was scattered
with iron crowsfeet. These wooden spikes varied in
thickness and in height from one to three feet, and
each belt was about fifteen feet wide. Beyond the
spikes and ditches, the whole was encircled by an
abattis.

Soon after the forts were occupied, all the wounded

Chinese were collected and put into a hut inside the south fort, whence they were afterwards removed to larger quarters at Tangkoo, soon after our own wounded had been carefully conveyed on board the hospital ships, where every comfort that skill and invention could supply was prepared for them. In this impromptu Chinese hospital we had a display of the various sub-divisions of the great Mongolian race well worthy the contemplation of an ethnologist, albeit the majority of its subjects were more or less contorted with pain. Here were men, on the one hand, giving vent to their feelings in the different dialects of China's northern provinces; and here, again, others lamenting in the short guttural of the Mongolian, and in the more liquid Mantchoorian. On that stove-bed, lying side by side, are represented these three sub-races; there can be no doubt about it, for their speech betrayed them; but there all mark of difference ceases, and I would defy the most accomplished physiognomist to point out which was which.

There is a certain amount of variation in the faces of the Canton men, when compared with the Fuhkeenese or the natives of Shanghai. These variations are somewhat constant, and more charac- teristic than any marks of difference we could observe between the northern big-boned Chinese and the Tartars that San-kolinsin mustered against us from the wilds of Mongolia and Mantchooria. All were alike ugly, with thick yellow skins; all alike dirty and odoriferous. One Chinese boy had nine bayonet pricks in his body. "Ah! sir," said the hospital sergeant to me, "that must be a brave fellow to have got so many wounds before he would give in." I thought to myself that the number and lightness of his wounds was rather a proof to the contrary; so, turning round to him, I asked him their cause. He thereupon told me that he was a cakeseller, who had gone into the fort on the night before our attack, to sell some cakes to the Tartars, and was not allowed to leave again; that on the 21st, as soon as the firing commenced, he went and hid himself under a mat in one of the huts inside the fort. Our troops entered the fort, and some of them, rushing into the hut, pricked him through the mat under which he was hidden. He did not, however, cry out, so they left him; but, soon after, others rushed in and repeated the operation so many times that the unfortunate cakeseller was obliged to betray his hiding-place, and was hauled out in a most unceremonious manner, trembling for his fate; but, to ·his utter astonishment, the devils showed him mercy, and, instead of killing him outright, took him under their friendly protection.

10

A few days after the capture of Takoo, General
Napier reviewed his Division, and in an open-hearted,
frank manner thanked his officers for the assistance
they had so cheerfully afforded him in carrying out
his plans during the late attack, and complimented his
men on the endurance and individual gallantry each
had displayed; and, in conclusion, congratulated one
and all on the successful issue of the struggle which
had so gloriously vindicated the tarnished honour of
our arms.

CHAPTER VII.

. . Bring me into your city,
And I will use the olive with the sword:
Make war breed peace; make peace stint war; make each
Prescribe to other, as each other's leech.

Timon of Athens.

Entrance to the Peiho.—Arrival at Tien-tsin.—Appointment of a
Commission to inspect the Captured Forts.—Head-quarters of
San-kolinsin.—A Ludicrous Scene.—Denizens of a Chinese
Swamp. — Going to Market. — A garrulous Chinaman. —
Chinese Vehicles.—Advance of the Main Body.—Camping
Grounds.—Chinese Villages.

AFTER the capture of Takoo, the gunboats set to
work to clear an entrance into the river. This was
no easy task, as the obstacles that barred its mouth
had been most cunningly contrived. They had first
to remove a row of heavy sharp-pointed iron stakes,
each several tons in weight, which had thin ends
firmly imbedded in the mud beneath. Then came a
large boom, floated by earthen water-jars, and succeeded by iron stakes again ; then a row of boats,
filled with combustible materials, moored right across
the stream ; and, lastly, a second large boom. Two
small hulls, dismantled of all their masts and gear,

10—2

were pointed out in the low-tide mud as the wrecks
of the *Lee* and *Plover* gunboats, which were destroyed
in last year's catastrophe; but of the third missing
boat, the *Cormorant*, no trace was visible.   As soon
as passage-room was procured, the Admiral entered
the river; and on the following day, taking Mr.
Parkes on board, continued on his way to Tien-tsin
in his steam-tender, the *Coromandel*, accompanied by
five gunboats.   The people in the villages on the
banks of the river turned out to stare at the passing
vessels, and showed no signs of hostility, but, on the
contrary, did their utmost to assist their advance.
The forts at the village of Shwang-cheang were passed
and found to be deserted.   In the evening, the
squadron anchored about ten miles below Tien-tsin,
and were visited by a deputation of respectable merchants from the city; from whom they learnt that
the extensive defences lately thrown up by San-
kolinsin for the protection of the city had been
deserted, and that there was no intention to oppose
the march of the victorious allies upon that place.
They were further informed that on the evening of
the 22nd, San-kolinsin had been observed riding past
the city with a few dirt-stained followers, and had
taken a circuitous route in order to avoid entering
the town.   Next morning, the gunboats pushed
on, and, landing small parties of Marines at each

of the forts below Tien-tsin, proceeded up and cast anchor before the city. The viceroy, Hang-fuh, upon invitation, came off to the *Coromandel*, bringing with him the two Commissioners, Hangke and Wantseuen, who had been delegated by the Emperor to escort Lord Elgin to Pekin. They were told that Tien-tsin must be considered in the possession of the allies, but that the local mandarins would be allowed to continue their functions and the people protected. Meanwhile, a party of Marines, who had been sent on shore to take possession of the eastern gate of the city, unfurled the English and French flags on the top of that portal, and posted up a proclamation in the archway, announcing to the people the change in their position. Mr. Parkes then made arrangements with the Committee of Supply, composed of certain well-to-do merchants of Tien-tsin, who had before been employed to cater for San-kolinsin's forces, to bring together provisions for our people, who were shortly to be expected at the city.

The Cavalry Brigade soon received orders to march to Tien-tsin. They started from Sinho on the 25th, with Mr. Wade as interpreter, and, keeping along the north bank of the Peiho, arrived on the following day at Tien-tsin, to which they crossed by the bridge of boats which spans the river just above the junction of the canal from the Pehtang river. They reported

the road moderately good and broad, the only village
of importance passed being the Cheun-leang-ching,
some six or eight miles above Sinho, and that the
country, apart from the orchards that lined the bank
of the river, presented one dreary aspect of bog and
marsh, relieved alone by conical tumuli.

On the 25th, Lord Elgin also pushed up to Tien-
tsin in the steam-sloop *Granada*, whence he shortly
afterwards changed his quarters into a large princely
establishment on shore, situated on the waterside,
and owned by a wealthy Chinese family surnamed
Han. His lordship was soon visited by the Governor-
General of the Province, and informed by that
worthy that he and Kweiliang (who had negotiated
the treaty of 1858) had together been appointed by
the imperial will to treat for peace at Tien-tsin.

I must now request my readers to leave diplomacy
at work, and return with me again to camp. On the
23rd, a commission of English and French engineers
were sent to inspect the captured fortifications, and
note the number and size of the guns that had
fallen into our hands at Takoo, with a view to
dividing them between the allies; two-thirds to the
English and one-third to the French. Mr. Morgan
and myself were desired to accompany the party as
interpreters. We accordingly embarked in a gun-
boat at Tangkoo, and proceeded up the river to

Taleangtsze, a village on the south bank, nearly opposite Sinho. On landing, we found the houses of the hamlet deserted, and the place in the hands of a few French troops, who took us through the orchards in which the village was ensconced, and showed us the few important guns; one of which, of rather larger calibre, was quartered on a housetop, while others, of smaller size, pointed out of holes made through the old mud walls at the back of the hut, and thus formed an impromptu casemated battery. On leaving this village, we walked across the partially-dried mud swamp, some three miles, to the crenellated wall that encircled in rear the long village of Takoo, and connected it with the large southern fort. A French colonel rode after us, and inquired if we had not better be accompanied by a regiment, in case any of the Chinese troops might still be lingering within this long wall. We thanked him, and said there was little fear of that, as we felt pretty sure that it was very un-Chinese for any paid soldier to linger long in a place which his general had abandoned. A ditch occurred between us and the crenellated wall, which we were some time bridging before we could cross over. We found the place deserted, as we had opined. A few villagers still remained, and these did their best to show a friendly feeling.

The task before us was a long and tedious one,

and we found that the evening had set in before we had half done the work. The party had divided into two; the one taking the wall on the right, the other the defences along the river; and it had been agreed to meet at sundown, at a two-storied pagoda in the centre of the village, commonly known as Tan-ga's Yamun, but to the Chinese as the Hai-shin-meao (or Temple of the Spirit of the Sea), where San-kolinsin had held his head-quarters. Not far from this place was a shot factory, and a forge, where the Prince's cunning craftsmen had wrought the iron chains and spikes which were used for the barrier at the river's mouth. On both sides of the temple were improvised huts for the accommodation of the gene-ralissimo's Tartar guard and menials. At the back was a row of storehouses and offices, in the former of which we found, amongst various Chinese warlike implements, numbers of iron crowsfeet, and some wooden dummies, carved and painted, and made to represent native soldiers, their arms and legs working on hinges, and each having a large wooden spike below, for the purpose of fixing it on the walls of their fortresses to scare away the poor ignorant bar-barians. It was laughable to see these figures, some already set in defiant attitudes, and to hear the use for which they were intended. One room was marked " The Prince's study," but it contained little except a few old papers and documents, none of which were of much interest. On telling the villagers that we intended passing the night there, they soon supplied us with enough provisions for a supper, and we made ourselves very jolly. But our jollification did not last long, for soon the snorting of a gunboat off the village intimated to us that we were to return for the night to the camp. The General, in the plenitude of his heart, had got the mistaken notion that we did not know how to take care of ourselves. We were accordingly obliged to return; and next morning steamed down to the south fort, where we commenced our labours again. The examination of the forts occupied the whole day; and as we had got permission this time to pass the night at Takoo, we repaired, at near sundown, to the temple again.

The only green spot in this neighbourhood is within the sacred walls, where, in the courtyard garden round the pagoda, a few bier-trees flourished, with unripe berries hanging from their branches, and a few trellised vines formed leafy bowers, but presented no clustering offerings to the god of wine. The Chinese *Tsaou*, called Bier by the Anglo-Indians, is a somewhat cylindrically shaped fruit, about an inch and a half long by three quarters in diameter. When arriving at maturity, it turns from a light green to a pale yellow, and then dries to a rich chesnut brown.

It contains a long seed or kernel, pointed at both
ends. When fresh, it is hard and slightly sweet;
but boiled in sugar, and then dried, it forms an
excellent conserve, called by the Chinese, *Me-*
(Honey) *Tsaou*, and known to Europeans in China
as the *Shanghai date*. The leaves of the tree on
which the fruit grows are small and annual, and the
flowers diminutive and of a pale yellow. Small as
this patch of garden was, it was curious to note the
number and variety of the birds that gathered there at
roosting time: flycatchers of three species, warblers,
yellow wrens, gold-crests, buntings, and sparrows, all
busily engaged procuring their last mouthful, before
the setting sun withdrew his farewell ray and bid
them to their roosts. We took the hint ourselves,
and setting some men to work with the culinary
department, looked about for a suitable place to
deposit our limbs during the hours of darkness.
There was an upper floor in the two-storied pagoda,
full of large ugly josses, which offered the advantage
of planking instead of tiles to lie upon, and, procuring
a few bundles of hay from San-kolinsin's store-rooms,
we soon made ourselves soft couches, not very inviting, it is true, to those who have been nursed in
the lap of luxury, on account of the filth and insects
below and the numerous mosquitoes above; but do
such things trouble a weary man? The villagers

brought us a sheep, and fowls, and some rice, and
left us to make ourselves comfortable, with a promise
to return next morning. Soon after dawn, as I was
preparing to go down below, with as little noise as
possible, for fear of disturbing my comrades, I met
an old man on the stairs, with some fish he had
brought for sale. He ascended, and raising his head
above the floor on which the sleepers lay, cried out,
" Great kings, arise! I have brought some fish!"
It was a ludicrous scene, and one that would have
tickled the most seriously disposed into fits of
laughter; the old man's head appearing above the
boards on the one side, with an expression of fear
and veneration, and the begrimed state and sleepful
attitudes of the great kings on the other.

This morning's search discovered to us a magazine
containing large quantities of powder, shot, sulphur,
and saltpetre, built on a small island encircled by a
ditch. Several of these had been blown up on the
night of the 20th, we were informed; and this
accounts for sundry loud explosions we witnessed in
the direction of Takoo, though many of the minor
flickerings of light, which continued almost every
minute during that portentous eve, can be attributable to no other than the electric effect of sheet
lightning on the distant horizon. One of the sufferers
from a magazine explosion was brought to us for

medical aid. His skin was almost entirely burnt off him, and his face presented a confused mass of raw flesh, in which it was difficult to distinguish any of the features. Several wounded were still lying about in some of the houses, and many a rotting carcase polluted the atmosphere, unheeded by the stolid inhabitants of adjoining houses. Bad smells they were accustomed to, and as the deceased or wounded was no friend of theirs, what did it concern them? When our work was over we crossed the river to the other bank. Carcases innumerable floated up and down with every tide, bringing forcibly to one's mind the frequent state of the Bengal Hooghly; but in the case of the Peiho there were no vultures to hasten the dissolution of the corrupting masses. We had noted in all between 500 and 600 guns, 50 or so of which were of brass, and many of a very large calibre.

The country between Tangkoo and Pehtang, consisting as it did of flat mud and alluvial ooze, occasionally subjected to inundations, and intersected with salt pools and ditches, afforded peculiar attractions to the large flights of wild fowl, which were at this time bent on their southerly migrations from the plains of Mantchooria and other inhospitable regions of north-east Asia. Between these two villages, moreover, the sea formed a shallow estuary, bringing with its advancing and receding wave abundance of food for beach-loving birds, who found here a quiet retreat from the rude gales that raged along the more exposed face of the shore. Farther inland, the low reeds and tangle that covered the harder ground, harboured innumerable hares, which would frequently start from close under the wayfarer's feet and bound away into the distance; while the rush-girt marshes and quaking bogs, which also occurred amongst the harder ground, invited the waders and scolopaceous birds. One ramble alone was sufficient to convince you how, at this season, this flat teemed with animal life, of which the evidence was also strong in the appearance of so many hawks and harriers, which were constantly seen sailing or hovering in the sky overhead. To a sportsman, equally as well as to a naturalist, the marsh held out amusement without end. The general reader, who probably believes that no water-birds exist except what are included by him under the heads snipe, woodcocks, ducks, and geese, and who would scarcely recognize even the plovers as " they scatter o'er the heath, and sing their wild notes to the listening waste,"—such a reader will not benefit by a list of the birds observed on this swamp. I will, therefore, reserve my notes on this subject for a separate publication to edify the more studious lover of nature.

The 3rd Buffs were left to garrison the Takoo
forts, and the rest of the army received orders to
advance on the march to Tien-tsin, the First Division
to start on the 29th, and the Second Division two
days after.   On the 28th I crossed over to the Takoo
village again with another officer on Sir R. Napier's
Staff, for the purpose of surveying the roads in that
neighbourhood, and for procuring carts for the
General's baggage.   We examined a walled Tartar outpost between the village and the main Tien-tsin road.
It contained no guns or warlike gear of any description, but abounded in dirt, filth, and insects.   A few
ragged villagers were now carrying away the dirty
mats and logs of wood that remained.   Along the
highway we then continued to a mud-built roadside
house, about two and a half miles from Takoo, which
supplied teacakes and tobacco to passengers.   On the
roof of this hut my companion mounted, while I
conversed with the people, and took note of what was
passing on the road.   Files of natives were wending
their way to the south forts, each man with a pole
across his shoulders, from either end of which was
suspended a basket containing fruit and vegetables,
or fowls and ducks, for the market already established
at the gate of the fort.   Rich water-melons, with
green coatings and juicy yellow or pink pulp; pump-
kins of various form, cabbages, onions, and garlic;

apples with such rosy cheeks, but alas! boasting no taste; pears, peaches, and gigantic apricots, and such delicious grapes, the large luscious purple, the long cylindrical muscatelle, and the small sweet Saxony. All these lay temptingly disposed in the baskets as I watched the market-men jogging past in their half-trot pace. Men with empty baskets, and strings of copper cash thrown over their shoulders, were on their way back, chatting and chaffing one another at the good bargains they had made. The people evidently had confidence established amongst them again; and cartloads of ugly damsels were hurrying back to the village which they had but lately left in such dire alarm, satisfied with the change of affairs, and apparently preferring the dollar-abounding barbarian to the thieving, niggardly Tartar. I entered into conversation with a pursy old gentleman with a fat, good-natured face. "Ah!" said this worthy, "your honoured country has given those Tartars a good thrashing." "Why," replied I, "you appear as if you were pleased at the event." "Pleased! surely I am pleased," said he; "was not the whole of this country groaning with the burden these Tartar rogues imposed on us? What need was there of squeezing the people to build forts for the purpose of driving you away? We felt sure that your object in coming here was for the purposes of trade, and surely that was a boon for both countries! But these Tartars, who acquired this country themselves by treachery, are naturally jealous of the advance of every other nation, because they are suspicious, and think that the main object of all other people is to wrest away from them by treachery what they won by the same base means."

"You do not, then, identify yourself with the Tartars?"   "I should say not; they are a wretched, filthy horde from the wilds of Mongolia, who love to oppress the people, and steal from them all they possess.   We were truly alarmed to see the change affairs took last year, when your ships retired defeated, and we naturally feared that you would return and wreak your vengeance on the unfortunate villagers, who were forced against their will to subscribe to the erection of the batteries that occasioned your treacherous repulse, when we knew you were coming on a mission of peace."

"But on the capture of the forts, you were agreeably disappointed at the treatment you met with at our hands?"   "We were indeed; and more astonished still at your magnanimity in releasing the prisoners you had taken at the forts, and in attending to the enemy's wounded that fell into your hands.   If reports are true, you treated the Tartar wounded better than they did themselves."   "Such is always

the custom among Western nations." " It is not so
here. It is the custom with the Tartars to torture
and kill all that fall into their hands. Most of us
that remained at Takoo watched from our housetops
the progress of the fight, and we were stricken with
wonder to see the way that your troops advanced
under fire. There was no dropping to the rear, and
halting at a distance, as with us. Your people
always seemed to advance in spite of the ravages that
the shot made in your lines, until the work was done.
Surely such gallant troops must eventually conquer
the world." I tried to explain to him that this daring
conduct was a good deal owing to discipline; but he
continued: " The Tartars were a good deal ashamed
of this defeat, and said that it was chiefly owing to
the accidental explosion of their magazines, which
took place inside the forts, and destroyed so many of
the garrison; that one of their big guns had killed
200 of your men, but that your numbers were so overwhelming that there was no standing against them."

I told him that the whole of our casualties were
scarce higher than that figure; and that we had comparatively few men killed, whereas the bodies of no
less than 2,000 Tartars lay about the field of operations, marking the havoc that had been committed
amongst them. He replied, that of course he could
not question the veracity of either party, but that he

11

could at least congratulate us on the successful issue
of that day's work, and felt sure that he spoke the
sentiments of all the villagers, when he thanked us
for our forbearance towards them, and only hoped that
now we were masters of the field we would maintain our mastery, and hold possession of the country
that we had so ably acquired.

The descent of my companion from the housetop
here put an end to the Chinaman's garrulity; and
having secured one of the country carts that passed,
we rode back to the village.   I have made no excuse
for introducing the above dialogue, as it gives a good
idea of the feeling of the people in that neighbourhood towards the conquering allies, as expressed in
numerous conversations that myself and others held
with them.   We asked our way to a baiting stable,
and there found only three carts.   Those we ordered
to be got ready; and my companions having to go
back at once to Tangkoo, I volunteered to accompany
them round over the floating bridge to Sinho. While
waiting about the stable, an old gentleman, who lived
a few doors off, came round and begged me to honour
his humble shed with my presence.   I accepted the
polite invitation, and discussed Chinese politics with
him over pipes and tea. He asked me if the General
would have any objection to their women returning to
the village ?   I replied, certainly not; that as long as

the people showed themselves peacefully disposed, our authorities would take care that no harm should befall them from any acts of violence on the part of the soldiers. He was so overwhelming with civilities, that I was not a little glad when the carts were ready to start. As our readers will feel a little interested in the vehicles used in this part of the country, from the fact of their having been the mode of conveyance by which the great American Minister was carried *in state* to the Chinese metropolis, it will be necessary here to make a few remarks on them.

Imagine, then, a narrow box with an arched roof, trellised over, and curtained in front, placed without springs on stout wheels, and floored inside with boards, without raised seat or cushions of any description. A shaft running out on each side, between which the pony or mule is harnessed, with a second pony at end tandem fashion, but attached by a long trace fastened to the axle-pole; all the harness or horse-gear made of rough leather and bits of brass and iron rings; the driver running alongside, or perched on the right on the side of a box between the shafts, with a long stick in his hand, from the top of which is hung a thin piece of twisted cord; and you have a picture of the simple rustic cart of the country. The private turn-outs, however, are lined with coarse cloth outside and sometimes inside, with

11—2

a blue awning projecting from the roof. It was first a question how to get in, as there were no steps; this the driver showed me was to be effected by a sprawling-out of my arms to the danger of upsetting the whole concern, while he pushed me up from behind. I had then to sit cross-legged within, and steady myself with a hand against each side; and off we started for the bridge of boats; but the roads were not of the smoothest, and before I was prepared for it down went one wheel into a rut, and bang went my head against the side of the box, from which I had hardly recovered when down went the other wheel into another rut, and thwack went my cranium on the other side. I felt annoyed, and tried to lean back, but the posture was uncomfortable. I then tried a recumbent posture, but the boarding was so horribly hard. I thought of poor Mr. Ward and staff, and groaned for the sufferings they must have endured. Fancy 160 miles from Pehtang to Pekin in such a conveyance! At last I got out, and dangled my legs from the shaft, as the driver was doing occasionally, having to jump out when a deep rut was encountered. This position was not so bad; yet it is not unusual in this country to see a couple of women and three children crammed inside one of these boxes, with a fat paterfamilias sitting in front, and the driver on the shaft. The tortures they must endure! To think that the

Chinese who enjoy such a savage invention should look proudly from its discomforts, and have the face to brand all other nations as " barbarians ! " I felt myself worked up into a mood, and would have felt much pleasure just then in being introduced to the veteran inventor of the article. But it was absurd to think of the possibility of such an event, as, if our sinologues were asked, they would possibly refer the date of his existence to some thousands of years B.C. ; and this antiquated style of equipage would afford another of the numerous proofs that the Chinese had progressed to this length of civilization during the period that other nations ranged wild in the forests, and that their inventive genius came to a standstill just when the Europeans began to develop theirs.

But enough : such antiquarian discussions are too abstruse for these pages. We at last arrived at the pretty orchards and hedgerows of " Seaou-leang-tze," a small village facing the floating bridge. It was slow work passing through the crowds of French and riflemen, who had already crossed the river. Just as we reached the bridge of boats, and commenced to cross over, the naval officer in charge desired me to halt the carts, as he was going to open the bridge to allow one English and one French gunboat to pass through on their way up to Tien-tsin. The Englishman went through all right, but the clumsy little French *Canonière*, with her forepart twice as high out of the water as her stern, answered badly to her rudder in so strong a tide, and charged to the right of the opening, breaking and crushing the planking of the bridge, and sinking one of the large boats that floated it. Then such a scene ensued—the Britishers not knowing a word of French, and the Frenchmen not a word of English, all hands vociferated and objurgated in their mother tongues without much effect on the understanding of either party. I retired from the scene, and got my carts stowed in a safe corner under a guard while I crossed in a boat to the other side to visit the camp of the First Division, near Sinho. I there heard that it would be midnight before the bridge could possibly be again passable, such mishaps having occurred no less than three times before, for the tide ran so strong in that part of the river that it required great management to steer the most easily-handled boat through the opening. General Michel very kindly asked me to dine with himself and Staff, so that it was past nine when I returned to the bridge. The accident had been made good, but the artillery of the First Division had already begun to cross, so I should have to wait until they had all passed over. The horses were all unharnessed from the gun-carriages and waggons, and these were then run down the wooden declivity from the bank by a swarm of Canton coolies. The impetus thus given to the curricle was easily kept up until the acclivity on the other bank was reached. As the heavy waggons charged over the bridge, the planking, which was by far too thin and narrow, rose on either side like a troubled sea, and had to be rearranged to receive the passage of the next waggon. The small portion of the bridge on the north bank which had been put together by the French showed far better execution than that entrusted to our engineers and sailors; but then it must be remembered that the materials our men had to work on were not of the best description. As soon as the waggons were across the river they had to be hauled up the acclivity, and this was no easy work, but had to be gradually effected by means of wedges and levers, accompanied by a great deal of screaming and cheering. It took about three hours getting the artillery of the First Division across, and then some French artillerymen, who had all this time been kept on the south side blaspheming at the lubberly slowness of the English, started their lighter waggons in drag of six horses at a trot across the bridge. They managed the transit very easily, but the first waggon as nearly as possible came to grief at the acclivity on the opposite side. My turn at last came; so hurrying my carters to harness in, I got across all safely, and rode briskly into Tangkoo by the moonlight at about two in the morning, much to the astonishment of the different sentries posted along the road.

The First Division broke up their camp on the 29th, and crossing the river commenced their march to Tien-tsin ; and the Second Division received orders to march two days after, leaving the 3rd Buffs to garrison the forts. The inhabitants of Tangkoo, when they heard we were about to leave, mustered in large numbers at the gates of the village. They were anxious to be apprised of the exact hour of our departure, as they feared that mobs of thieves from the surrounding villages would rush in on our leaving and plunder the houses of what little they now contained. They particularly desired, as it was against our rules to admit the householders into the village while we held it, that we would also keep out the low gang of thieves whom they were continually meeting laden with sacks of millet or salt fish stolen from the village. It certainly was true that while the sentries had orders to prevent Chinese from entering at the gate, nothing was done to keep out the ragamuffins that entered from the river front or over the crenellated wall in rear. The respectable inhabitants then begged that each householder should be allowed to station a man at his own house to keep out these thieves, but they were told in reply that this could not be permitted, as the men they would station in the village would probably be as great thieves as the others, and avail themselves of the opportunity of stealing from our baggage; that theirs was the fortune of war, and that they must bide the chance.

General Napier, however, in the goodness of his heart desired me to promise them, as a trifling indemnity for their losses, all the refuse ponies belonging to the Military Train, which had been pronounced unfit for work; but when it was found that a very large percentage was in that state, and that the Military Train and Commissariat made some demur to the promise, its fulfilment was deferred until the return of the army from Pekin. Upwards of ninety of these poor beasts, which through bad treatment and starvation had become reduced beyond all hope of recovery, had been shot; 150 more remained which would certainly be unfit for work for the next two months to come; but forage was cheap, and it was more expedient to feed up the animals and give them a chance of recovering themselves, than to throw them away on the needy villagers. Thus thought the Military Train, and to their persuasion the General yielded; but I must say I felt rather foolish when, after promising the present to the villagers, and assembling a lot of their magnates together to receive it, I had to tell them instead that the General thought better of his promise, and preferred keeping the horses until the campaign was over.

On the 31st August our division evacuated Tang-koo at 4 P.M., and encamped under canvas near the bridge of boats, with the intention of crossing over the first thing next morning. The clouds were gathering dark overhead, and threatening rain; each one, therefore, set to work to entrench his tent in and make it waterproof. Next morning, at gray dawn, the bugle sounded, and we were up, tents and baggage packed and secured on the tops of our carts or ponies, and the whole division soon streaming across the rickety bridge to the orchards on the opposite bank, where we were ordered to halt and pitch our tents. Beyond the few houses and gardens on the river's bank was a large grassy plain, stretching out southward to the broad road that led from Takoo to Tien-tsin, and blending on the other side of that highway with the marshy ground. On this plain the greater part of the division encamped, while a favoured few were allowed to occupy the orchards. The best of these was, of course, selected for the lot of the head-quarters, and it was no small pleasure to be recumbent on the fresh grass strewn beneath us for a couch, and watch the overhanging branches of fruit-trees swayed playfully to and fro by the gentle breeze, or rambling, gun in hand, among the leafy mazes of the orchards, when released from work before sundown, to study the ever-varying face of nature in so novel a locality. But one interpreter to a large division has not much time to devote to sylvan studies. On arriving at a new encamping ground, he has to parley with the natives, to try and calm their fears, and induce them to establish a market for provisions. He has then to procure guard-houses for the sentries, who are required to be posted at the different villages; and after that he has constantly to be at hand to interpret in any disputes or rows, which too frequently arise between the soldiers and natives. On breaking up an encampment, his services are again required by the commissariat, and, like the members of that body, after a long day's march, when the rest of the army are enabled to make all snug and take a quiet rest in gentle Morpheus' lap, the interpreter's work only then commences, and is accompanied throughout with much bustle and torment; and yet, at the outset of the campaign, the Commander-in-Chief ruthlessly refused to acknowledge them as mounted officers, and gave orders that they were not to be supplied with horses. On arriving at the encamping ground, I was at once despatched to the village of Seaou-leang-tsze,

about three-quarters of a mile up the river's bank.
The people were already much alarmed by the
appearance of some Punjaubees armed with big
sticks, whom they described to me as devils in loose
white garments.   This hamlet consisted of a few
dirty-looking mud-built houses, being hardly worthy
the name of a village.   The French had evidently
taken the place under their protection, as most of
the better houses had bits of red paper pasted over
their doorways, with inscriptions scrawled in French,
such as "Défense d'entrer;" and one inscription,
evidently done by some wag, ran thus—"Il y a ici
du beau gras; mais helas, Français! la place est
signée, ne touchez pas."   The people were dirty and
filthily clad, as usual, but in great fear, and anxious
to do anything whereby they might win our good
graces.   They readily promised to do their utmost
to bring fresh vegetables to a spot where I pointed
out the market should be; but their supplies were
short, owing to the frequent pillage of their gardens
by the French who were encamped near.   When I
spoke of a guard to protect them from straggling
soldiers, they were wondrous pleased at our consideration, and at once got ready a house to accommodate
it.   In the evening I took a walk along the river
bank.   The bed over which the river runs is formed
of clay, but the downward stream brings with it large

quantities of mud, which is partially deposited along
its rush-lined banks. The water is too muddy to
drink when first drawn, but is speedily rectified by
the application of a little alum, which soon deposits
the mud at the bottom, and leaves the fluid above
clear and colourless. The Chinese here were well
acquainted with this peculiar property of alum, and
a lump of this mineral was to be found in most
houses. Mr. Abbot, chaplain to the Marines, who
was attached *pro tem.* to the Second Division, used
generally to supply himself with a pocketful of alum
when going the rounds of the camp, and frequently
won the hearts of the simple soldiery by purifying
the filthy liquid they were drinking by the use of this
juggle, as they termed it, the chemical properties of
which were to them quite mysterious and inexpli-
cable. On the river's bank was a path used by barge
towers; then came a ditch and a hedge, and then
orchards, and gardens, and patches of corn; divided
again by hedges and ditches, and insterpersed with
huts. Many of the winter birds of South China
were here revelling in the congenial sunshine of a
Peiho summer. As I wandered along I heard the
loud uniform footfall as of a regiment marching over
wooden boards, and, looking to the bridge of boats,
observed the red coats of the 99th. They had come
all the way from Pehtang that day in order to join our

march. The men were much fagged and required a
day's rest after their long tramp ; and as the General
also wished the First Division to be well ahead of
us before we started, a halt was ordered for the whole
of next day. But a commissariat officer and myself
were despatched in the afternoon to the next encamping ground, to gather together supplies, and make
provision for the reception of the force there on the
following day. The General kindly provided me
with a horse from Milward's Battery; so starting
at 3 P.M., with four orderlies, we soon rattled over
the ground. We rode through the village of Seaou-
leang-tsze, and, deviating a little from the river's
bank, got into the main road from Takoo to Tien-
tsin. Along this we continued, the country still
maintaining its marshy character, and abounding in
water-birds. Snipe flushed up with a cry as we
passed; herons stalked about the reeds and gazed at
us with indifference ; while terns and black-capped
gulls hung in mid air over our heads, making game
of us, as if conscious that duty kept us from making
game of them.

The first village passed was " Hwang-chia-cheuen,"
consisting of a straggling series of mud houses of no
great extent. The road then carried us through a
larger and more thriving village of one long street,
called " Sin-ching," or the New City, in which the

temples and a few of the better houses were of brick
and tiled.   Then came a small place, by name
" Yang-hwey," a few miles farther on; and, lastly,
" Kih-koo," our destination ; the whole distance
being about nine miles. The First Division had,
probably, left word that we should shortly make our
appearance, for a large crowd of respectably dressed
villagers were awaiting our arrival; and, on our asking
to see the head man, led us to a large temple, where
accommodation was cheerfully supplied to our steeds
in the courtyard, and to ourselves in the numerous
houses adjoining. The magnates of the village soon
attended on us, and we informed them that we were
the precursors of the division, and had come to make
arrangements for the reception of the troops on the
following morning. They accompanied us to a plain,
about three-quarters of a mile beyond the village,
and showed us the ground previously occupied by the
First Division ; and having pointed out where we
wished the forage and fuel to be stored, and the
market to be held, we returned to the temple.
" Kih-koo " is a large and substantial village, with a
cleaner-looking class of inhabitants than the majority.
But its streets are narrow, tortuous, and dirty; the
main road crossing, by means of a wooden bridge,
a ditch from the river, on which the village stands.
A dinner had been prepared for us at the temple, and

a garrulous old man appointed to attend on us. This individual, by profession a cook, was short and stout, with a funny leer in his eye, and appeared before us naked down to the waist. On our giving any orders, he would turn round and repeat it, with a very loud noise, as if transmitting it to some other menial, who was invisibly waiting to carry it into execution; but as there were no others in the room at the time but the old man and ourselves, and as he went out at once to procure what we wanted, we discovered that it was a plausible attempt on the part of this grotesque individual to make us believe that we had no end of attendants awaiting our beck and call. We want some water to wash in, we would quietly say to the old man, who would at once turn round, and roar it through the hall, "The great kings want some water to wash in;" then out he would slip quietly and return with it. As soon as we had finished regaling ourselves, we were waited on by the heads of the village. These were as fine specimens of native opulence as you could find; and though rather noisy in conversation, did full justice to the many ceremonies of Chinese courtesy. But the society of Chinese is always repulsive to the European, owing to the frequent expectorations and other offensive habits which they too often indulge in: while they taint the air with the far from ambrosial fumes of their sickly-smelling pipes. We learned that our visitors were wealthy merchants engaged largely in the North China junk trade; and as there were no officials appointed by the government to control their large and flourishing village, they had formed themselves into a protective committee; and they were very desirous to provide us with all the necessaries our force required at a moderate cost, in order to enable us to pass quietly through without the risk of incurring our displeasure. The greater part of the evening was spent in arranging for the morrow's commissariat, till at last, thoroughly done up, we laid ourselves supine on the stove-couch, as a quiet hint to our friends that the night was fast waning. They politely rose, and ordered servants to supply us with pillows and coverlets, and bade us " Chin-chin."

Next morning at cockcrow we were on the encamping ground, superintending the stowage of supplies. In a few hours' time, the Quartermaster-General of the Division, accompanied by the Quartermasters of the different regiments, arrived and measured off the ground to be occupied by each regiment; and soon after the band of the advancing column broke on our ear, and the red coats burst into view from the narrow opening of the village. Then came the usual work and bustle before alluded to.

12

The ground selected for the camp was low and swampy. The General, therefore, wisely selected the raised road for himself and Staff, it being sufficiently broad to admit of carts passing, and the usual traffic going on, without interfering with the row of tents that lined the road. The road was flanked on each side by a wet ditch; on the left lay the camp, and on the right a series of corn-fields, with a few small mud huts under some stunted trees. Leaving his tent during the heat of the day, Sir R. Napier had a ladder placed across the ditch, and betook himself to the refreshing shade afforded in the huts. While indulging in the midday siesta after the fatigue of the march, he was favoured by a visit from the magnates of the village; and a native from Shanghai, who owned several junks lying in the river bound to that port, also paid his respects, praying the General to give him a letter to the Admiral that these boats might be allowed to pass out of the river. The General courteously received these visits, and, exchanging compliments with them, gave the Shanghai man the letter for which he entreated. A junk was then hired to carry some sick men down to Takoo, and some more boats to carry to Tien-tsin the packs of the foot-sore soldiers, as the men were found to suffer much during their short marches from carrying such heavy loads in addition to their other accoutrements.

In the afternoon, Mr. Wingfield, the Commissary, and myself were despatched, as before, to the next encamping ground. The raised road continued in a westerly direction through a dreary tract of marsh and swamp on either side, until we arrived at the village of "Heen-shuy-koo" (or Salt-water Mart), so called from its being the highest point of the river where the tidal influx of salt water reaches. This village was also touched by the river, which on leaving Kih-koo deviates a long way to the right of the road before it re-bends towards this spot. Mud houses, again, and little appearance of wealth, though the village enjoys a large junk trade. We rode through Heen-shuy-koo, and emerged into more cultivated land: the farther we advanced the larger grew the waving fields of coarse millet (*sorghum*) and maize, until we arrived at the pretty grove of willows, with a terrace of clean-looking houses, that marks the entrance to "Peh-tang-kow." We rode boldly into the village and asked for the head man. A neatly-dressed juvenile represented himself as the person we sought, and conducted us to a public hall, which was a small, neat, little room, with tiled floor, and decorated with old saws and fine sayings on red fancy paper that glittered from its walls. On our asking to be conducted to the ground where the First Division had encamped, he called a

12—2

cart, and sprawling in, with one dandy-stockinged leg hanging out, rattled away before us, leaving us to follow on our animals after him. About a mile from the village, we arrived at five small forts, now dismantled, that formed the defence of the river at "Shwang-chiang," which village was situated a little farther on, across a wooden bridge that spanned a creek from the river. "Shwang-chiang," or Double River, earns its name from its position on the angle of the river, which trends to the right and left, and thus gives the appearance of a double river. The villagers at Peh-tang-kow showed much more alarm at our appearance than those at Kih-koo, and, as we traversed its streets, our friend in the stockings, who rode in advance, shouted out to the "ladies," as they loitered, with true feminine curiosity, to have a peep at the "barbarian," to run and hide themselves. I accused him afterwards of his want of courtesy in so doing; he replied that he had no intention of being discourteous, but, on the contrary, was afraid of hurting our delicacy by a rude display of the weaker sex in the public thoroughfares through which we were passing. Rain had fallen during the night, and the ground was, consequently, wet and slippery next morning when we appeared at the camping ground. After all arrangements had been made, and still no arrival, we grew impatient, and rode to meet the troops. Back to Heen-shuy-koo, and yet no sign of the advancing column. Here, leaving Wingfield to return to his commissariat preparations, I rode on, and, before reaching the camp, met a couple of Seikh troopers (orderlies to the General), who had a letter for me, inquiring after the state of the road. I galloped on, and found the camp still standing, the march being deferred till my answer should be received. Much more rain had fallen in the neighbourhoood of Kih-koo, and the ground on which the tents stood was all but a complete swamp. The General was anxious, therefore, to proceed, and orders were soon circulated to strike tents. The Commissariat was, as usual, in difficulties in settling with the villagers for provisions supplied, and I found my return most opportune.

We were soon again on the march, and arrived before evening at the forts, the total distance being about eleven miles. The large fields of tall millet so encroached upon the open plat of ground in rear of the forts, that the troops had to be distributed in the forts as well. The next march would bring us to Tien-tsin, where all arrangements had already been made for the reception of our Division; and we were not, therefore, required to go in advance.

At 4 o'clock next morning, the bugle sounded the "reveille;" tents were struck, and in an hour we were on the march. Villages were more frequent, and cultivation general; the total distance being about ten miles. My services were not required in the front, so the horse I was favoured with was no longer lent, and I had to trudge the distance on foot.

We passed through Hwey-tsin, Chin-tang, and then Too-ching. At this latter village a halt was called, while the advance officers rode on to head-quarters to receive orders about the encamping ground. This occasioned a most tedious delay, of two hours' duration, in the hot sun. Every one was nearly driven crazy. At last the advance bugle sounded, and on we went through Leang-chia-yuen and Ma-chia-kow, and then deviating to the left, wended our way along lanes, through unceasing fields of towering maize and millet, till the large grassy plain in front of the walls of Tien-tsin opened to view, with the distant gathering of tents of the advance army. The bands of our Division struck up as in high glee, and we soon sought refuge from the sun's burning glare, lying prostrate in our tents, sipping at intervals the cooling iced drink which our "cupid" served to us, and at intervals puffing the fragrant smoke from our weed, as we contemplated the numberless swallows playing with airy evolutions over our heads, and dealing destruction among the incessant plague of flies that blackened with their numbers the inside of our tents, and kept buzzing incessantly in our faces.

CHAPTER VIII.

. . . . Hast thou not,
Beneath thy sovereign's name, basely presum'd
To shield a lie ? . . . . .
. . . . But know,
This poor contrivance is as weak as base.
* * * *
Had my resolves been wavering and doubtful,
This would confirm them, make them fixed as fate.
This adds the only motive that was wanting
To urge them on through war and desolation.

Tancred and Sigismunda.

San-kolinsin's Tactics. — Description of Tien-tsin. — A Scientific
Mission.—" Own Correspondents."—Chinese Duplicity.—Ad-
vance of the Allies.—A Topographical Department.—Russian
Secretary.—Description of the Country.—Yang-tsun Village.—
Flag of Truce.

THE approach to Tien-tsin from the river, as we
before remarked, was defended by a small fort on
each bank of the Peiho, situate about two miles below
the city. Inland from these forts on either hand
extended long crenellated walls, which, taking a semicircular sweep, girded the town, its suburbs, and a
portion of the adjoining plain, and was only divided
again by the course of the river above the city. The
whole length of this wall was estimated at fifteen
miles, and, had it been defended by sharpshooters,
it might have given considerable annoyance to the

advance of the Allies. This mud wall was of recent construction, and had been thrown up, as we learnt, at the cheap rate of 15*d*. the current foot. The forts showed signs of recent occupation, but the wall bore no marks of mounted guns, and was evidently raised as a bugbear to frighten at a distance, with the probable intention of beating back light-armed troops; an idea having prevailed among the Chinese that we were a peculiarly maritime race, who could only manœuvre large guns on shipboard, and who were quite unpractised in field artillery. The foretaste, however, which the Tartars had of our Armstrongs on the seaboard induced them to change their views, and to yield passively to our army the fortresses which were intended only to compete with our navy.

San-kolinsin had proved himself a good engineer by the masterly manner in which he had constructed the forts, and made them impregnable from the sea; as a general he was hardly to be blamed for having miscalculated his enemy. He had hitherto only contended with a naval power, and had shown himself fully equal to the command and trust bestowed upon him; and, indeed, had done wonders, considering the *matériel* and the *personnel* he had to ply into use. But when he found a powerful army and good fieldguns opposed to him, his calculations wrong, and his enemy quite the contrary to his preconceived ideas, he resolved on the most prudent measure that could possibly have occurred to a man placed in similar straits—namely, to allow the victorious Allies to advance as far as they wished in force, and then to call in the assistance of diplomacy to delay their further progress in numbers, and to inveigle them forward only in small parties, under the blinding title of guards to the foreign Ministers, while he might have time to retire and take his final stand near Pekin, where he hoped to rally his troops and prepare them to meet in the field such small parties of the enemy's superior soldiers, and make them an easy prey to his overwhelming numbers.

This, no doubt, was San-kolinsin's policy; and though an amusing story was prevalent in the camp that the Prince was a runaway Irishman from the corps of Royal Marines, whose proper designation was Sam Collinson, and that his policy was perfectly characteristic of his descent from the land of Erin; yet to an impartial observer the Tartar general's last resource admitted of considerable plausibility. He felt sure, from the hard-earned experience he had acquired within the last few weeks, that it would be madness to venture his army against the whole of ours in fair field; he therefore determined, by the aid of diplomacy, to have recourse to treachery, and win back his reputation by exterminating our troops piecemeal.

However we might repudiate such conduct between two powers desirous of making peace, yet in war we are told all means are fair to gain the desired ends.

That the Chinese government believed that our object in making this expedition was with a view of wresting the country from them, there may be some little doubt; but they were at all events sure that our desire was to humiliate them; and, finding themselves too weak to resist us by force of arms, they had appeal to treachery, and by making pretence of their anxiety to concede to us all we demanded, they had hoped to inveigle our Ambassadors to the capital, under the plea of exchanging ratifications, accompanied by only 1,000 men each as guard; and to have conducted them instead into the trap that they had instructed San-kolinsin to prepare for us. Most of the officers from India, who had been there well initiated into the treacherous character of Asiatic politics, drew long faces, and recommended caution when it was given out that it was the intention of the Plenipotentiaries to leave the army at Tien-tsin, and proceed with only a small guard to Pekin; and, indeed, the natives themselves on this intelligence, though they treated us with courtesy, betrayed occasional hints that our visit would prove fruitless, and our prosperous career be but of short duration.

The camp life before Tien-tsin was very tedious

and uncomfortable. We were encamped on a large grassy plain to the east of Tien-tsin, and our bell tents afforded little protection from the scorching winds that swept over the open tract,—so much so that, had I not had leisure to repair each day during the midday heat to the friendly shade of the Hai-kwang monastery, situated a mile and a half to the left, or to the streets of the town, it would have been impossible to have existed. Fortunately for the troops, the large airy Indian tents were soon substituted for their accommodation, and every measure was adopted to maintain the hitherto good health of the army. Tea was plentiful and cheap, and so were provisions of all descriptions; and a first-rate market was established close to the camp. Sheep were purchasable at 12s. 6d. a-piece, and bullocks varied in price up to 5l., according to size; while flesh of both was retailed at small cost—mutton at 4d. and beef at 3d. per lb.; but even these rates were much higher than the prices ruling in the native markets in the town. The most relished luxury during that hot season among the natives as well as the Europeans was ice, and hawkers were running about the camp all day long with this much-desired article. Among the Chinese themselves it is much used *to lie upon* during the heat of the day. The ice for this purpose is crushed and scattered over the stove-couch, whereon it is then covered with a mat, on which the native casts his body as soon as he has divested himself of superfluous integuments; and, thus released, refreshes himself with a cool siesta until the sun partially withdraws his midday heat, and enables man again to renew his energy. For though the noon is hot and enervating, resembling in this respect that of the southern parts of China, yet the nights are cool and refreshing, and a coverlet almost necessary. Long stay in a hot climate, it is often affirmed, acclimatizes an individual, and enables him to endure the heat; and yet the northern and southern Chinese are very impatient of heat,—in fact, nearly as much so as the newly-arrived European. Even in the Takoo Forts, surrounded as they are by a wilderness of mud and saltpans, ice was found in large quantities, as though San-kolinsin himself had been of opinion that it was necessary for the health of his troops.

At the rumour of the success of the Allies and their intention to advance on Tien-tsin, great numbers of the inhabitants retired from that city; yet as we passed through its streets we observed no material change from the usual crowded thoroughfares of a Chinese town. The ordinary business of the street-vendors and stall-keepers continued with the usual alacrity, and the lower classes laughed, grumbled, and scolded one another, clad in frowzy old rags, yet happy withal. The more respectable inhabitants, however, dressed in their long blue frocks, might be seen grouped together, looking anxious and unhappy, and the principal shops were shut. The crowd increased as we reached the water-side, and became insufferably large in the neighbourhood of the " Han" establishment, where a large throng was gathered, their occupation gone, lazily eyeing the sentry, or watching the barbarians as they passed to and fro. This large house of the wealthy corn-merchant, surnamed *Han*, was conveniently divided into different series of apartments, with two doorways leading out on to the bund, or river's bank. The higher of these led to two suites of rooms, one of which was occupied by Lord Elgin and Staff, and the other by Sir Hope Grant and Staff. The lower door formed the entrance to the French General's quarters. These separate suites merely consisted of clusters of low Chinese houses, each divided into two or three small rooms, and connected by series of courtyards and galleries in perfect labyrinth. Some of the rooms had boarded floors and glazed windows, with carved pillars and hangings, and a few of the courtyards were ornamented with grotto work and plots of flowers. There was some style and show of wealth about this place nevertheless, and it was, without doubt, the finest house in the town; and our high authorities added no little to their dignity in the native eye by fixing their head-quarters in this place. The Hai-kwang ('Glory of the Ocean) Monastery, near our camp, which I have before alluded to, was the place prepared, in 1858, for the reception of our Ambassador, on the occasion of signing the treaty. It was a large, spacious temple of an antique appearance, but in the ordinary temple style. Its monastic apartments now afforded roomy accommodation to the Commissariat Department.

On the river's bank a few doors above the Han establishment, was a house occupied by the French *Mission Scientifique,* as certain letters chalked conspicuously over the doorway certified. I congratulated myself on the discovery, and felt rather hurt that the French Government should have been in advance of our own in thus associating scientific researches with modern warfaare. I at once paid a visit to that learned body, to ascertain the particular object of their mission, when, to my astonishment, I found the whole establishment consisted of one man (!), who informed me he had been appointed as head of the mission, but through some mistake in its organization the various scientific members required to complete the whole had not been forthcoming. This gentleman further informed me that the pecu-

liar part he took in the explorations was the study of
political economy as developed among the Chinese.
But before I took my leave, he made a statement
which rather shook my faith in the leading member
of this scientific body, viz. to the effect that he had
been only three months acquiring the Chinese spoken
language, and could now speak it fluently, and that
he felt convinced that a further three months' study
would perfect him in the written language. I would
not, however, have dared to question the boast of this
master of political economy, had he not betrayed his
want of proficiency in the language by discoursing
with a Chinese in my presence.

I was agreeably surprised to hear that there was
a zoologist in the French camp, to whom I next
repaired. This gentleman was an amateur, who had
procured permission to accompany the French army
throughout the campaign. M. Yill was a colonist of
Algeria, who, during his residence in that country,
had paid considerable attention to the Fauna of the
Atlas range, a subject which has of late years attracted
numbers of enterprising naturalists from our own
islands to the North African coast.

He was a man of mature years, but possessed of
that zeal for his hobby which overlooks all signs of
decay that man's enemy Time impresses on the body.
During his residence at Chefoo, the French rendez-

vous, he had carefully worked up the zoology of
the promontory of Shantung, but unfortunately the
exposure concurrent with the subsequent campaign
at Takoo, had confined him to his bed with rheu-
matism, and he had consequently done little since
the landing at Pehtang. He was a guest among
the members of the *Bureau Topographique,* in company with another distinguished amateur in the
French camp, the correspondent of the *Moniteur.*
M. Yill complained much of the rude treatment
he had received from the French soldiers, who were
inclined to look upon him as an interloper, and he
told me that many of his expensive illustrated works
on natural history had come to grief owing to their
wilful carelessness. When he complained of their
conduct, they retorted, "*Nous sommes soldats, nous
ne sommes pas porteurs de bagage.*"

We have thus shown that the French had one paid
scientific man only in their camp, and he was a political economist. But, shame to our Government, we
had none. Our Government always works on the
utilitarian principle, and leaves scientific investiga-
tion in nearly every case to private enterprise. A
well-known and learned zoologist, in the person of
Mr. Blyth, of Calcutta, proffered his hard-earned
thirty years' experience in Asiatic zoology to illu-
mine the North China campaign, on the part of Great

13

Britain, with a scientific lustre, but the niggardly
policy of our Government unhesitatingly rejected so
noble an offer. Thus the fine opportunities presented
by the success of our arms in a comparatively new
field would have been entirely lost, had not the zeal
of certain private individuals actuated them to bestow
their leisure hours to the acquirement of those facts
in natural history which always form so essential a
part in the geography of any country.

The newspapers were better represented, for besides the intelligent correspondent of *The Times*,
Mr. Boulby, who was a guest of the Embassy, the
camp had the honour of sustaining the editors of the
North China Herald and *China Mail*, both of which
gentlemen had been brought there by their love of
enterprise and party spirit, the one in principle
befriending the English, and the other the Chinese,
and both anxious to see fair play.   One of these
personages, much respected by all who knew him,
with locks prematurely white, and quite a specimen
of the rare old English gentleman, was frequently
mistaken for Lord Elgin, and sometimes in a most
laughable manner.   On the morning after the first
night out at Sinho, while this gentleman was sitting
quietly on a haycock regaling himself in the refreshing beams of the early morning sun, a padre
stepped up to him, and taking off his hat inquired,

" My lord, will you take a cup of chocolate ?" The person accosted courteously declined the disinterested offer, and the padre went away chuckling to himself at the happy opportunity he had just had of showing some little attentions to his lordship. Another similar mistake, which was somewhat more ludicrous, took place at Tien-tsin. The Russian Ambassador, on hearing of our advance, had come down to Tien-tsin to meet us, and quartered himself in a house in one of the back streets, at the door of which a Cossack guard was mounted. Our friend the editor had taken up his residence a few doors off this Embassy, and was quietly walking down the street when the Cossack spied him, and being under the impression that a venerable looking gentleman in plain clothes must be Lord Elgin, he rushed into the guard-house, and kicking up his drowsy comrades made them turn out and present arms to our friend, who quietly acknowledged the salute, though inwardly feeling nettled at having to receive an honour which was intended for a greater man ; and in returning to his room he took advantage of a back alley to escape the notice of the officious sentry.

The whole army had now been mustered under the walls of Tien-tsin, with the exception of the small force left to garrison the Takoo forts, and the 44th Regiment, which had been despatched to Shanghai

13—2

soon after the fall of the forts on the arrival of the
news that the settlement there was under menace by
a large body of Nankin rebels.　Odin Bay in Talien-
wan had been abandoned, as, from the abundance of
supplies procurable at the field of operations, it was
no longer needed as a commissariat depôt, and the
19th Punjaubees and remnant of Royal Artillery
were ordered to the front.　It was given out that
the Chinese commissioners had acceded to all the
demands made by Lord Elgin and Baron Gros; that
the convention would be signed in a few days, and
that then the Allied Ambassadors would proceed with
their escort of 2,000 men to Pekin for the purpose of
ratifying the Treaty of 1858.　Our demands were
modest enough it was true.　Beyond what the ultimatum contained it was required that Tien-tsin
should be opened to foreign trade, that the indemnity to be paid by the Chinese Government should
be fixed at eight millions of taels (about two millions
and three-quarters sterling), and that the Takoo
forts be held until the money was paid.　Half the
amount of indemnity should go for the Canton losses,
and the other half to defray the expenses of the war.
The French claimed the same amount of indemnity
as ourselves, whereas their Canton losses amounted
to scarce two millions, and their warlike preparations
were on a far more moderate scale than ours.

At this pacific intelligence all parties were made to believe that the war was at an end, and that ere long the camp would be broken up. Indeed, the 1st Royal Regiment, which had served for some years at Hong Kong, and had been almost decimated by sickness, received their orders to prepare for immediate departure for England, and many of the officers sold off their horse-gear and much of their heavy baggage by public auction. But suddenly, like a clap of thunder, came the news, on the 6th September, that Messrs. Parkes and Wade had had an interview with Kweiliang and Hang-fuh to arrange for the signature of the convention on the following day, and that on the Chinese Commissioners being invited to show their credentials it was found that they were insufficient, and that they really had no power to sign the convention. They had told a barefaced lie in the hope that the interpreters, trusting to their honour, and not examining too deeply into their assumed powers, might be led to induce Lord Elgin to go through the formality of signing a convention at Tien-tsin, and then to proceed to Pekin with only a small guard, under the plea of exchanging ratifications at the Imperial Court, when his lordship would be quietly led instead into the meshes of the wily San-kolinsin. Such, doubtless, was their shortsighted policy, but, thanks to the acuteness of our trusty Chinese secretary and his colleague, the enemy's hope was blighted in the bud. This want of good faith was at once reported to his lordship, who at once communicated the whole to Sir Hope Grant, and requested him to commence the march on Tungchow, where he informed the Commissioners he would confer with them as soon as they had received sufficient authority from the Emperor to sign the convention. Next day Sir Hope Grant pushed out an advance guard on the road to Tungchow, and encamped them some miles beyond Tientsin, at the same time giving orders that the march should commence on the following day. Accordingly, on the morning of the 8th, I was roused from my slumbers at an early hour by the band of the Rifles playing " Old Folks at Home," and, turning out, saw that the march had commenced. The First Division, under Sir John Michel, were on their way to Tungchow. Mr. Gibson, their interpreter, was too sick to accompany them, so he was left behind, and Mr. M. C. Morrison, also of H.M.'s consular service, who was absent from his post at the Amoy Consulate on sick leave, and had volunteered his services to the Commander-in-Chief, was appointed interpreter to General Michel. After breakfast that morning, as I accompanied General Napier into the city and passed the baggage of the First Division, still struggling

through the crowded thoroughfares, I was selfish
enough to envy the better luck of my fellow in office
in having been appointed to the advance while I
myself was destined to remain behind with the Second
Division. But imagine my joy when, on reaching
head-quarters, I learned that the fates had had something better in store for me, and that Sir Hope Grant
had attached me as interpreter to the Topographical
Department under Colonel Wolseley, whose duty it
was to follow in wake of the advancing columns and
survey the roads. The neighbourhood of the "Han"
establishment presented a scene of bustle and confusion easier imagined than described. Rows of carts
and waggons lined the way, all carrying little flags
with numbers on them, preparing for the morrow's
departure. Colonel Wolseley kindly procured me an
order on the Military Train for a horse, and desired
me to join him next day, and I returned to camp
rejoicing.

"A pony or a horse?" inquired Captain Gray of
the Military Train, as I presented myself before that
gallant officer of the white stripe on the following
morning. "I hope not the former, as we have no
animals of that description worth choosing." On my
informing him it was one of the latter animals I
sought, he sent a groom with me to inspect the lines.
The horses were picketed in three or four rows, and

as the syces uncovered them for my inspection it was a hard matter to choose from such a number of tall, gaunt scarecrows. I passed up and down the lines in despair, and felt half inclined to give it up as a bad job, when a Military Train trooper returned with a gray he had ridden out on an errand. This beast did not " handsome," as our American cousins say, but he could boast a little more flesh than the others, and was free of sores, from which most suffered. I fixed on him at once, and having satisfied *red tape* with my receipt, rode in triumph to where the servants were packing up my tent and baggage. They had engaged native porters, and all was in readiness for the start; so, taking an affectionate farewell of General Napier and Staff, I posted off to join my new master, and commence a fresh career.

The topographical department, newly organized, consisted of three individuals — Colonel Wolseley, Deputy Assistant Quartermaster-General; Lieutenant Harrison, of the Royal Engineers; and myself. It was on a Sunday morning, the 9th September, when we commenced slowly to move along in rear of the French baggage with our three carts and servants through the streets of Tien-tsin; it was slow work, and accompanied by numerous stoppages as we gradually progressed through the street of " Everlasting Prosperity," and curious it was to hear the strange remarks of the various shopmen who stood at their doorways watching the uncouth procession of carts, attended by men of all shades, sizes, shapes, and costumes. " They surely must be composed of a great number of nations," said one; " see how black some are, and how fair are others." " No," said another; " they are only from two countries, France and England. Those black devils are their slaves." Numbers admired the large size of our horses, and were extremely puzzled at our foolhardiness in riding stallions. And as our department rode three abreast, and all had gray chargers, many a " hai-ya" of admiration was expressed. We at last emerged from the streets on to the boat bridge across the junction of the Peiho river and the Grand Canal, or Yu-ho; then through a street, and over a small bridge across the Seaou, or Hia Se-ho (Little or Lower West River). The road then led over a stone bridge, the Hung-cheaou (or Red Bridge), which spans the Ta, or Shang Se-ho (Great or Higher West River), alias When-ho, and then past a cluster of houses on the bank of the Peiho, known as the Se-chwang, or West Village, until a little farther on we reached the village Ting-tsze-teoo, so called from the river here taking the form of the character " Ting," or the letter T. To the left of this a grassy flat offered a nice encamping spot, and as Colonel Wolseley did not wish to proceed too far the first day, we had our tents pitched. I was dubbed commissary of our small camp, and went to parley with the villagers, which soon resulted in a supply of ice, fowls, and fruit, and we were thus enabled to regale the officers of Sir Hope Grant's and Lord Elgin's Staffs, who hailed us on their ride out to join the advancing column.

We made inquiries about the names and courses of the different rivers in the neighbourhood; but the Chinese never understand a river as a whole, each portion being christened separately by the inhabitants of the towns and villages through which it runs, and often the same portion having different names applied to it by people living at no great distance apart from one another. This was most perplexing. Thus the Peiho below Tien-tsin is known along its banks as the "Peiho," or North River; at Pehtang it is distinguished as the "Nan-ho," or South River, from the Pehtang River, which is there called Peiho. At Tien-tsin the Peiho, flowing seawards, is spoken of as the "Hai-ho," or Sea River, and the portion above the city towards Tung-chow bears the name of Peiho, or "Ta Peiho," Great North River.

The Grand Canal, "Yun-leang," or "Yu-ho" (Grain-bearing or Imperial River), flows in a southerly direction, till it meets the "Hwang-ho," or Yellow River, through a long list of towns and villages, whose names and distances we procured, but I fear they are not very reliable and scarce worth insertion here. It is still navigable for 400 or 500 miles of its length, and for perhaps more, but information on this head was obtained with difficulty. Every one knew that the Yellow River had burst its dykes, and destroyed the navigability of the Grand Canal; but as to the extent of the damage done no one could speak with certainty.

The Little or Lower West River is a small stream winding in a southerly direction, and is navigable for flat-bottomed barges as far as the departmental city of " Ning-tsing," distant about 150 miles from Tien-tsin.

The Great or Upper West River, alias " When-ho," that joins the Peiho at the Red Bridge, runs almost due west to the Great Salt Marsh, or " Ting-hai," east of Pekin, passing which it continues its course to the large prefectural city of Paou-ting-foo.

Next morning I rose early, and walked in a southerly direction towards a cluster of masts about a mile distant. These belonged to some junks anchored before a village on the When River. Other junks were moving down the river under sail, laden with sacks of salt. Traffic appeared to continue, notwithstanding the advance of the enemy. I was separated from the river's bank by a creek running through a

bed of rushes, and finally losing itself in a marsh of
no great extent. This creek abounded in wild-fowl,
and I only regretted that our stay would be of too
short a duration to admit of my returning to the
spot.

The British column had halted after the first day's
march at "Poo-kow," and on the following day (10th
September) advanced to Yang-tsun. The French
column kept a day's march behind, and though they
marched out of Tien-tsin on the 9th at the same
time as our department, they had only proceeded as
far as "Se-chwang," where they had encamped close
in rear of us. We were, therefore, obliged to delay a
little in order to let them pass. The small camp of
our department consisted of one Indian tent, which
accommodated the colonel and the lieutenant, and
served as well for our common hall—and two bell
tents, one belonging to myself, and the other to
Wolseley's soldier servant and a corporal of Engineers.
The Chinese servants and carters generally built huts
of mats and millet stalks, and the two nigger servants
were accommodated with a *tente d'abri*. Besides our
three horses picketed in row, there were the six
baggage ponies belonging to the carts, and the carts
themselves, and in a group hard by the eleven Seikh
troopers detailed to us as guard, with their tents and
horses. The whole made quite a conspicuous little

group to the observation of the passers by, and many
were the questions asked by the French officers as to
who we were, and what was our particular commission?   Among others, a Russian, attended by two
Cossacks, rode up to us, and complimented us on the
neat appearance of our camp, and the wonderful condition of our horses, which looked so strong and
healthy, notwithstanding the long voyage they had
undergone.   He said what struck him as particularly
marvellous was the Seikh Regiment, with their fine
Arab horses.   " When you reach Pekin, you will
astonish the people," he said.   " I assure you that the
Emperor rides on just such a pony as I am now
mounted on" (pointing to the native galloway he
bestrode.   " But your Seikhs are magnificent.   To
think that from a country of black savages you could
have produced so fine a troop of mounted soldiers !"
The secretary to Count Ignatieff (for such he proved
to be) was candid in his remarks ; and indeed it
could not have been deemed arrogant for a British
officer to admire the drill and turn-out of these
Seikhs, as compared with the wretched Sipahis from
Algeria of the French lines, who too often showed
themselves impatient of discipline, as the French
officers acknowledged, and were mounted on the most
wretched of Manila ponies, lank and half-starved to
look at.

As soon as the French had got well ahead we struck tents and commenced our duties on the road. Harrison took the course of the Peiho for his part of the survey, while Wolesley continued to track the road; and as my duties were to inquire the names of villages and to procure any required information, I was directed to accompany the latter officer. The river, as Captain Sherard Osborne observes, is fenced in on either side with artificial dykes, and the villages on its banks are larger and more thriving than those farther inland, whose inhabitants depend entirely on the fruits of agriculture for their livelihood. But the story of the paved road said to exist by that same author between Tien-tsin and Pekin, is all a myth, as we before supposed. He must surely have intended the paved way between Tungchow and Pekin, which other writers have before commented on.

The face of the country was covered for miles, as far as the eye could see, with fields of tall millet, and were it not for the occasional brick-kilns and watch-towers that occurred, an accurate survey of the road would have been most arduous. As it was, Colonel Wolesley felt that he could not ensure accuracy without pacing the road. The distances so noted were afterwards compared on the return march with the revolutions of a perambulator, and their accuracy

verified. We rested at a pretty wayside temple called
Taou-hwa-she (or Monastery of the Peach-flower),
where the priest had fitted up a little room for the
accommodation of travellers. On the benches within
were gathered a motley group of Chinese rustics
enjoying their cup of tea and pipe. By the side of
these we seated and cooled ourselves, after the hot
walk, under the friendly shelter of the temple's roof,
while our companions the Seikhs brought us apples
and peaches, by way of accompaniment to the hot,
refreshing beverage. The sky, which had hitherto
continued cloudless, now began to lower, and before
we had continued much farther on the road, showered
a deluge over our heads, while lightning gleamed with
vivid flashes, and the thunder vibrated through the
air with terrific roar. We were compelled to seek
shelter in a small mud-built village on the bank of
the Peiho until the contention of the elements was
somewhat abated. Lieutenant Harrison here joined
us, and having received a coat apiece from our trusty
followers of the swarthy complexion, which they insisted on our accepting, we slipped along the slimy
road, converted by the deluge of rain into a sea of
mud; but very fortunately we had only a couple of
miles to go farther, for our servants, who had proceeded ahead, on observing the threatening state of
the weather, had pitched our camp in a delightful

little grove of willows close to the village of Lower Poo-kow, about two miles nearer than Poo-kow itself, where the French were encamped. We were thus enabled soon to make ourselves comfortable, and prepare for the worst, whereas many of the French baggagers only a little in advance of our carts were brought up short by the muddy state of the roads, and compelled to halt where they were, and brave the fury of the drenching storm. One Frenchman, with his wife, a pretty little *vivandière*, was in this difficulty on the road close to us, and we were sorry we could give them no assistance further than tent-room for the night. The lady herself, however, did not partake of the hospitality at our hands, for a French officer who shortly afterwards came up assisted her to their camp. Many of our Seikhs were Mussulmans, and it was, therefore, difficult to supply them with provisions, as they would not eat pig, the only animal that abounded in the village. We at last succeeded in procuring a few fowls for them, and a moderate supply of wheaten flour.

Next morning the sun rose again in all his splendour, and evaporation of the earth's surface commenced with vigour. We were, however, determined to take it easy till near noon, and I was consequently enabled to stroll about the precincts of the village. " Hia " (or Lower) Poo-kow is a village of no great

extent, consisting entirely of mud huts, the home-
steads of farmers. Near these was an abundant
supply of forage of several descriptions. Fine hay and
straw were built up into ricks, supported off the
ground on poles, stacked in with millet stalks, and
roofed with mushroom-shaped tops of mud, and in
some cases coated all round the sides for a couple of
feet from the ground with the same material. Many
of the houses were deserted, by the women at least,
and the greater part of the cattle had been driven
away. By the way, the hospitality we tried to show
to the French stragglers was met by an act of ingra-
titude on the part of one man, who quietly, in the
dead of the night, unloosed my baggage-pony and
carried him off to his camp, without leaving me any
chance of ever recovering the animal.

There were several handsome trees in the neighbourhood of our grove, whereon the birds were particularly lively in the cheering sunshine of the morning.
The wet night succeeded by a clear, bright morn, with
the sun slowly rising and shedding his beams of light
and warmth on saturated nature, was a gladdening
sight to us mortals as well, and while the drenched
and drooping bushes began to hold up their heads,
the birds to shake their moistened feathers and prune
them into order, we ourselves felt a peculiar pleasure
in lounging idly in the sunshine. Here woodpeckers

14

(a pied species) first made their appearance, and ran their giddy run up and round the bark of overhanging trees, while the gorgeous yellow plumage of the Chinese oriole showed conspicuously among the leafy foliage.   Little flycatchers kept darting into the air to catch the passing fly, and the merry trill of the gray caterpillar-catcher told us that he, too, was busy overhead.   The cheerful twitter of buntings, finches, and wagtails, and the heavy brushing through the branches of the clumsy cuckoo gave notice of our lively companions in the willow-grove, and made us mindful of our acquaintances of South China, which, to wage their insect war, had arrived before us, and were already at their summer haunts to welcome us to the hitherto unexplored northern regions of the Celestial Emperor's domains.

A few hours of sunshine works wonders on the mud-formed roads of this country, and, before noon, the highway was sufficiently dry to admit of our proceeding in our carts.   As before, Harrison took the course of the river, and started first with two Seikh orderlies, and Wolseley and myself continued along the road with three Seikhs, leaving the other six to accompany the baggage; but before we had gone far one of these dark followers came to grief, his horse having slipped and fallen with him bodily into a mud pool; which accident necessitated his return to the baggage and his place being supplied by one of the others.

We soon arrived at the village of Poo-kow, situated on the river's bank. One long and dirty street through which we rode was partly occupied by the French Ambassador and his guard, but the French camp was pitched in a millet plain some little way beyond. Their advance was deferred till the following day at the request of Sir Hope Grant, who had sent back from the British camp at Yang-tsun.

Not far from the French camp we encountered two French sportsmen, who had availed themselves of the halt to have a day's shooting, and I was glad to recognize in one of them my friend M. Zill. They were beating the millet-fields for quail, and had procured as yet only one button quail (*Turnix Dussumieri*).

Poo-kow, the first halting place on the march, is distant twelve and a half miles from Tien-tsin. Several villages of minor importance occur between this village and the city; these I have not thought it worth while enumerating here, as such lists of meaningless Chinese names would have little purpose in this narrative, while they are accessible to the inquiring reader in the lately published Government Survey, the fruits of our department, planned by the indefatigable and painstaking Colonel Wolseley and Lieu-

14—2

tenant Harrison, in which they are all carefully
noted.

From Poo-kow a farther travel of seven and a half
miles brought us up before evening with the British
camp at Yang-tsun, where our baggagers had already
pitched our tents and made all snug. Yang-tsun is a
large, flourishing village occupying both banks of the
Peiho, with several brick-built houses of the better
class. It falls within the Hien, or department, of
Woo-tsing, and holds the residences of two civil
mandarins, a " Che-Heen " and a " Heen-ching,"
both of the seventh rank, with gilt buttons. These
worthies, it is needless to add, had decamped before
we arrived. The drivers of the carts hired at Tien-
tsin to carry the baggage of the Embassy and that
of the Head-quarters' Staff, had run away during the
night's stormy darkness, carrying with them many of
the baggage animals ; so a number of junk-boats were
seized and manned by sailors to carry the *impedi-
menta* by the river.

The carters had doubtless been frightened by the
threats of the Government underlings, many of whom
we heard were hanging about the camp at this place,
and, notwithstanding the vigilance of our Seikh sowars
in keeping an eye upon the carters attached to our
own department, two out of three managed to escape
during the night we spent at Yang-tsun.

A flag of truce had arrived in the early part of the day borne by two mandarins of the fourth class, who announced that "Tsai-wan," President of the Imperial Court of Punishment, who was the leading member of the war party, and "Moo-hien," President of the Council of War, had been appointed to treat with the Ambassadors, and were now on their way down to Tien-tsin. The flag-bearers were dismissed with the reply that there could be no treating till we had arrived at Tung-chow.

Next morning (the 12th) at daylight the troops were on the march, but our department did not start till 10 A.M.

Several villages were passed; the country maintained its alluvial character, vast tracts being covered with tall millet and maize as before, but trees became more numerous the farther we advanced.

By the evening we reached Nantsai, the next stage on the march, seven and a half miles from Yang-tsun, where we halted again in the British camp. Next morning the march continued, and we followed somewhat later; but this time Colonel Wolseley took the survey of the river, which soon after leaving the village takes a long bend to the northward, and the road was left to Lieutenant Harrison.

As we approached Ho-see-woo the soil became more sandy, the village itself being situated in some sandy hills, or rather undulations on the river's bank, but the rest of the country as far as our vision reached was still one large flat, moving with a sea of undulating millet speckled with woody hamlets and here and there a brick-kiln or watch-tower.

The Head-quarters' Staff had taken up their quarters at a gaudily painted Confucian temple just outside the village, and we pitched on the hill hard by. I took a walk along the bank of the river, here only thirty yards broad, in which numbers of the troops were luxuriating, the average depth of water being up to the waist, with occasional deeper spots occurring, and the current very fresh. I could not resist the temptation, so, throwing off my clothes, I plunged in, and for a while forgot the heat and dust of the road and the discomforts of a marching camp in the cool, refreshing bath in which I revelled.

CHAPTER IX.

Being carelessly encamped,

* * * * *

And but attended by a single guard,
We may surprise and take him at our pleasure.

SHAKSPEARE.

Chinese Committee of Supply.—Looting.—Encampment at Ho-see-woo.—Negotiations.—Conference at Tung-chow.—Baiting a Trap. — Chinese Deserters. — Mandarin Spy. — An ominous Expedition.—A Llama's Grave.—Chinese Fox-Hunt.—The " Black Prince."—The Noise of Battle.—Engagement near Matow.—Reconnaissance to Tung-chow.—Gallantry of Colonel Walker.—Mr. Parkes' Account.

Ho-SEE-WOO, as you ride through its main thorough-fare, presents no very attractive appearance. The houses are mostly of brick, and perhaps rather better built than those already passed, but their doors are closed and barred within, and the larger part of the inhabitants have fled.

The men deputed by the Committee of Supply at Tien-tsin to provision the army on the march, here fell short of their engagements, and attempted to make off. The consequence was that the most responsible of them was kept close prisoner, while the others were sent to hunt up caterers for the commissariat. The supplies provided were not equal

to the demand; hence the houses had to be broken
open to search for grain, the commissariat undertaking that nothing but the necessaries of life should
be abstracted from them.   Grain was found in
abundance, but labourers to grind it into flour scarce.
The few villagers left in the place did not care to
exert themselves to pulverise their own staff of life,
though it were under the condition that the rest
of their property should be preserved.   Soldiers were
sent to bear a hand, and *looting* followed as a consequence.   The pawnbrokers' shops were soon discovered
by their conspicuous sign-boards, generally dragons'
heads, carved of wood, and painted with green and
gold, protruding over the doorway, and the mischief
once commenced, not the utmost vigilance and
frequent use of the rod on the part of the provost-
marshal could put a stop to it.

The town of Ho-see-woo is walled, and has rather
a decent little gate under a quaint old tower porch
at each end; but the road the carts had to pursue
led up a sandy hill, through a small suburb on the
right, on the bank of the river, and toilsome work
it was for the carts to drag their slow lengths up this
undulation, with axle half embedded in the sand.
But on opening the farther side of the village, the
eyes are greeted with quite a picturesque view: low
green hills, with a pretty pagoda, a gaudily painted

Confucian temple, and a square-walled monastery, besides other tasteful-looking buildings, groups of handsome trees, and groves and woods speckling the country away in the distance on both sides of the river. Lord Elgin took up his abode in the monastery, and, as I remarked in a previous chapter, the Head-quarters' Staff dwelt in and about the Confucian temple, while the army was encamped in the plain, and among the groves in front of us. On the following day the French arrived and pitched their camp beyond ours. Ho-see-woo, without doubt, is the finest village on the road to Tung-chow, and in a military point of view, the undulating ground in its neighbourhood would have enabled the enemy to have considerably impeded our progress. They might have originally had such intention, for a large store of bows and arrows and other munitions of war were discovered in an old hall; but there were no other signs of defence. We learned that a " Seun-cheen," or small magistrate, of the ninth gilt button, had a residence there, as also another civilian, the Tung-chee of Tung-loo, of the fifth rank crystal button.

On the day of our arrival, Messrs. Parkes and Wade pushed on with a small escort to Matow, where the commissioners had reported themselves waiting for Lord Elgin's reply to their letter which had reached his lordship at Nan-tsai. A letter had been

received from the same parties at Yang-tsun couched
in rather defiant terms, and expressing astonishment
at his Excellency's moving forward from Tien-tsin.
The first letter having deservedly met no other reply
than that expressed by a continuation of the march,
another despatch, in milder terms, met the Ambassador at Nan-tsai, in which the commissioners calmly
suggested, "If, therefore, the British Minister will
withdraw his forces to Tien-tsin, the prince and his
colleague will have it in their power to repair at once
to Tien-tsin for a conference for the consideration
and despatch of business. But if his Excellency be
apprehensive that time will be wasted by their movements to and fro, there would be no objection whatever to his halting his force at Yang-tsun, and select-
ing some place midway between that town and Matow,
near enough to suit his convenience, at which business
might be discussed and disposed of. Let his Excellency decide whether it shall be Ho-see-woo or Ngan-
ping," &c.

As his lordship, however, was not so easily to
be taken off the scent again, he preferred carrying
the troops with him to Ho-see-woo, and thence sent
on Messrs. Parkes and Wade with his reply. Meanwhile, the prince and his colleague had got wind
of the advance of the troops, and with true Chinese
caution had retired to Tung-chow, whither the two

interpreters followed them after an uncomfortable night passed at the wretched village of Matow. In the reply, Lord Elgin signified his determination to continue the march to Tung-chow, and that if the Chinese gave sufficient security for their good conduct, he would halt the army " at a point within an easy stage of that city, and proceed from there with an escort of 1,000 men to Tung-chow for the signature of the convention, and to Pekin for the exchange of the ratifications of the treaty of Tien-tsin."

At noon on the 14th, Messrs. Parkes and Wade arrived at Tung-chow, in the neighbourhood of which they saw signs of a large force encamped near. They took up their abode in the residence of the chief civilian, and went at 4 o'clock to the temple outside the east gate to meet the commissioners. Mr. Wade describes Tsai, Prince of E, and his colleague in the following words :—" The former is a tall, dignified man, with an intelligent countenance, though a somewhat unpleasant eye ; Muh-yui, President of the Board of War, softer and more oily in his manner, but also intelligent. Both were extremely polite, the prince especially, and without condescension or affectation."

After the prince had engaged to produce authority for his exercise of plenipotentiary powers, a copy of the convention was shown to him, which, with the mendacity for which the Chinese are justly celebrated, he ignored, "although," writes Mr. Wade, "in two of his despatches already written he had promised to sign it." And when this fact was brought to his memory, he ventured objections to nearly every stipulation contained in it. A spirit of friendship appears to have pervaded the whole conversation, and from it we learn that the actual government of the country is not vested in the three Tartar princes only—to wit, Prince Hwui, Prince of Ching, and Prince of E; but that there are others of Chinese extraction that share with them the control. The Prince of E desired that the army should be encamped one mile and a half to the rear of Chang-chia-wan. This point was ceded to him, and he engaged to meet the ambassadors at Tung-chow in the manner proposed by Lord Elgin, to which we have previously referred, stating distinctly in the letter he returned to his lordship—"To the inquiry made on behalf of the ambassadors as to what security can be given for the faithful execution of the engagements now entered into, the prince and his colleague have to reply that no comparison can be drawn between the authority vested in them and that held by other ministers who may have been charged with negotiations, and that this fact affords a positive assurance of the future observance of good faith on the part of their government." We shall see, in the course of the narrative, what the words " good faith" are worth in China. With this reply Messrs. Parkes and Wade returned to the camp at Ho-see-woo, having observed " numerous cavalry videttes" at Chang-chia-wan, and " long lines of very wretched cavalry " at Matow. They were well assured of the good intentions of the Chinese diplomatists, and looked upon the presence of men in arms near our camp merely as evidence of the neighbourhood of San-kolinsin's *peaceful* forces. The military officers they conversed with were all inclined for peace, and signified their joy at a settlement of the difficulties that embroiled the two countries. Thus, the way was smoothed, and in a few days our force would advance to its final camp at Ho-see-woo, to provide Lord Elgin with the escort of honour that was to conduct him to Tung-chow, and thence to Pekin.

Meanwhile the natives of the neighbourhood spoke ominously of the success of our advance, and intimated in strong terms to my Chinese attendants that San-kolinsin was carefully baiting his trap, and that his soldiers were loud in their brag how they were going to surround us on our march and cut us to pieces: for their Commander-in-Chief had determined that not one of the " Hats" should return again to Tien-tsin alive. The term " Hats" was very generally applied to the French and English troops, owing to the strange and conspicuous *solar topees* of pith they wore to protect their heads from the sun. Among others who brought this intelligence were two deserters from San-kolinsin's army, whom we employed to cater for our department during these times of comparative scarcity of provisions at Ho-see-woo; for the villagers had deserted the place in alarm, and showed none of that readiness to bring supplies into the camp which they had hitherto done at previous stoppages on the march. For some time I was not aware of the suspicious character of our caterers, and on one occasion took one of them with me for a shooting ramble, giving him my gun to carry. He seemed quite up to the manœuvres of the fowling-piece, and showed himself so intelligent that I took quite a liking for the fellow. My servants at last came to me in dire alarm, and communicated the news they had picked up from the villagers and from these two men; and as I had to go round to the Embassy's quarters with a prisoner caught conveying a letter through the camp from a mandarin residing at Ho-see-woo to the commissioners at Tung-chow, I mentioned what I had heard to Messrs. Boulby and Wade. These gentlemen laughed and said that they were only idle tales sprung up among the rabble, and that they wondered at my listening to such nonsense; that they fully believed in the sincerity of the commissioners, who had behaved in such a friendly spirit in their late interviews, and that we should shortly see how smoothly all difficulties would be arranged. At this repulse I sent the deserters away, and tried to think no more of the matter. The writer of the letter we had intercepted had lately been taoutai, or chief magistrate, of Shanghai, and had had much intercourse with foreign officials at that port. He was, therefore, selected as a spy on our proceedings, and quietly sent to take up his quarters at Ho-see-woo. He had several times attempted to get an interview with Lord Elgin, but without success, and was now stating in the letter to the commissioners, after a detailed account of our doings at Ho-see-woo, the amount of the force we had with us, and the intention we had in view of advancing in a few days, and of encamping near Chang-chia-wan, whence an escort 1,000 strong would be supplied to Lord Elgin, to accompany him to Tung-chow. In speaking of the troops, the term "Hats" was invariably used. The bearer of this letter was detained, but the mandarin managed to make his escape. It was not to be expected that one mandarin writing to another would speak of a hostile force in courteous terms; but, perhaps, fearing the chance of the document falling into our hands, the writer had avoided making any allusion which might throw light on the uncertain state of our existing relations.

Lord Elgin communicated the success of his envoys to the French Ambassador and to the Commander-in-Chief, and it was determined that the army should move forward to the camping ground proposed, five *le* this side of Chang-chia-wan. Mr. Parkes was then commissioned to proceed in advance of the army to Tung-chow for the purpose of making preparations for the reception of the Embassy at that place, and also to procure means of transport for the Ambassadors and Staff. A letter was entrusted to him by Lord Elgin to deliver to Prince Tsai and his colleague on arrival at Tung-chow.

The camp broke up at daylight on the 17th, and commenced their march to Matow, the first stage, leaving a regiment, however, at Ho-see-woo, where Lord Elgin had decided for the present to remain. Mr. Parkes started in advance at a very early hour, "accompanied by Colonel Walker, Quartermaster-General of the Cavalry Brigade; Mr. Thompson, of the Commissariat Department; Mr. Loch, private secretary to Lord Elgin; Mr. De Norman, one of Mr. Bruce's attachés, who volunteered to go with him as assistant; and Mr. Boulby; and escorted by five men of the King's Dragoon Guards, and twenty of Fane's Horse, under the command of Lieutenant Anderson."

Our department followed some hours afterwards; as before, Wolseley and myself continuing along the road, and Harrison on the river's bank. The country was very beautiful, with luxuriant crops of millet and numbers of umbrageous woods roundabout the villages. Two curious tombstones attracted our attention on the road, and afforded a good landmark. They stand off the village of Wa-woo, on a grassy flat surrounded by cultivated fields. The most conspicuous of these monuments is a narrow column of marble about ten feet high, written all over with Thibetan characters, and surmounted by a conical top. We were told that it marks the grave of a Llama priest. At Gnan-ping, the midway village, consisting of a large cluster of mud houses, with here and there a temple, I talked with the proprietors of a few of the shops still open; these men told me that a force of a thousand Tartar cavalry was stationed there three days ago, but had since been withdrawn. They said that these troopers were insubordinate in their bearing to their officers, and, in defiance of their orders, ill-used and plundered the villagers. They were mostly Tartars, and only a few knew a smattering of Chinese. The rest of the road was all but deserted, and many of the houses of the small villages

15

were quite cleared out. We had, therefore, much difficulty in procuring information for our survey, for as soon as a native spied us, even at a distance, he made off as fast as he could go. In such cases the only plan was to give chase, so I generally had to proceed in advance, accompanied by a Seikh orderly, and as soon as he saw a native we separated and gave chase to cut him off whichever way he ran. When once caught the quarry was easily tamed by a few words of ' his familiar lingo, and the information we sought easily procured. But in one instance I was tired, and sent the sowar alone on a chase, and after waiting some time, and the man not returning, I followed his track and discovered him halted in front of a house belabouring the door with the butt end of his spear. He grinned and gave me to understand in a mixed jargon of Hindustani and Patan that the fox had taken earth through that entrance, and as he spoke I descried a native clambering over the housetop to escape. I shouted to him in Chinese not to be alarmed, and he soon became tranquillized, and told me that the grim appearance of the " black prince " with a spear had frightened him.

The camp was pitched beyond Matow, in a very sylvan locality, and we erected the tents of our department in a field, in which the millet had been just cut down, close under the shade of a stately

willow of gigantic proportions. Matow, or "Landing-place" (literally "Horse's Head") is a poor,
straggling village on the banks of the narrow stream
of the Peiho. Its wretched mud huts were then
tenantless. The distance from Ho-see-woo to Matow
was twelve miles, but we had got over the ground
rather quicker than usual, and I was tempted by the
brightness of the sky and the loveliness of the scenery
round to take a ramble. The millet was cut down in
this neighbourhood, but still it was unpleasant walking over the fields, as the stalks, a foot and a half
high, were left uncleared, hard, and stiff, and seldom
yielding to the pressure of the foot; but the numbers
of quails that lurked about the ground induced one to
brave the risk of bruising one's shins. A village I
passed through, as the sun was setting, presented an
enchanting though melancholy sight. Lately, no
doubt, the scene of so much alarm and confusion,
its inhabitants all hurrying away elsewhere for protection, it now rested in tranquil repose by the side of
a brook, with a green lane, through hedges passing
from it, to the fields. The branches of the overhanging trees, that threw a pleasant gloom over the
mud cottages, rocked about almost noiselessly in the
gentle evening breeze. I stood and gazed for some
time charmed into a peaceful reverie, when the noisy
curs—the only guardians of the deserted huts—spied

15—2

me out, and, setting up a noisy barking, reminded me
of the approaching darkness, and of the necessity of
my return to camp.

Next morning (the 18th) at daylight, the troops
resumed their march to the encamping ground near
Chang-chia-wan, and we resolved to do as we had all
along done, to let the army get well in advance before
we struck tents.   It was a bright, clear morning, and
we were preparing to take it easy after breakfast,
when a King's Dragoon officer came riding back, and
told us that the General had sent orders to the rear-
guard to move up all the baggage as fast as possible,
as there was a large body of Tartar cavalry ahead.
He did not know whether the order applied to us, but
he thought it was his duty to inform us of it.   We
thanked him, but, thinking it was a precautionary
measure on the part of the General, paid no further
attention to it.   Shortly after we distinctly heard the
noise of distant cannon, and seeing four mounted
French riding back along the bank of the river,
Colonel Wolseley desired me to have my horse saddled
and ride across to them, and inquire what the cannonade was about.   They coolly replied that they
were on their way back from Tung-chow to Ho-see-
woo, and had just passed through the Chinese camp
and the French and English lines, with as much
safety as if they had strolled through the streets of

Paris, and that they had heard no firing. I asked them if they could not hear it now, for while we were speaking together the rumbling noise continued. To my astonishment they replied, "No, not at all. But that if there really was any firing, it must be an engagement between the Allies and the Tartars."

On this I turned away from the two mounted officers and their orderlies to return to our tents, where I found Wolseley and Harrison, both on the raised road watching for signs of smoke. We soon saw balls of white smoke in the air, indicating the explosion of shells, and clouds of dust, such as would be raised by the charge of horses. This at once convinced us that hostilities had certainly recommenced, and the danger we were in so long as our white tents afforded a conspicuous mark to the enemy's eye. We at once struck tents, and assisted in packing the carts. It would have been madness to have pushed on towards the belligerents at once, and to have left our baggage to the mercy of any of the enemy's stragglers; so we determined to keep by it, and gradually creep on as fast as the carts would let us towards the rear of the British column, which we judged could not be many miles in advance. It was a long, anxious four miles we had of it. At times the mules would pull different ways, and at others the cart-wheels would stick in the ruts, whence it was difficult to extricate them; while all the time the noise of cannon increased, and the clouds of dust appeared closer and closer. We at last got up with the baggage, which was halted at a village in charge of the rear-guard, from whom we learnt that, had we been half an hour sooner, we would have been cut off by a party of the enemy's cavalry, who had passed the road in rear of the village, and thence crossed the river. Leaving our baggage with the rest, we galloped along the road, turned off to the left along the bank of the Seaou-ho (Little River), the raised causeway of which had afforded a natural curtain to the enemy's guns, and thence through Chang-chia-wan, and across country to a spot where the Commander-in-Chief was resting under the shade of some trees. Sir Hope Grant and Staff were all dismounted, and all apparently much exhausted from excitement and fatigue. The General expressed his disgust at the turn affairs had taken, and appeared much alarmed for the safety of the prisoners whom the enemy had treacherously detained while passing through their lines. We then learnt that Messrs. Parkes and Loch, and several others, had been captured. The General added that the enemy seemed to be innumerable, and could not have numbered less than 80,000 in the field. Sir John Michel and the

troops had captured all the camps in the neighbourhood, and were now engaged in destroying them by
fire, which accounted for the frequent puffs of gun-
powder smoke that we saw repeatedly rising into the
air all around us. When this duty was accomplished,
orders were sent to withdraw the troops into Chang-
chia-wan, where they would be quartered in the
deserted houses. We accompanied the General on
his return, and, fortunately passing an orchard on
the way, we were enabled to quench our almost in-
satiable thirst with the refreshing juice of the rich
ripe grapes, which clustered so luxuriantly in its
bowers. The baggage was meanwhile moved up to
the village, and the houses being apportioned out to
the different regiments and officers, we were soon
housed in our new quarters.

As I was not present at the spirited engagement
of the 18th September, when the small band of
British and French troops encountered and put to
flight the overwhelming foe, I will, in order to satisfy
my readers with an account of the affair, extract
a few portions from a letter published in the *North
China Herald*, adding thereto any further particulars
I may have gathered from the verbal statements
of parties present. The force that marched from
Ho-see-woo, under Major-General Sir John Michel,
consisted of the Cavalry Brigade, to wit, the King's

Dragoon Guards, Probyn's and Fane's Seikh Horse, with Sterling's half battery, Brigadier Pattel commanding; two field batteries under Captain Desborough, and the two brigades under Brigadiers Sutton and Reeves, viz. 2nd Queen's, 15th Punjaubees, Royal Marines, and 99th Regiment, with detachments of Royal Engineers and Military Train. One French regiment (the 2nd Chasseurs de Vincennes) and one field battery followed. The army marched from Matow on the 18th, and had advanced about four miles, " when the enemy's piquets were observed, which, at their approach, leisurely retired to a large camp, distant about a mile farther. While halted, to enable the column to form up, a flag of truce was brought in by a few mounted men, which was soon followed by a mandarin in a green chair wearing the pink button and peacock's feather of a first-class official, who was recognized as the former Hoppo, at Canton, and late Commissioner sent to Tien-tsin to negotiate with our ambassador. While he was making the usual Chinese excuses, Mr. Loch arrived."

It appears that Messrs. Parkes and Loch, accompanied by Colonel Walker and Commissary Thompson, with a few orderlies, left Tung-chow at an early hour that morning to arrange about the encamping ground for the army; that on the road

they met large bodies of Tartar troops, who were
drawing guns into position, and apparently preparing
for an engagement. The Tartars behaved at first
civilly, but were decided in their tone; and Mr.
Parkes, finding he could only get evasive answers
from their officers in reply to his questions, returned
to Tung-chow to remonstrate with the authorities for
their breach of faith. Colonel Walker and Commissary Thompson rode on with a Tartar escort to
inspect the appointed spot for the camp, while
" Mr. Loch sought the Commander-in-Chief, to
whom he reported the state of affairs, and by whom
he was requested to rejoin Mr. Parkes, and to warn
him," with the rest of the gentlemen, to return at
once to the main column, and Captain Brabazon,
Quartermaster-General of the Royal Artillery, was
requested to accompany him. " The mandarin left,
after impudently assuring Sir Hope Grant that the
Tartar cavalry, whom we now saw assembled in
hundreds, were merely collecting the supplies we
required." Large bodies of them were seen moving
to the left, who were said by this worthy to be going
for provisions for the allied troops; while others that
were moving to the right in the direction of the
river were going to draw water (on horseback and
without buckets!) " Meanwhile, the troops were
formed up in contiguous close columns of corps, and

awaited during three hours the return of the party from Tung-chow. While enjoying the shade of a clump of trees, some 500 yards from the camp in which the Tartars were now busily stirring, I was suddenly startled" (writes this correspondent) "by hearing a volley of gingals and a round from numerous guns along their entrenchments: a few horsemen enveloped in a cloud of dust galloped up. These proved to be Colonel Walker, Assistant Quartermaster-General of Cavalry, Assistant Commissary-General Thompson, and two dragoons." I spoke with Colonel Walker on the subject afterwards, and gathered from his account that he and the Commissary were shown to a spot set aside for the camp right in the centre of the Tartar files, whereupon he shook his hand to his guide and tried to make him understand that a place must be chosen nearer the water. His guide, was a low white-buttoned mandarin. While waiting in anxious uncertainty for the army to move up the Chinese soldiers began to increase in numbers, and pressed round himself and companions; they were not openly rude, but rather overbearing in their manner, and betrayed that impertinent curiosity so often shown by Chinese to a foreigner. Some time after a red-buttoned mandarin rode past with a military retinue, who, the guide intimated to him, by raising his thumb, was the chief, probably San-kolinsin himself. The functionary in passing by turned his head away, as if he did not see the British officers. Presently a man came on one side of the colonel and snatched his sword from the scabbard. The man, however, was reprimanded for his rudeness, and the sword returned to its owner. At last the crowd, who were composed of armed men, all in similar uniform and most of them neatly dressed, began to get excited and rude; and a great commotion seeming to take place at a little distance off Colonel Walker rode up to see what it was, and found that the Tartars were attacking a French officer. The officer was badly cut about the neck, and seemed to have lost all sense. The colonel interposed and tried to ward off the assailants, when they turned upon him; one snatched his sword from its sheath, cutting the colonel's fingers in his attempt to save it; others attempted to drag his feet out of the stirrups; and another came behind Commissary Thompson and made a lunge at him with a spear, but fortunately his belt warded off the blow and he only received a flesh wound.

Seeing the unpleasant turn affairs had taken, and deeming it no longer safe to remain in such dangerous company, the colonel cried out to his party to charge for their lives through the midst of the enemy. At the word of command the party bent down to their horses' necks and spurred their chargers through the Tartar ranks, which gave way at once before them. The enemy discharged every available matchlock at the fugitives, and several guns opened fire upon them, but fortunately the gauntlet was run without any serious casualty; one dragoon receiving merely a flesh wound in his thigh. The British column was soon reached and the General acquainted with the particulars of the affair.

The assault was undoubtedly more premature than the Tartar general had intended, for it is plain their intention was to beguile the Allied troops to encamp peacefully in the midst of their numbers, and then to attack them unawares. Their plans were, at all events, foiled; for " there being no signs of the return of Mr. Parkes and his companions, Sir Hope Grant made arrangements for the immediate advance of the Allied forces. The disposition of the troops was as follows:—the French on the right, with Fane's Horse and Desborough's and Barry's batteries, supported by a squadron of King's Dragoon Guards and 15th Punjaubees in the centre. The Second Queen's, with the cavalry and Stirling's battery, on the left; the remaining regiments in reserve. The enemy at once opened a heavy fire, and showed their position to be behind an entrenchment several miles in length crossing the high road, which was defended by a battery of sixteen guns,

their left thrown forward and resting upon a village
in a grove of trees, their right extended as far as the
eye could reach over the millet fields, the crop of
which had been recently cut some two feet from the
ground, forming a disagreeable impediment to the
troops, especially the cavalry. After a sharp engagement which lasted for two hours, the enemy, who
could not stand against the fire of our artillery,
gradually advancing to within 500 yards, gave way,
and spirited charges were made by our cavalry. Fane's
Horse on the right pursued them through the village;
the King's Dragoon Guards and Probyn's Horse on
the left drove them several miles, and were only
obliged to desist on finding themselves at a considerable distance from the main column. The Seikhs,
headed by their officers, did great execution. One
old sowar was heard describing the Chinese army as
so many *moorgee* (*anglice*, fowl), very difficult to
overtake and entirely harmless when caught. Following up the enemy, the 15th Punjaubees and 99th
Regiment entered the walled city of Chang-chia-wan.
It was estimated that the force opposed to us numbered 30,000 men; the Allied troops were under
3,500 men."

The field of operations extended over so large a
space of ground that it is impossible to form a guess
of the number of the enemy's slain. Indeed, as we

rode into the batteries, skilfully constructed amidst
clumps of trees, and masked with freshly chopped
branches, we rarely came across a Tartar corpse.
The raised road which strikes off at right angles to
the main road and follows the course of the *Little
River* formed one long battery and had some fine
brass guns in position, a few of which had been
dragged on their clumsy carriages half way through
the shallow stream and there deserted. Seventy-four
pieces of cannon were captured on this occasion and
all destroyed. We had very few casualties; but the
French lost the colonel commanding their cavalry
in a dashing charge on the Tartars, in which they
were assisted by a company of Fane's Horse. General
Montauban, in a letter of thanks to Sir Hope Grant
for the assistance of the Seikhs, spoke very highly of
their behaviour during action, and recommended the
lieutenant commanding that company for the Legion
of Honour.

Lord Elgin, at Ho-see-woo, had during the day
heard the sound of distant artillery, but it was not
until after midnight that he was apprised by a letter
from Sir Hope Grant of what had taken place.
Betimes in the morning his lordship started for the
front, and, on arriving at Chang-chia-wan, proceeded
with the Commander-in-Chief to the quarters of the
French General to confer on the best means of

recovering the prisoners; where "it was agreed that a reconnaissance of British cavalry should proceed forthwith to Tung-chow, and that Mr. Wade should accompany it with a notification to the chief mandarin of that city, to the effect that the Commanders-in-Chief of the Allied armies required all English and French subjects to return to the head-quarters of their respective armies, and that if any impediment was put in the way of their return, the city of Pekin would forthwith be attacked and taken. It was added that Tung-chow would not be molested if the inhabitants kept aloof from all resistance to the Allies." Mr. Wade first attempted to communicate with the Tartar camp on the east of Tung-chow, but his flag of truce was fired upon; he then tried the city of Tung-chow itself, and managed to get an interview with the mandarin on its walls, who calmly replied, in answer to the questions on the welfare of the prisoners, that "he believed a party of upwards of twenty had left the city some time before the firing on the 18th had commenced." On the day following, however, Major Probyn, in the course of a further reconnaissance, secured a native, who asserted that he had seen some foreigners being conveyed to Pekin in a cart on the day of the fight.

Much disgust was at this time entertained among the officers in the army at the obtuseness shown by the diplomats, in the easy manner in which they had been beguiled into a trap by the treacherous Chinese, and many invectives were launched forth against Mr. Parkes for having tamely submitted to sue for a pass from San-kolinsin, instead of charging the cowardly crowd that thronged around him with the band of trusty companions in his train. Had they trusted to their weapons and charged, the majority would have escaped, in all probability; whereas, now they were all completely at the mercy of their cruel enemies. At the same time, loud were the praises in favour of Colonel Walker, who had so gallantly, in spite of the great odds against him, ridden through the Tartar ranks, and delivered the whole of his small band with only a trifling casualty. This ill-feeling was chiefly based on conjecture, the true particulars of the capture not having transpired. The public have since been favoured with Mr. Parkes' own story, from which we gather, that having returned to Tung-chow to remonstrate with the authorities against the warlike preparations he had observed on the road, Mr. Parkes was returning, with the whole of his party, to the British lines, as desired by Sir Hope Grant. "We had just passed Chang-chia-wan," writes Mr. Parkes, "and were hoping to be clear in ten minutes of the Chinese lines, when a fire of Chinese artillery opened along their front, and showed that the engagement had begun. As soon as we were observed, a number of Tartar horse moved into the road to intercept us, and, halting the party, I informed an officer who we were, and asked him to allow us to pass on. He desired me not to proceed until orders arrived from a superior officer close at hand; upon which I suggested that time might be saved if I visited that officer myself. He assented; and I therefore rode towards the spot, accompanied by Mr. Loch and one sowar carrying a white flag. The remainder of the party, namely, Major Brabazon, Lieutenant Anderson, Messrs. De Norman and Boulby, one dragoon, and, I believe, eighteen sowars, remained on the road, and were also provided with a white flag." The interview with this *red-button*, and then with San-kolinsin, resulted in Messrs. Parkes, Loch, and the sowar being treated as prisoners, and carried off to the Prince of E.

The rest of the party anxiously awaited the return of Messrs. Parkes and Loch. "The Chinese," writes Sir Hope Grant, "crowded round them in great numbers, to disarm them. The position in which they found themselves precluded any attempt to cut their way out with any chance of success, upon which Lieutenant Anderson very properly determined to trust to the protection of the flag of truce, and ordered the sowars to make no resistance. They

16

were accordingly disarmed and taken to the rear, being permitted to retain their horses."

Thus we see how apt men are to hastily prejudge cases before they are fully acquainted with all the points bearing upon them. A perusal of Mr. Parkes' tale, subsequently published in *The Times*, must have induced many to change their opinions on the subject of the capture, and to give him, at least, his due, for the noble behaviour he bore towards his captors while completely at their mercy.

CHAPTER X.

Brave followers! yonder stands the thorny wood,
Which, by the Heaven's assistance and your strength,
Must by the roots be hewn up yet ere night.
SHAKSPEARE.

City of Chang-chia-wan.—Wanton Destruction of Property.—Deserted Chinese Women.—Advance from Chang-chia-wan.—Another Encounter with the Tartars.—Dashing Charge of the Dragoon Guards.—Various Conflicts with the Enemy.—Yungleang Canal.—Ruffianism of the Coolies.—A Grandee's Monument.—Arrival of Reinforcements.

CHANG-CHIA-WAN is a city of the past. Its lofty walls are crumbling with decay, and moss-grown; and the little river that flanks it on the east, and forms the connecting link between the Peiho and the Great Marsh, or Tunghai, with its tributary, the Pan-chia-ho, flowing northwards to Tung-chow, were probably once important rivers, conducting the wealth of commerce to her gates, but now have dwindled to insignificant streams, to whose cooling ripple our horses lowered their lips as they waded, side-deep, into the shallow water, hot and thirsty after the long day's gallop. A stone bridge spans the little river, crossing which you enter, through a gateway, the old

16—2

city, and almost immediately find yourself in its chief
street, lined on each side with shops, which, soon
after the capture by our troops, presented a very
forlorn appearance. No steps were taken to prevent
looting, as the town was a capture in war, and hence
lawful booty. Grain and other necessaries of life
were handed over to the Commissariat, but everything else fell as plunder to the discoverer's hands.
An immense store of brick tea was found in one
warehouse, estimated at about half a million pounds
weight. Some of this was taken for the use of the
troops; for, coarse as it was, it was much superior to
the stuff provided for them from home; but the
greater bulk of the commodity was left untouched.
This was rather a pity, and caused much grumbling
in the camp; for it might afterwards, when convey-
ances were plentiful, have been carried down to Tien-
tsin, and there disposed of for the benefit of the
army. As it was, one energetic young officer loaded
several carts with the tea on his own account, and
despatched them to Tien-tsin; but his little game soon
reached the ears of the Commander-in-Chief, and as
peace had been then declared, an order was issued
that the tea should be returned to its rightful owner.

A great rush was made, as usual, by the Canton
coolies and idlers to the pawnbrokers' shops. One
very wealthy one occurred, filled with articles of every

description; large quantities of Sam-shoo (Chinese spirits), piles on piles of strings of copper cash (the currency of the country), and large quantities of old clothes done up in bundles. These dresses were soon scattered with other articles about the streets, and coolies and niggers vied with each other in gay and fantastic apparel. Some hairy old Seikh, attired in feminine costume, would stroke his beard and strut in long boots before the admiring eyes of his surrounding comrades. One cared not so much for the destruction of dirty, foul-smelling shops, but when it came to works of art and taste you could not help feeling annoyed. Thus a rare old house, with its exquisite carvings and hangings, and its rooms filled with curiosities too big to carry away, was completely ransacked and destroyed internally, the roof and walls merely being left. No one would grudge a man's taking what he could carry away, but why ruthlessly destroy what had cost years of labour, and great outlay of money, to collect together? Our people were, in this case, the destroyers; but the greatest thieves were the natives from the surrounding villages, who crowded into the town all day long, and made off with whatever they could lay their hands on. In a walled enclosure several of the cavalry horses that had escaped from their riders during the engagement were found; and, curious enough, in a house hard by

lay Colonel Walker's much-valued sword, which had
been snatched from that gallant officer, as before
related.

The house in which our department was quartered
belonged to an old man, whom we found on entering
still standing by his property. He could not at first
understand what right we had to usurp possession
of his domain, and seemed inclined to be uncivil,
until I mildly assured him that if he conducted
himself properly we would allow him to occupy one
of his own outhouses; for that had his house been
allotted to the troops, he would have found little
mercy from them, and would in all probability have
had all his furniture destroyed or carried away;
whereas now, if he attended to our wants, and did
as he was told, we had no intention of making him
too great a sufferer.   Upon this, he immediately
killed some fowls, and set himself to work to prepare
a dinner for us, and continued his attentions with
right good will to the day of our departure.   This
old individual was not the only one that was found
at home after the capture of the town.   A few doors
off was a large house, evidently containing valuables,
from the number of coolies that clambered over the
housetops to peep into its courtyards.   My curiosity
incited me to walk along the top of the wall, and
learn the cause of the stealthy visits of the coolies.

On looking down into the yard, I saw a stout native gentleman of a middle age and his two sons, all armed with spears, and prepared for the worst. They had barricaded their doors, and looked much excited. I at first thought that the fair sex was in question; and feeling somewhat inspired with a spirit of knight-errantry, spoke to them, and asked them what they had to fear, and why they were so armed. They, on the other hand, judging from the fact of my being on the wall, that I also had sinister intentions, replied defiantly that they were standing by their property, and would defend it to the last; and that if I ventured to jump down into their yard, they would despatch me with their spears. I complimented them on their show of pluck, and told them that I was led there chiefly by curiosity to see what was going on, and to offer my assistance if their ladies were in any danger of being insulted.

Poor men! their pluck was of usual Chinese consistence; for that evening, in spite of their spears, their house was entered over its walls, their boxes broken and scattered over the yard, and all the money and other valuables carried away. The following morning, Mr. McGhee, chaplain to the forces, came to procure my assistance in forming an asylum for the numbers of native women who had been left behind in the town deserted by their male relatives. We first went to the adjoining house to have an interview with my friends of the spears, whom we apprised of our intention to turn their house into an asylum for their unfortunate countrywomen, and we hoped that they would show them some attention for the present until the return of their husbands or relatives. Mr. McGhee had previously marked the spot where the forlorn damsels were to be found, and had provided a covered cart to convey them to the asylum. The cart stood at hand, and, jumping on one side of the shaft, he invited me to seat myself on the other side, and away we went through the town. The first house visited presented indeed a sickening spectacle. A group of females of all ages, from the grey-haired beldam of fifty to the lisping child of two, were huddled together, with small tin boxes of liquid opium by their sides; some leaned on their hands; others were prostrate on the floor in unbecoming attitude, their faces ghastly yellow, and their eyes rolling wildly in their sockets, while their hands and mouths, besmeared with opium-juice, told the shocking tale of their attempt at suicide. The more conscious among them started at our entry, and beating their breasts condemned the opium for its slow work, crying out, "Let us die; we do not wish to live." They were at once conveyed to the asylum, and placed under charge of some of the regimental doctors, who kindly volunteered their assistance, and remedies were at once applied to frustrate the effects of the poison. Water was sprinkled on the faces of the wretched patients, and they were kept continually moving about, and before long the majority of them began to give signs of resuscitation. The old gentleman who owned the establishment was quite assiduous in his attentions on his self-poisoned countrywomen, and half induced us to change our ideas on the lack of generosity and charity in this heathen land. He rushed about for hot tea and water, and called in an excited manner on his sons to assist him. We left these half-dead wretches under care of their kind host, and sallied out after another batch. These were much more lively: three dames and some eight little girls all crying out most lustily when we entered their small apartments. The leader of the lamentations was a stout middle-aged lady, who asked us in a loud voice what we wanted, and told us in plain terms they did not want any of our company. I tried to quiet her fears by explaining to her that we meant well, and that we had come there to assist them to a house provided for them, where they would be attended to by their own country-people. She answered, " Go away ! how can I believe you ? Your heart is not good ; your intentions are evil." With that she set up a howl, and all the other voices, great and small, joined in concert. Again and again we tried to pacify them, but in vain. I then suggested to Mr. McGhee that we should take them by force to the asylum, where the sight of their fellow sufferers would help to quiet them. So, seizing the leading dame in our arms, we deposited her in the cart, and helped two or three of the little ones in after her. Thus laden, we drove off, notwithstanding the cries of the frightened women inside, who kept shouting all the while, " Great princes, forbear! Oh! save our lives! We are women in distress. Save us, great princes!" &c.

We hurried on through the crowds of troops that were attracted by feminine cries to gaze on female beauty until the cart drew up before the asylum door. Here I desired the women to get out, and went forward to assist them. On looking into the cart I discovered the elder woman with a string round one little girl's neck, at the ends of which she was tugging with all her might, with the evident intention of strangling the poor little creature. We soon hurried the old brute out of the cart, and finding the child, who had been enduring the pain so patiently without muttering a cry, was not much hurt, set her down and commenced helping out the rest of the children. When all were out we turned to enter the house, and to our horror found the brutal mother was again in the act of strangling her child. We rushed to stop her, and led them all into the house, where the old man took charge of them. The rest of the females were brought to the asylum without much ado, and we soon had quite a collection of forlorn damsels under the charge of the master of the house and the kind-hearted medical attendants. Those suffering from the effects of opium were put into rooms by themselves, and constantly attended, while the others stowed themselves away as best they could in the numerous apartments of the house. Tea was served to those that could drink it, and ample food supplied by the generous-minded chaplain, who, true to his cloth, was ever foremost in the relief of suffering. In fact, everything was done for them that humanity at such a season could suggest, and yet the women's fears were not to be allayed; some still wept and mourned their fate, and when the hours of darkness enabled them to slip out unobserved, several of them—the old beldam and child among the number—made their escape, and were observed wandering away along the banks of the river; but whether they committed suicide, or what was their ultimate fate, we never succeeded in learning. Thanks to the skill of our doctors, only one opium-poisoned patient succumbed; the rest all recovered.

The 21st was fixed for our next move; so on the 20th we rode back to Matow, and completed the survey of the road and river from that place to Chang-chia-wan, the whole distance along the road being nine miles and a half. The village near which Mr. Parkes and party were taken prisoners is marked by a low pillar, and called Kopo-chwang. It was close in rear of San-kolinsin's works, and about two miles from Chang-chia-wan.

The two days' halt had enabled the French to add to their strength by marching to the front 1,000 men and a field battery from their force left at Ho-see-woo; so orders were issued to strike camp on the 21st. At daybreak all were astir in the town, and soon an unbroken stream of men issued forth in a north-westerly direction. Major Probyn had been sent on a reconnaissance two days previous, and had, with the assistance of Mr. Dick, interpreter to the Commissariat, succeeded in securing three natives, who were versed in the whereabouts of San-kolinsin's camp; these men were taken along as guides.

At the Kaowle village, some two miles from Chang-chia-wan, a halt was called, to enable the French to move up. I had been directed before starting to report myself to Sir Hope Grant, and accompany him as interpreter in place of Mr. Parkes, who had hitherto held that important position. The General was dis-

mounted and conversing with several officers of his
Staff in a wood, under the shade of which Probyn's
Seikhs were also taking it leisurely.   Shortly after,
Lord Elgin and Staff, with their escort of dragoons,
arrived, accompanied by sundry amateurs, and
amongst others Lord Robert Grosvenor.   At last
the French, who had been encamped in rear of
Chang-chia-wan, and had in consequence been obstructed in their progress through the streets of the
town by our baggage, moved to the front, and took
the right hand of the advance.   General Michel
marched his division to the left, and the Cavalry
Brigade, with the Marines and 2nd Queen's, took
the extreme left.   All were ready for starting, and
the advanced guns of the French had already opened
fire, when Sir Hope Grant, followed by his Staff, rode
towards the French lines to confer with General
Montauban as to the order of the attack.   A few
words were exchanged, and the British General
moved slowly forward in advance of the column,
apparently engaged in thought, and without taking
heed of a line of Tartar cavalry drawn up ahead on
the farther side of a long mound.   The mandarin in
command was observed riding up and down in front
of his men, and inspiriting them to the charge ; and
when we approached to within 200 yards, the Tartars
gave a series of yells, and leaping the bank, charged

furiously at us, discharging their matchlocks. The
General and Staff at once galloped to the right and
left, disclosing the Armstrongs, which wheeled round
in hot haste and unlimbered, giving, however, to the
Tartars the impression that all hands were panic-
stricken and turning tail. They, therefore, galloped
forward the more boldly, cheering and uttering their
war cries, but before they had proceeded far the case
shot poured in among them, and the rifles of the
2nd Queen's saluted them with a shower of bullets.
Their cheers soon yielded to yells of despair as they
hastily withdrew to a more respectful distance. Sir
Hope Grant led the cavalry yet farther to the left,
and gave the First Division room to advance. The
King's Dragoon Guards chose their opportunity, and
cantering up to a large body of Tartar horse suddenly
charged.   Both parties were withdrawn from view
by the cloud of dust that enveloped them, and nought
could be seen of the encounter save an occasional
gleam of the uplifted sword, or puffs of gray smoke
from the discharged carbine or pistol. In a minute,
as it were, the cloud of dust was swept away, and the
gallant dragoons appeared drawn up in line, as if
nothing had happened.

We soon moved over the ground. One private lay
dead of a matchlock-ball wound through the heart,
and a captain of dragoons dropped to the rear with

a bad cut on his arm: but the ground was strewn with dead and dying Tartars. I stopped with the Commander-in-Chief's doctor to look at the dead private. As his face was turned upwards, one dragoon that stood near remarked to another, "Why, Bill, if it ain't old Charley! Poor fellow! he has gone to his long home!" Several riderless ponies were rushing about the place; these were caught, and taken along as trophies. Some of our people were rather given to examining the enemy's dead, in search for curiosities, and it so happened that on one occasion rather a stout individual dismounted with this object in view, close to what he took to be a dead Tartar. He stooped down to turn over the body, when, to his horror and fright, the supposed corpse turned its head and peeped at him through the corner of its eye. The spoiler leapt back as if shot, jumped on his horse, and galloped away as hard as he was able. After this little adventure the individual in question was never again so eager to examine the bodies of the fallen foe. The fact was that many of the unhorsed Tartars, on finding that the enemy were upon them, and that they could not run away, feigned death to elude the chance of being taken prisoners. The Cavalry Brigade had now moved some way to the right, and had lost sight of the First Division; but we could hear constant

cannonading from their direction, and could see the
legions of mounted Tartars that fled from before
them towards us. The enemy seemed innumerable,
but they showed hesitation, and would not admit of
nearer approach than 1,000 yards. At this distance
the Armstrongs occasionally got a few shots at them,
and emptied a few saddles. One shell was distinctly
seen to burst in the midst of a group of the enemy's
horse, emptying three saddles, and cutting two horses
almost asunder. Probyn's Horse then took a circuit
well to the left, and tried to get round the enemy.
We at first lost sight of them. Presently a line of
serried pendants appeared in the distance, with a
peculiar quivering motion. They moved nearer and
nearer, and soon we could make out that it was the
gallant Major and his trusty sabres, 700, all told.
They made for a large party of Tartars bustling
about under some trees, and charged at them. The
Tartars scuttled away in confusion until the Seikhs
were halted, when they showed face again, and discharged matchlocks at them at long range. Brigadier
Pattel then sent word that he had drawn up the
Dragoons before an entrenched camp on our left,
which he was unable to enter without the assistance
of infantry. We soon reached the camp, and the
2nd Queen's were ordered in to drive the enemy from
it, a few of whom still remained near the tents, while

others had fled for refuge to an adjoining village. The camp turned out to be the head-quarters of General Paou, commanding the Tartar cavalry. It was very beautifully arranged under a grove of handsome cedars; the tents of fine American drill, all well pegged down, and erected at equal distances apart, with the pavilion of the commander in the centre. This camp had every appearance of being deserted in a hurry: the clothes and bedding in the tents remained unrolled; a table stood in the General's tent with a lamp upon it, and also his bowls of rice and chopsticks, showing in what hurry he must have taken the field. In rear of this small picturesque camp several fine mules were found browsing, and, together with some carts, were made booty of.

We then rode into the little village adjoining, in the houses of which some Tartars had ensconced themselves, and kept taking "pot" shots through crevices at our troops. Orders were at once given to fire the houses, and as the enemy attempted to escape over the walls of the burning buildings the troops retaliated by taking "flying" shots at them. The temple and enclosed houses were spared, but their rooms were searched for the lurking foe. Two priests, "all shaven and shorn," were taken prisoners, who might or might not have been soldiers, for a Chinese soldier has a most convenient method of throwing off

17

his numbered doublet and powder waist-belt, and assuming the meek look of an ordinary native, whom in other parts of his attire he much resembles. Some Seikhs were then sent to fire the camp. The village at which we found ourselves was called Yu-chia-wei, distant south-east from Pekin about eight miles, and in the dim distance we could just see one of the gates of the City of the Emperors. A proclamation was posted up on the walls of the village in the name of General Paou, telling the villagers not to be alarmed at the presence of his camp, as his soldiers had been strictly warned against committing any acts of injustice on the natives of the place; and at the same time giving them to understand that all provisions supplied should be honestly paid for. General Michel and Brigadier Sutton here joined Sir Hope Grant, bringing the intelligence that the First Division was in possession of the bridge of boats and the toll-bridge, and all the country in their neighbourhood this side of the Yung-leang canal. The Commander-in-Chief, therefore, resolved on retiring from Yu-chia-wei, and fixing the camp on the banks of the Yung-leang canal. I was then sent with an officer and a guard of Seikh troopers to bring up the baggage, which was halted at a village some way in the rear of the camping ground. We found the baggagers in great alarm, as they had mistaken us at a distance for a squadron of the enemy's cavalry. They were soon, however, reassured, and eventually reached in safety the groves of trees that marked the picturesque spot on the banks of the canal where the camp was to be fixed.

We had no sooner arrived on the ground than the enemy opened fire with heavy guns from the cover of woods on the opposite side of the canal. The 15th Punjaubees and two howitzers were ordered to cross the river and put a stop to the annoyance. They came upon a camp of troops robed in imperial yellow, with silk banners of the same colour. These soon decamped, and their camp was destroyed; but our troops soon afterwards came to close quarters with some Tartars in a village, and committed great havoc among them. One gallant Punjaub officer, forgetting the use of the sword that hung by his side, engaged a Tartar with closed fists, and had succeeded in flooring him, when a Punjaubee private thrust the man through with his bayonet. Meanwhile the French had had an exciting engagement with the enemy at the stone bridge, over which the paved way runs between Tung-chow and Pekin. This is the famed Pa-le-cheaou (or Eight Le bridge), so called because it marks the distance of eight le, or two miles and three quarters, along the paved road from Tung-chow; and on the opposite side the enemy had planted some heavy guns. These the French carried in a

17—2

most gallant manner at the point of the bayonet, and in the hand-to-hand skirmish that ensued General Paou was mortally wounded, and carried off the field by his own men. In the midst of his sufferings, it was afterwards reported, he had given orders for the decapitation of Captain Brabazon and the Abbé de Luc, two of the unfortunate gentlemen that the Chinese had so treacherously stopped while returning to the allied lines under a flag of truce. The loss of the Chinese at this bridge alone could not have been less than 300, and we set down their total loss at 500, though in all probability it was considerably more. The Tartars, on the whole, seemed less afraid of coming to close quarters with the French than they were with our troops; but this may be owing to the fact that the French had scarce any cavalry.

In one of the charges of the Seikh cavalry I was informed that a trooper lost the management of his horse, and was carried among the enemy, who first gouged his eyes out in a most barbarous manner, and then cut him to pieces, limb by limb. But the Seikhs themselves were by no means sympathetic towards the suffering foe; and it was a common practice among these gentlemen, when riding over the field after an engagement, to murder the wounded. As they rode past a prostrate wounded man, one would prick him with a spear's point, and, if the unfortunate sufferer cried out or writhed under the pain inflicted, some of the party would dismount and deliberately saw his head off. The French encamped on both sides of the stone bridge, and the British to their left on the east bank of the canal between the two bridges they had captured. Soon after erecting our tents, I observed a small boy in plain clothes, mounted on a pony, dragging a blue-buttoned mandarin along by the tail. I advanced to inquire who he was, and learnt that he was a naval officer's steward, who, having lost sight of his master during the engagement, was quietly riding through a field in which millet stalks were stacked in separate heaps; out of one of these the prisoner had rushed and deliberately fired his matchlock at the boy, but fortunately missed him. The mandarin then drew a knife from his pocket, and attempted to cut his own throat, but the blade was too rusty to have the desired office. The boy at once ran at him, and, seizing him by the tail, brought him along prisoner. The mandarin said that he was a lieutenant of the cavalry under General Paou, and had got unhorsed during the engagement; but he positively denied having fired at the boy. He was soon after released, and told to go about his business.

The country here was very beautiful, tope after tope of lofty and magnificent trees occurring frequently, and in their neighbourhood several large though dilapidated temples. In one of these near our camp Lord Elgin and the Commander-in-Chief found quarters, while their staffs encamped under the shade of the adjoining trees. General Montauban occupied another near his camp. The villagers were for the most part wretched, and showed little signs of wealth. The camp of our department was pitched in the middle of a parched-up field close to Probyn's cavalry, and the dust raised by the horses going backwards and forwards all day long was anything but agreeable.

On the 22nd the camp was alarmed by some shots fired by an outpost at a party of approaching Tartars, who thereupon halted, and an official came forward with a flag of truce and presented a letter addressed to Lord Elgin. This was from Prince Kung, brother to the Emperor, who informed his lordship that, in consequence of the mismanagement of affairs by Prince Tsai and Muh, he had been appointed imperial commissioner, to treat with "the ambassadors; and he proposed an armistice, with a view to the re-establishment of peace." In reply, Lord Elgin referred him to the notification which had been already delivered to the chief mandarin of Tung-chow in the names of the Commanders-in-Chief, and informed them that, until the British subjects detained in

Pekin were restored, no steps could be taken to stay military operations.

The Yung-leang canal, on the banks of which we were encamped, connected Tung-chow with Pekin. The waters were all but stagnant, and of a yellow hue, which no doubt was heightened by the taint of numerous Tartar corpses that floated about its surface. It was fringed along each bank with reeds and rushes, and averaged in breadth twenty-five yards, its depth varying from one to twenty feet, and its total length perhaps thirteen miles from town to town. The Peiho just below Tung-chow divides, the main stream keeping a little away to the north, and a branch skirting the foot of the town and trending somewhat north-easterly; two miles, however, above the city, these two branches are connected by a narrow tortuous canal. The Yung-leang canal reaches to within a few yards of the Tung-chow branch of the river, but does not flow into it; consequently goods intended for water carriage to Pekin are transhipped at Tung-chow into large flat-bottomed barges on the canal. These boats are pulled up to and under the stone bridge, or Pa-le-cheaou, and onwards a couple of miles farther, till they are drawn up before a stone pier or dam extending across the canal and bridged over. The portion of the canal above this pier is some ten feet higher level than the portion below, and the goods have, therefore, again to be transhipped, by means of a roller and pulleys erected on the bridge above, into other barges on the higher water. Close to this obstruction stands a toll-house, for the levy of toll on goods so transhipped. As soon as this stoppage is passed the goods may continue on without further obstacle to where the canal ends, under the walls of Pekin.

Before our arrival, traffic on this canal had apparently ceased, and the barges on the upper water had been moored side by side, and formed into a bridge of boats, which, together with the weir bridge, had fallen into the hands, as I before stated, of the First Division. This water communication afforded great convenience in supplying the camp with provisions and other necessaries during the delay that ensued until reinforcements, and heavy siege guns, arrived from Tien-tsin. Captain Dew, R.N., who superintended the water carriage, found no difficulty in moving up the commissariat and other boats from Ho-see-woo to Tung-chow, and thence the numerous barges on the river brought up supplies right to the camp. The Governor of Tung-chow had been informed that if he made no hostile demonstrations against us, his city would be spared, and the people protected, and he accordingly showed his good will by instructing the townspeople to open a market on the stone bridge.

The small suburb just outside the north gate of Tung-chow was at once occupied by 400 marines and an equal number of French soldiers, but the citizens took good care to keep the gates that opened in our direction closed, and had the portals manned by city braves. This, however, was purely a precautionary measure, in order to keep straggling soldiers and followers of the camp from entering the town for plunder, as on all occasions when the Commanders-in-Chief demanded admission, the gates were at once thrown open to them. One class of plunderers, however, could with difficulty be kept out, and these were the Canton coolies. There were several complaints of the mischief these ruffians impudently committed, until at last the townspeople determined to retaliate on them, and on an occasion of a party of six coolies entering the town and setting to plunder a shop, the people rose, and, murdering two of them, handed the other four to the British authorities, who to show their disapproval of the wrong they had done, had them publicly flogged.

But, on the other hand, the citizens were scarcely justified in taking the law into their own hands, and dealing so harshly with the other two; the General, therefore, deemed it expedient to demand possession of one gate of the city, and ordered the marines to occupy the north gate. The few braves that guarded the entrance were soon dislodged without a blow, and the marines in occupation. The coolies were in the frequent habit of slipping away from camp and prowling about the neighbouring villages, big sticks in hand, in search for plunder, and it was absurd to see the large brawny sons of the soil cowed down by these southern Celestials, so much inferior to them in size and physical strength. The natives of this neighbourhood, however, almost entirely deprived of implements of defence, and continually governed by the paternal rod of iron of the mandarins, were a more submissive and abject race than the half-independent tribes of South China, who league together in clans, and too often set the government at defiance.

While alluding to the loose acts of the Canton coolies, I may record a flagitious act committed by some of their number near the camp, and the punishment awarded. Some officers out for a stroll, hearing loud shrieks in an adjoining field, went to the spot to ascertain the cause, and caught three coolies in the act of taking rude liberties with an unfortunate woman. The officers laid hands on the miscreants and dragged them before the General. One was proved to be more criminally concerned than the others, and was condemned to be hanged, while his abettors in the crime were sentenced to 100 lashes each. At the time appointed for the execution of the sentence, all the coolies of the camp were assembled to witness it. The two first received their castigations under the cat of the provost-sergeant, in the presence of the third, who then suffered the extreme punishment of the law. The condemned man looked perfectly calm before his execution, and did not evince the slightest fear or trepidation, not even when the rope was being adjusted round his neck.

During the delay at this camp, our department had ample time to survey the country back to Chang-chia-wan, and I had frequent leisure to make notes and observations on the natural history of the place. I visited the *Bureau Topographique* of the French camp, and made the acquaintance of Colonel Dupin, who was fond of sporting and a first-rate shot; and with that officer and M. Zill, the French amateur naturalist, I had several very pleasant excursions.

About four miles from the camp, in the direction of Chang-chia-wan, occurred a very handsome marble monument to a governor-general of Paou-ting-foo. A small marble bridge, with pillars of the same material on each side, conducted you to a wall-enclosed greensward, in the centre of which stood a marble arch, handsomely carved, and written over with Chinese characters; passing under this, you entered a grove, girt all round with a dense line of small cypresses; and at the farther end of the grove were erected, side by side, three grass-covered mounds, the tumuli of the grandee, his wife, and his son. Adjoining the grove was a temple-like house, tenanted by the appointed guardians of these tombs. I was on a visit to this spot with a military surgeon, a friend of mine, and had left him outside while I entered the grove to note its peculiarities. Suddenly he shouted to me, in dire affright, " Come out, man! make haste, and bring your gun. We must fight for our lives. Here is a Tartar riding towards us full pelt." I hastened out, and soon descried the object of alarm. The doctor's short sight had led him to mistake a mounted Punjaubee officer, with a turbaned head, for a live specimen of our valiant foe.

On the day of the engagement, the Tartars had made somewhat of a stand at this tomb, and eight or nine carcases of their small ponies, with a few mangled corpses of the riders themselves, lay to the left,—

> " Fiery steeds, with wounds transfixed,
>   Floating in gore, with their dead masters mixed."

Near these corrupting masses, I was much surprised to find an emaciated native sitting, like a spectre among the dead. The unfortunate man was quite bereft of sense, no doubt through wounds and

starvation, and was plucking up the grass by hand-
fuls and eating it. I spoke to him, and tried to get
him off the place; but, in reply, he returned me a
vacant stare, and shrieked menacingly at me. For
miles round indications still remained of sites of
Tartar encampments: these seemed to have been
legion, but, according to returns picked up in a
tent, their force appears to have amounted to 80,000,
chiefly mounted men.

On the 24th September, General Napier and Staff
arrived, and through the energetic measures of Sir
Hope Grant our army was reinforced by the following accessions:—a battalion of the 60th Rifles,
the 67th, the Royals, and wings of the 99th Queen's
and 8th Punjaubees; and the siege guns and several
8-inch mortars had reached Ho-see-woo by river, and
would soon be at Tung-chow: so there was every
prospect of a speedy advance, at which no one felt
regret, as our camp life had some time past been
rendered miserable by the fearful gales of wind from
the north-west, that threatened incessantly for hours
at a time to bring our tents down about our ears,
and carried with them clouds of dust, that most pro-
vokingly covered everything, both inside and outside
the canvas. A day or two's rain then ensued, followed on the 1st October by sharp fresh weather; so
that the thermometer, which ranged during noon, a

few days previous, at 90° to 100°, now suddenly lowered to 40° and 50°. The commissariat arrangements were all this while eminently successful, and the army consequently in excellent health and spirits.

CHAPTER XI.

The sun shines hot, and if we use delay
Cold biting winter mars our hoped-for hay.

SHAKSPEARE.

A refractory Mandarin.—Punjaubee Couriers.—Letters from Prince
Kung.—Advance of the Allies.—Letter from Mr. Parkes.—
Chinese Mahommedans.—Bivouac.—Flight of the Tartars.—
Chinese Mendacity.—French Advance on the Summer Palace.
—A Celestial Funeral.—Friendly Feeling of the Natives.—
Outside the Palace.—An Imperial Eunuch.—Description of
the Palace.—Rare Loot.—The Summer Park.

MR. MONGAN of ours, who was stationed at Tien-tsin
as interpreter to the force left there, found much
difficulty in dealing with the prefect, or magistrate,
of that place. This functionary was several times
called on to exercise his authority in various ways,
but returned evasive answers, and at last became
insolent. General Napier, therefore, hit upon the
plan of taking the prefect under his charge, and
holding him close prisoner in the camp before the
walls of Tien-tsin. The interpreter called upon the
mandarin with a strong guard, and requested his
attendance at the camp, but he refused compliance.

He was at once seized and put into a chair, despite his struggles, and carried to the camp, where a tent was allotted him close to the General's, and a sentry posted at the door to guard him. For the first few days he sulked, and would scarcely eat anything; but, finding he gained no object by adopting such a course, he soon became more cheerful, and issued whatever orders he was bid. He told the interpreter that his impression before, with regard to foreigners, was that they were a set of unruly barbarians, and that he had no previous conception that such nations existed as France and England. He expressed much surprise at the equipment of the British force, and much admired their horses; but what particularly astonished him was the untiring attendance of the sentry. He said, "Those men are wonderfully disciplined. When a man is posted at my tent's door, there he remains until he is relieved; he never thinks of going away, except to attend me when I move out. Why, if it were one of our soldiers, the scamp would run away, as soon as the officer's back was turned, to smoke his pipe, or to gamble with his comrades. I cannot make out how you teach your men such discipline."

The capture of this mandarin, and his detention under guard, had reached the authorities in the capital, and was afterwards quoted by Hangke to Mr. Parkes in prison as one of the reasons why the Prince of E concluded that we were not sincere when treating for peace at Tung-chow. It was most essential to keep open a road communication with Tien-tsin; and for that object, detachments of the 31st had been stationed at Ho-see-woo and Yang-tsun, so that travellers between the camp and the city were enabled to find a safe halting-place on the road either way. For the conveyance of mails, to and fro, the Seikhs were usually employed, and their hardihood and indifference to the sun made them the best suited for the work. A couple of them were wont to be despatched on these errands, and they found no difficulty in performing the journey in two days. On one occasion before the camp at the canal broke up, two of these trusty troopers were fired on by some villagers as they rode through a village some miles in rear of Chang-chia-wan. The circumstance was at once reported to the General on their arrival in camp; and the matter being promptly taken up, the 8th Punjaubees were despatched to destroy the village by fire. This lesson had a lasting good effect on the roadside villages, and no folly of the like kind was again attempted.

Reconnaissances of cavalry had several times been sent from the camp right to the walls of the city, and these had brought back word that the enemy

18

had a strong position within an embankment on the north-east angle of Pekin.

We have before stated that a communication had been received from the Prince of Kung, announcing his appointment as commissioner, and Lord Elgin's reply that no treating could be thought of until the prisoners were returned. We will now briefly summarize the correspondence that followed. Prince Kung, in his second letter, acknowledged that the Chinese Government did hold certain British subjects prisoners, but as they were taken after the fighting had commenced, they could not be released until the convention had been signed and the allied armies withdrawn from the country. The reply to this was that the prisoners must be given up, or the army would advance, and then his lordship would not be responsible for the consequences, which might prove of a very serious nature, leading, perhaps, to the destruction of the capital, and possibly to the overthrow of the dynasty; and that if the Chinese Government preferred it, the restoration of the prisoners and the signing of the convention might be made simultaneous acts. Three clear days were given to Prince Kung to determine the course of the allies. The letter was written on the 25th, consequently, unless an answer was returned on the 29th, hostilities would be resumed on the 30th. The term

would have been shorter had the allied forces been
ready to advance at once; but the French reinforcements of infantry had not yet arrived, and our siege
guns were still on the way from Tung-chow. Ere
the term had expired, again and again did Prince
Kung write, using every imaginable argument to delay
the advance of the troops, but the question of the
surrender of the prisoners he always evaded. On
the 29th, we were cheered by the sight of a card,
written in Chinese and English, in Mr. Parkès' own
hand, and bearing a late date, enclosed in one of the
Prince's letters, and from this testimony we were
delighted to learn that one of the prisoners at least
was alive. For, previous to this, since the capture,
nothing reliable had been heard of the prisoners, and
we laboured under the fear and suspicion that they
had been barbarously murdered, as is too often the
treatment dealt by the Chinese to their captives
in war.

The three days' term had expired, and no satisfactory answer being returned from the Chinese,
the army would have advanced at once, had the
French infantry arrived; but as they had not yet
made their appearance, the march was postponed.
The General, however, kept his word, in so far that
he pushed on a party of Rifles to take possession
of a village on the other side of a canal, close to the

paved highway, where it was proposed to establish a depôt.

On the 2nd of October a note was received by Mr. Wade from Mr. Parkes in Chinese, stating that he and Mr. Loch were well, and both together, and had received permission to send for some clean clothes, which they much required; but not a word was said about the other prisoners, to whom the Chinese themselves did not allude. The reticence on this subject naturally filled us with much anxiety as to their safety. Mr. Parkes' letter spoke in high terms of Prince Kung's kindness and ability, but in a forced language which did not bear the stamp of sincerity; and that such was the case was verified by a few words in Hindustani written by Mr. Loch over his signature, which certified that the letter was written by order of the Government. To this note Mr. Wade returned an answer the same day in Chinese and English, and forwarded a bundle of clean clothes, among which one handkerchief was inserted with Hindustani words printed in Roman characters round the initials, to the effect that in three days the heavy guns would open fire and breach the walls of the city; and a shirt was also similarly marked in a conspicuous part.

At noon on the 3rd we struck tents, crossed the canal, and advanced to the Mahommedan village of

Chang-ying, close to the advanced outposts of Rifles.
Lord Elgin and Sir Hope Grant and Staffs took up
their quarters in a handsome domed mosque, while
the army, some 6,000 strong, encamped round about
in the adjoining fields. The village was small, and
composed of mud huts, but at the time not altogether
tenantless. Its inhabitants were all of the Mahommedan faith, and were at once to be distinguished
from other natives by the singular conical caps they
wore on their heads, into which the queue was folded.
The interior of the mosque contained numerous inscriptions in large Arabic, as well as Chinese letters,
and several printed books and manuscript writings in
the Arabic character lay about. Many of the Chinese
followers of the Prophet could spell out a few words
of these books, but in a very few instances could they
explain their meaning. They were, however, often
acquainted with prayers and passages from the Koran,
and used to repeat them to the Seikhs; the repetition
of such prayers often drawing tears from the eyes of
these tried warriors of Ind, and not unfrequently the
silver from their pockets, which latter sympathy the
Celestial Mahommedan knew better know to appreciate. In the afternoon letters were received from
Messrs. Parkes and Loch in English, saying that
they were well; but again making no allusion to the
other prisoners.

The French reinforcement had now arrived at the camp at Pa-le-cheaou, and it was arranged to march on the 5th and storm the Tartar encampment supposed to exist within the great earth embankment near the north-east corner of the Pekin wall. The baggage was all to be collected together and left at a large marble monument, the tomb of some grandee, and the troops to set out, with three days' provisions in their haversacks, in light marching order.

On the 5th the French arrived from their encampment at an early hour, and the whole force of the Allies, over 10,000 strong, started on their Tartar-hunting expedition, the French keeping to the left, the British to the right. It was quite a pretty sight to watch the movements of this compact little army as it stretched away over the country. Now the whole would be visible, moving uniformly along over an extent of cultivated ground; and now some portions would be lost to view, as they filed through a village or diverged on one side to avoid a wall-encircled grove.

> "Behold in awful march and dread array
> The long-extended squadrons shape their way."

We had proceeded about four miles when a halt was sounded close to some grass-grown brick-kilns, from the tops of which we got our first view of the long-secluded capital of the Celestial Empire. The

city lay at a distance of some six miles on flat
ground, and almost entirely hidden by its long line
of wall; but the towers over its gates, and its larger
corner towers, loomed conspicuously through the clear
atmosphere. The General and staff officers assembled
on the top of the mound, and deliberated on the
plan of attack; and the prospect of a collision, aided
by the cheering sunlight which succeeded a damp,
chilly morning, invigorated all to a speedy advance,
when word came from the French Commander-
in-Chief desiring a deferment of proceedings till
the morrow, as his troops, which had marched four
miles farther than ours, were fatigued, and required
rest. A general order was, therefore, immediately
circulated for the British troops to bivouac where
they were. A few huts only, and those of the most
wretched description, occurring on the spot, some of
the more favoured officers were enabled to find quarters; the rest, in company with the soldiers, made
what arrangements they could with the straw and
millet stalks they could find, to make a comfortable
bivouac. The French, however, were more fortunate.
Having marched with the greater part of their heavy
baggage, they soon pitched tents, and made themselves snug with all the ordinary comforts of camp
life. The few rustics to whom these straw and mud-
built tenements belonged had, in nearly every case,

decamped, leaving behind them, however, a few fowls
and other poultry. One would have thought that,
midst all other discomforts, to say the least, one was
entitled to appropriate these to cheer the dejected
spirits with the prospect of good fare. But not so!
The provost-marshal was at work, and many an unfortunate " black " was summarily chastised while employed in catering for his master's table. Forage
was plentiful, and the horses were allowed to supply
themselves without dread of falling into the hands
of the ruthless provost. Colonel Wolseley selected
an old broken-down homestead for the accommodation of himself and department. A very deaf old
lady, full of years, was the only occupant, and she
appeared too imbecile to take much heed of us.
During that afternoon we heard from some Chinese
who straggled through the camp, that the Tartars
at the north-east corner of the city wall were fast
making off, and removing their camp; they could
or would not tell us whither.

Next morning betimes we were again in the field.
It was damp and raw as we rode up behind the
General, who was issuing orders for the disposition
of the march. Sir Hope Grant called me to him,
and ordered me to attach myself to the Cavalry
Brigade, who were well away to the right. I forthwith galloped away in the direction I was told, and

on opening a clump of trees found the brigade halted, and awaiting the signal for general march. I reported myself to Brigadier Pattle, commanding, and rode by his side as the troopers advanced through the pretty wood-abounding country of this neighbourhood. The infantry were on our left at no great distance, and we rarely lost sight of them, except where a grove or a village intervened. At eleven, a halt was called, and a staff officer came riding across with orders for Brigadier Pattle to attend on the General. The halting place was close to a glaring red wall, which partly closed in the mausoleum of one of the Emperor's sisters. The structure was still unfinished, and did not display much taste. Some unwholesome-looking pools supplied the horses with ample water, and the troops refreshed themselves with a snack from their wallets, and a few whiffs from the ever-cheering pipe.

The Brigadier soon returned to his brigade with orders to proceed, after half an hour's halt, in a northerly direction for a few miles, and then to strike due west, and halt at any convenient place on the broad northern road leading to the Tih-shing, or second gate of the north face of the city, as in all probability the Tartars would retreat along the north road, when their encampment was being attacked by the British and French infantry from the east; and thus an opportunity would be afforded to the Cavalry

Brigade to intercept and cut off their retreat. The cavalry were advancing to the north-west, when the videttes reported large bodies of Tartars moving north. The brigade was halted, and a squadron of Probyn's sent to observe the fugitives; but the Tartars sighted its approach, and made off.

We at last reached the broad road to which we were directed, and the brigade was drawn up in a grove on an eminence on the other side of the road, commanding open country on both right and left. The place was well adapted for a hiding-place, as the superabundant foliage covered the force from view of any passing enemy. Among some fir-trees at a distance we could see several men mounted on mules, scuttling about, but most of them were carrying bundles under their arms, and had the appearance of villagers escaping with their valuables. A cart was observed passing with what appeared to be a gun in it, and a few Seikhs were at once sent to capture it. The formidable-looking instrument turned out to be only some household chattels, which the native was hurrying off from a house in the neighbourhood. The Brigadier then sent me away with Captain Fane and a guard, to make inquiries along the road in the direction of the city as to the whereabouts of the Tartar camp. We had proceeded about two miles when we heard the report of muskets, and learned from a passing native that the Allies were already in the enemy's camp.

With this intelligence we returned to the Brigadier, who determined to march towards the Allies. On the way we met a half-nude Chinaman with a sheepish look, who tried to avoid us. I was sent to seek for information from him; the man stopped at the sound of my voice, and when questioned stoutly denied having seen or heard anything of the Allies; but instead of standing still and giving straightforward answers, he kept sidling away the nearer I approached, and at last made a run for it. An officer immediately gave chase, and, seizing him by the tail, swung the poor wretch in the air, and hurled him prostrate on the ground; he picked himself up sharply, and again matched the swiftness of his heels against the pace of the officer's horse, but without avail. The second grasp at his tail was a more firm one, and he was led back much humbled. He protested against this rough treatment, and swore that he was only a simple villager, and no Tartar. The coat rolled up under his arm, with the soldier's badge and regimental ticket attached to his girdle, however, belied his affirmation. These, he insisted, he had picked up on the road, together with a roll of fine-powder-tubes, which he held in his hand—another ordinary accompaniment of the Chinese soldier's accoutrements, which added more convincing proofs of his barefaced mendacity. The fellow was handed to the charge of a guard in the rear, and we advanced. We arrived at the large Peh-ting temple, some three miles from Tih-shing gate, close to which we found the French halted, and making anxious inquiries after the British infantry. The Brigadier spoke with General Montauban, who said that he suspected Sir Hope Grant had moved on to the Summer Palace, where he had appointed the rendezvous at the close of the day. The French General then intimated his intention of advancing at once on the Palace, and begged that the cavalry would move off his line of march. The Brigadier thought it very odd that the French, who were only a short way on the left, should have lost sight of the British troops, and, thinking that they might have pushed on to the Summer Palace, he directed his brigade thither also; but to avoid impeding the way of the French, we went some way up the north road before we struck across country for the Summer Palace in a north-westerly direction.

We came suddenly up with a procession of Chinese travellers. The chief personage was a pale young man seated cross-legged in a large sedan, carried by two mules, the fore and aft cross-poles resting on the respective shoulders of these animals. A large coffin, covered with blue cloth, was carried in a similar manner on two other mules. If the beasts were at all inclined to be troublesome, this mode of conveyance would be made far from agreeable, but they were attended by a groom apiece, who soon corrected any show of evil inclination on their part. The young man was greatly alarmed at our appearance, and continued knocking his head against the bottom of the chair. He prayed us to let him pass, as he was only a civilian engaged in escorting the coffin of his father to his native village. The Brigadier desired me to tell him not to be alarmed, for that he would see that none of his people harmed him; and this gallant officer really believed that none of his officers would take the mean advantage to plunder a harmless disarmed man; but, to my surprise, I afterwards heard that the coffin was seized for the sake of the mules that carried it, and these latter being properly secured, the former was thrown into a ditch.

The country was so thickly wooded, and the view so intercepted, that we were at a loss what direction to take. Just in the nick of time up rushed a Chinese in a most excited state, saying that but a short while ago parties of rascally Tartars had plundered his house in retreating, and run in the direction of the Summer Palace, and he prayed us to be avenged on them for plundering his all. If we would give them a good beating, he continued, he would be only too happy to show us the way. We were but too glad to avail ourselves of his guidance. A couple of miles or so brought us to the barracks of the Blue Bannermen. Our guide showed us these, adding, " There are soldiers inside ; go and murder them all." He then ran off. These barracks consisted of a large cluster of low houses, enclosed by an eight-feet wall, and entered by a large wooden gate, through the chinks of which we observed faces looking at us. To the right of the gate, and outside the wall, were a few houses, about which some respectable-looking villagers clustered with offerings of tea and cakes. Colonel Walker, the Quartermaster-General of the cavalry, and myself, went to them, and questioned them as to the inmates of the barracks. They replied that they only consisted of the wives, old folks, and children of the soldiers, the able-bodied men being all away with San-kolinsin. This was reported to the Brigadier, who demanded that the gate should be thrown open that we might go in and inspect the place. This they objected to, as they said our appearance would frighten the women and children ; whereupon, to alarm them into compliance, a gun was quietly unlimbered, and made to face the entrance, and word was sent to the inmates that unless some of the veterans immediately came out to parley with us, and the gates were thrown open, we would force our way in. The threat produced the desired effect, and soon a deputation of old men attended on the Brigadier, dressed in long white frocks in token of respect.   They protested a warm friendship for our cause, and prayed we would not hurt them.   We then questioned them as to whether they had seen any of the British infantry pass that way.   They said they had seen plenty of Tartars passing during that day, but that we were the first of the Allies they had encountered.   As we continued our course, in vain did we seek to gain information of the whereabouts of the British infantry.

The Brigadier thereupon resolved to move towards the French column, which was advancing on the Summer Palace.   We found them on the road, as we had suspected, and the Brigadier offered his co-operation in the capture of the Palace.   To this the French General assented, and begged that he would keep well to the right round the walls of the gardens to cut off the retreating Tartars, while he attacked the central gate.   The French then advanced through the central road of the large village of Hai-teen in front of the Palace, while we moved round by the right.   A few skirmishers were on ahead as we struck through a straggling series of the outermost houses.

> " Now sunk the sun ; the closing hour of day
>   Came onward mantled o'er with sober gray ;
>   Nature with silence bid the world repose,
>   When near the road a stately palace rose."

We were at the walls of the Palace, but we were completely closed in on our rear by the large populous village, and should the imperial gardens be well defended by Tartar skirmishers, as it was reported to be, it would be no place for mounted troops in the fast fading twilight. The Brigadier, therefore, determined to defer entering the grounds till the morrow, and now made inquiries of the natives for a spot of ground supplied with water to pass the night on. We were led to a clear space of turf of a rectangular form, made by the receding line of wall that encircled the Summer Palace; but this did not suit military taste, as only one end was open, and should the Tartars please to treat us with a night surprise they would catch us in a complete trap. We, therefore, turned our steps to the right, and sought an open spot in the fields beyond the village. As Colonel Walker and myself proceeded in advance we suddenly came upon a party of some twenty mounted men, who were in a field raised above the level of the road. These made off as fast as they could go, and the Brigadier selected the ground they had left for the bivouac. The troops had orders to stand by their horses, and not to light fires until the moon rose at eleven.

It was a clear fresh evening, and a bivouac *sub jove* would not have been so unpleasant, had we been provided with something at least to cheer the inner man. I had been despatched that morning with short notice, and had not had time to supply myself; but, thanks to the large holsters of the Brigadier and his Staff, I managed to procure a snack before resigning myself to sleep. We found ourselves close to a floor on which there was a pile of chaff, which yielded a most luxuriant mattress; and being provided with one of those fur coats, of which the doctor carried a goodly store (having had—true to his profession—an eye to the requirements of others), I soon succumbed beneath the fatigues of the day.

Atone o'clock we were roused by the arrival of an officer with a prisoner. The moon was well up, and shed her mild light around; numerous fires glimmered throughout the camp, and, aided by the hum of voices, gave quite a cheerful appearance to the spot. A large fire blazed merrily close to our roost, and round it we soon recognized the Brigadier and several officers standing, and by their side an unfortunate native trembling with fear, and gesticulating most grotesquely to his captors. The captive was a withered old man, dressed in the garb of an official menial. He told me he was one of the Emperor's eunuchs, who had been left behind to look after the Summer Palace. The Emperor had left for Ge-hol some fifteen days before, carrying with him his thirteen wives, and a large retinue. They had left in

19

a great hurry, but Prince Kung had stayed behind till the evening previous, when the intelligence was brought that the Allies were marching on the place. The Prince took a precipitate leave of the premises, giving directions to the eunuchs, some 300 in number, to stand by in its defence. At sundown the French burst open the doors, and on the eunuchs opposing their entrance to the holy precincts of the Dragon Hall two of the eunuchs were killed, and others wounded. Seeing no hope of defending the place, our prisoner then mounted his pony and ran for it, and in his hot haste to escape he had run into our lines.

The Emperor, he said, was a very sickly man, and had lately suffered much from dropsy in one leg, which had necessitated his using a crutch. He had thirteen wives only. The first wife, or Empress, was barren, but two of the junior wives had blessed him with issue, one a boy now four years of age, the other a girl of five. His children, as well as his wives, had accompanied him to his retreat at Ge-hol, some hundred miles distant from Pekin. The total number of eunuchs employed by the Emperor amounted to about 480, and these were distributed throughout the different palaces and imperial grounds. Eunuchs were usually selected from families where there were three sons, the youngest being selected to the honourable post. He himself was the youngest of three in the ·

family of a farmer, and at the age of eighteen was taken from the bosom of his family, and a bonus of fifteen taels of silver paid to soothe his bereaved parents. At that age he was totally emasculated, and then placed to serve in the Royal Imperial Hall of Medicine until within a few years, when he was promoted to attend on the Emperor. He had been twenty-seven years an eunuch, and would at the expiry of three years more be entitled to a gold button. The next step to a gold button was a white one, which appointment was a reward for good behaviour. From the white buttons was selected the controller of the eunuchs, decorated with a blue button, the highest rank attainable for this class of officials, his duty being to attend on the Emperor's person. The gold buttons were very numerous, but there were only some twenty or so white-buttoned eunuchs. In former days the eunuchs were a far more honourable class than at the present; they were then empowered to hold appointments under Government, and could attain the highest official rank of the red button; but, owing to the frequent intrigues in which they had taken a prominent part, their position in life was now degraded to the simple menial.

Soon after daylight we were startled by the sound of heavy guns, and at first we thought that the bombardment of Pekin had commenced; but the reports continued uniformly until we had counted twenty-one, and then ceased. We listened in vain for more, and as no other sound of firing struck the ear, we felt convinced that the cannonade was intended for a royal salute, and that the city had either surrendered, or, what was more probable, it was done to give the missing cavalry notice of the direction of the British camp. Soon afterwards Colonel Wolseley found us out, and told us that the General had quartered the troops in the suburb outside the Tih-shing gate. It appears that Sir Hope Grant had diverged a little to the right in his line of attack on the earthwork, and had sent word to the French General to do the same, but that the latter had made a more decided turn to the right, and, crossing the rear of the British column, pushed after them, always thinking that he was behind them, until he reached the Summer Palace. The British had seen a considerable body of infantry falling back, but were unable to get up with them. They, however, had had a slight skirmish with a picket of Tartars at the Tih-shing suburb, which accounts for the reports of musketry we had heard. From this suburb they drove the Tartars into the gate, and as the troops were tired, and it was getting late, the General deemed it expedient to bivouac where he was. Colonel Wolseley, upon exchanging a few words with us, returned to the

General; and the brigadier, accompanied by a couple of his officers and myself, at 7 A.M. paid a visit to the French at the Summer Palace, taking the captive eunuch along with us.

A paved roadway leaves the Palace inside Pekin, and emerging at the Se-che gate on the west side continues with a few windings in the direction of a group of villages of different names collectively called Hai-teen. The stoneway runs through this group of ugly hovels on to a broad road with the pavement through its centre. Stone garden walls stand to the right and left as you advance, enclosing the grounds of nobles and imperial connections. You advance, *suivant le pavé*, across a stone bridge, take a sweep to the left, and the road brings you between two large pieces of water in front of the grand entrance to the Palace of Yuen-ming-yuen. It was here under the trees that the French were encamped.

After the capture of the entrance the French posted a guard at the gate, and bivouacked under the trees; the French General reserving a large space of ground for the British cavalry, whom he expected to return to him after their peregrinations in search of the retreating Tartars. The ground of their camp was shut in on all sides by walls and houses, and the men appeared to have been tired and in low spirits; for, twice in the night, a panic seized

them, and the French troops were almost uncon-
trollable on both occasions, and would not listen to
the calls of their officers.   General Montauban led
us into the Palace, solemnly protesting all the while
that he had strictly prohibited his troops from entering within its walls, as he had determined that no
looting should take place before the British came up,
that all might have an equal chance.   We entered
through the central gateway upon a large paved
courtyard, whereon the bodies of two Chinese officials
were lying dead.   The French assured us that these
were two of the Tartars, who had opposed their
entrance on the previous evening, and had succeeded
in wounding two of their officers.   The so-called
Tartars turned out to be eunuchs. They were dressed
in the usual official costume, and had red tasselled
hats on their heads.   On the centre of the pavement,
and facing the gate, stood the grand reception hall,
a large Chinese building, well adorned exteriorly with
paint and gilding, and netted with iron wire under
the fretted eaves to keep the birds off.   We entered
its central door, and found ourselves on a smooth
marble floor, in front of the Emperor's ebony throne.
The carvings on the throne consisted of dragons in
various attitudes, and was quite a work of art ; but
the material, on closer examination, proved to be
some inferior wood painted to imitate ebony.   The

floor of the throne was carpeted with a light red cloth, and three low series of steps led up to it, of which the central series was the widest and intended for kow-towing on before the Emperor. The left side of the room was covered with one extensive picture, representing the grounds of the Summer Palace. Side-tables were covered with books in yellow silk binding and articles of virtu. There was somehow an air of reverence throughout this simple but neat hall, and we could well imagine the awe that it was calculated to inspire on the chosen few who were privileged to draw near on ceremonial days, and render their obeisance before the much-dreaded Brother of the Sun and Moon.

Imagine such a scene. The Emperor is seated on his ebony throne, attired in a yellow robe wrought over with dragons in gold thread, his head surmounted with a spherical crown of gold and precious stones, with pearl drops suspended round on light gold chains. His eunuchs and ministers, in court costume, ranged on either side on their knees, and his guard of honour and musicians drawn up in two lines in the court-yard without. The name of the distinguished personage to be introduced is called out, and as he approaches the band strikes up. He draws near the awful throne, and, looking meekly on the ground, drops on his knees before the central steps. He removes his hat from his head, and places it on the throne floor, with its peacock's feather towards the imperial donor. The Emperor moves his hand, and down goes the humble head, and the forehead strikes on the step three times three. The head is then raised, but the eyes are still meekly lowered, as the imperial voice in thrilling accents pronounces the behests of the great master. The voice hushed, down goes the head again and acknowledges the sovereign right, and the privileged individual is allowed to withdraw. The scene described is not imaginary, but warranted by the accounts of natives. How different the scene now! The hall filled with crowds of a foreign soldiery, and the throne floor covered with the Celestial Emperor's choicest curios, but destined as gifts for two far more worthy monarchs. "See here," said General Montauban, pointing to them, "I have had a few of the most brilliant things selected, to be divided between the Queen of Great Britain and the Emperor of the French."

Behind the grand hall was rockery, and in rear of that again a large pond, so that a pebbled path leading over a bridge and taking a semicircular sweep of half the water, had to be traversed before you visited the next hall. The distance was about 500 yards. This hall was smaller, and not got up with such care : yellow sedan chairs and one mountain chair stood close to the throne ; on the right and left were small rooms adjoining, with images of Bhuddha. Behind stood another reception hall, and in rear of that again a third ; and on the left the Emperor's private rooms, beautifully got up, the tables spread with all manner of precious articles, many of which were English or French.   The house was small, and consisted chiefly of one moderately sized room, with a large double-seated throne, covered with gaudily coloured cloth, and having red drapery in rear, which formed a curtain to a waiting recess.   A large glass chandelier hung from the roof, and large ornamented clocks and statuettes stood about the floor.   Opposite the door was a carved wooden wainscoting, which formed by partition from the hall a narrow passage leading on the left to two small rooms with a spiral staircase in the rearmost of them, conveying you to two other small rooms above, which appeared from their shelves of books to have been the Emperor's studio.   A window in each of these rooms, of large single panes of glass, enabled you to look down into the hall.   On the right of the passage were the Emperor's two retiring rooms.   A hanging blind over the entrance being withdrawn, you could enter the foremost of these rooms, which communicated again, by means of a doorway and another hanging blind, with the room in rear,—his Majesty's bedroom. A large niche in the wall, curtained over and covered with silk mattresses, served for the bed ; and a sloping platform enabled his Majesty to mount into it. A small silk handkerchief, with sundry writings in the vermilion pencil about the barbarians, was under the imperial pillow, and pipes and other Chinese luxuries were on a table close by. The English treaty of 1858, with its covering envelope, lay on a table ; and large quantities of vermilion pencillings were packed up, most of which had reference to the Allies. The greater part of the curiosities lay about these rooms, and we proceeded to examine them as we would the curiosities of a museum, when, to our astonishment, the French officers commenced to *arracher* everything they took a fancy to. Gold watches and small valuables were whipped up by these gentlemen with amazing velocity, and as speedily disappeared into their capacious pockets.

After allowing his people to load themselves as fast as they could for about ten minutes, the General insisted upon them all following him out, and kept on repeating that looting was strictly prohibited, and he would not allow it, although his officers were doing it without any reserve before his own eyes. He then told the Brigadier that nothing should be touched until Sir Hope Grant arrived.   Just as we were

walking out of the chief gateway an officer accosted
the General, and informed him that they had caught
a Chinese stealing a pair of old shoes out of the
imperial grounds. "Bring him here!" said the
indignant General. "Have we not said that looting
is strictly forbidden?" The prisoner came forward
trembling, and the gallant General exhausted his
wrath with his cane about the shoulders of this luck-
less scapegoat. The Brigadier,then went to breakfast
with General Montauban and Staff, and I sought my
friends of the *Bureau Topographique*. The French
camp was revelling in silks and bijouterie. Every-
body had some rare curios to show me, asking
me their worth, as, being an interpreter, and having
the eunuch with me, they looked upon me as quite
a connoisseur. One French officer had a string of
splendid pearls, each pearl being of the size of a
marble (this he afterwards foolishly disposed of at
Hong Kong for 3,000*l.*); others had pencil-cases set
with diamonds; others watches and vases set with
pearls. Indeed, it would be an endless task to
enumerate all the valuables already appropriated from
the Palace, and yet the French General had asserted
that nothing had been taken, as looting was strictly
prohibited!

After breakfast the correspondent of the *Moniteur*
got me a pass to accompany him into the palace

again, and we had not been long in before Sir Hope
Grant and Staff arrived. General Montauban wel-
comed him, and positively assured him that nothing
had as yet been taken from the palace; but as Sir
Hope Grant walked through the French camp his
own eyes plainly told him the falsehood of such a
statement. Looting still continued, but more surrep-
titiously; and a French officer, alluding to General
Montauban's prohibition, said, " It places us quite
in a false position. The General says you must
not loot, and yet he allows it to take place before
his own eyes." Lord Elgin next arrived, and strongly
protested against the looting, saying, in plain terms,
" I would like a great many things that the palace
contains, but I am not a thief."

The *Moniteur* correspondent, myself, and the eunuch,
continued our rambles through the palaces. On the
extreme left were the Empress's two rooms and several
smaller ones for the sundry wives, but none of them
in style at all approaching those of the Emperor's.
Several baskets of fruit and sweetmeats lay on the
Empress's table, showing that her departure was of
no long date. On the right of the grand hall were
houses after houses well stored with silks, curios, and
luxuries of all kinds, such as birdsnests, tea, tobacco,
dried fruits, &c. Then followed the houses of the
retainers. Narrow painted galleries connected all

the imperial rooms "in endless maze intricate, per-
plexed."

Behind the chief building came the summer park,
the extent of wall surrounding the whole being about
twelve miles. Pebbled paths led you through groves
of magnificent trees, round lakes, into picturesque
summer-houses, over fantastic bridges. As you wandered along herds of deer would amble away from
before you, tossing their antlered heads. Here a
solitary building would rise fairy-like from the centre
of a lake, reflecting its image on the limpid blue liquid
in which it seemed to float, and then a sloping path
would carry you into the heart of a mysterious cavern
artificially formed of rockery, and leading out on to
a grotto in the bosom of another lake. The variety
of the picturesque was endless, and charming in the
extreme ; indeed, all that is most lovely in Chinese
scenery, where art contrives to cheat the rude attempts
of nature into the bewitching, seemed all associated
in these delightful grounds. The resources of the
designer appear to have been unending, and no money
spared to bring his work to perfection. All the
tasteful landscapes so often viewed in the better class
of Chinese paintings, and which we had hitherto
looked upon as wrought out of the imagination of
the artist, were here bodied forth in life. I will
not, however, venture on too minute a description,

as it would doubtless prove tedious to the reader. Such spots can be better imagined than described.

Just within the walls that encircled the grounds on the right and left were large handsome llama temples with yellow tiled roofs.

In the afternoon the Brigadier called me away, and we returned to our bivouac, where we had to spend another night; but this time we spent the dark hours stowed away in a rude straw hut close to the threshing-floor. The farmer to whom it belonged appeared to have been a bird-fancier, for two cages hung to the roof of the hut, the one containing a hawfinch, and the other a pair of redpoles, both old acquaintances of our boyhood's early days.

The next morning we found our way to the British camp before the Tih-shing gate, where the Cavalry Brigade took possession of the quarters set aside for them, and I returned to my old position in the Topographical Department, and put up with Colonel Wolseley.

CHAPTER XII.

Perjury, foul perjury, in the highest degree;
Murder, stern murder, in the direst degree;
All several sins, all used in each degree,
Throng to the bar, crying all, "Guilty, guilty!"
Richard III.

Release of Messrs. Parkes and Loch.—Looting the Summer Palace.
—British Share of the Spoil.—Discovery of Secret Documents.
—Preparations for attacking Pekin.—Surrender of the An-ting
Gate.—Restoration of other Prisoners.—Spirit of Retaliation.—
Funeral of Murdered Prisoners.—Lord Elgin's Reasons for the
Destruction of the Summer Palace.—Firing the Yuen-ming-
yuen.—General Description of the Palace and Grounds.

ON the day after the advance, Mr. Wade received a
note from Mr. Parkes, dated the previous day (5th
October). It was enclosed in a letter from Prince
Kung, written from the Summer Palace. This note
announced the intention of the authorities to release
the prisoners confined in Pekin, on the 8th. Shortly
after, Mr. Wade had an interview with Hangke, who
had been appointed Assistant Commissioner with
Prince Kung, and acquainted him of the demand
of the Commanders-in-Chief that one of the gates
of Pekin should be surrendered to the Allies. The
mandarin of course protested against the possibility

of such an act, but eventually promised to refer the matter to the Prince. When questioned with regard to the prisoners who were said not to be in the capital, he replied he would do his best to secure their return; but not knowing whither they had been conveyed, he could make no positive promise.

On the 8th, Messrs. Parkes and Loch, and their attendant sowar of Probyn's troop, together with the Count L'Eskayrac de Lauture, of the French scientific mission, and four French soldiers, were released. These eight were all the prisoners, the Chinese positively asserted, that they had inside the city; and we naturally felt much anxiety as to the fate of the other unfortunates in their hands, especially as we believed they had been handed over to the tender mercies of the Tartar soldiers.

> " For none so cruel as the Tartar foe,
>   To death inured, and nursed in scenes of woe."

Messrs. Parkes and Loch, fortunately for them, had been held rather as state prisoners, and though at the first their treatment from the mandarins was brutal in the extreme, yet latterly, when matters were brought nearer to a crisis, their chains were taken off them, and they were properly housed and attended. The adventures of these two gentlemen, as related in their letters to Lord Elgin, having been already placed before the public, I cannot do more than

allude to them as extremely interesting.   Their
constancy and courage throughout their imprison-
ment, and their high determination not to submit
to acts which might in any way involve the honour
of the country, merit admiration; but much as
we sympathize with their sufferings, we cannot help
feeling gratified at the information with regard to
the internal working of the Pekin jail-system, which
their trials have eliminated for the benefit of those
interested in Chinese topics.

On Sunday the 7th, every one that could get permission to leave the camp repaired to the Summer
Palace, as the General now made no objection to
looting.   Soon after breakfast I mounted my horse,
and galloped across country alone, on a promise to
meet some officers there.   It was a bright, fresh forenoon, and the sunlight gave a youthful brightness to
the decaying foliage of the groves that marked the
way.   A few villagers stood watchful at the doors of
their domiciles, but disappeared sharply on spying me.
The French camp still lay before the palace, and the
French sentries at the gate; but no pass was required
—the place was open to ravages of any and all.   What
a terrible scene of destruction presented itself!   How
disturbed now was the late quiescent state of the
rooms, with their neat display of curiosities!   Officers
and men, English and French, were rushing about

20

in a most unbecoming manner, each eager for the acquisition of valuables. Most of the Frenchmen were armed with large clubs, and what they could not carry away, they smashed to atoms. In one room you would see several officers and men of all ranks with their heads and hands brushing and knocking together in the same box, searching and grasping its contents. In another a scramble was going on over a collection of handsome state robes. Some would be playing pitch and toss against the large mirrors; others would be amusing themselves by taking "cock" shots at the chandeliers. Respect for position was completely lost sight of, and the most perfect disorganization prevailed.

The love of gain is most contagious, and in every sense the *incitamentum malorum,* as the Latin grammar rightly teaches us. No one just then cared for gazing tranquilly at the works of art; each one was bent on acquiring what was most valuable. That scene afforded a very good proof of the innate evil in man's nature when unrestrained by the force of law or public opinion. Licensed theft soon displays the love of greed natural to every heart; and its concomitant vices, jealousy and dissension, speedily follow. The silk warehouses on the right were burst open, and dozens rushed in over the piles of valuable rolls of silk and embroidered dresses. These were thrown out in armfuls. There were piles on piles of them; and though plunderers were conveying them away by cartloads, still the ground was strewn with them, and there was yet more in the houses. A commission of prize agents had been formed by Sir Hope Grant for the purpose of collecting together curiosities to dispose of for the benefit of the army; and the officers composing it were busy all day in making their selections from what yet remained undamaged; while hundreds of others were looting on their own account. New rooms were constantly being found as the marauders extended their researches, still untouched and filled with old bronzes, clocks, enamelled jars, and an infinity of jade-stone curiosities. To these the plunderers rushed with eagerness. The booty was plentiful, but the means of conveyance scarce. Chinese from the surrounding villages crowded in and added their numbers to the vivacious looters, and hundreds of them were going backwards and forwards all day laden with bundles of spoil. After the spoliation had continued some time, light portable valuables became more rare, and the natives were soon seized upon as porters for the larger curios. An officer would be seen struggling under the weight of old jars, furs, and embroidered suits; he would meet a native similarly laden; the native would be made to open out his pack, and the choice contents being

20—2

added to the officer's load, the native would be compelled to relinquish the remainder of his spoil and undertake the freight of the officer's burden. Soon the rumour spread that treasure had been discovered, and an excited crowd ran about to seek for the spot, but very wisely a guard had been placed over it, and the money was made over to proper hands for fair division between the English and French armies.

At the close of the day's loot it was found, as was to be expected, that much dissatisfaction occurred among the different members of the army. Numbers of the officers, and nearly the whole of the men, had by their duties been deprived of participation in the spoil; and among those that were there several had fallen across articles of great value, while others had only procured trumpery gewgaws. Some of General Napier's staff officers, moreover, had stripped off and brought away with them the roof of a neglected cottage, which had been mistaken for brass, but which turned out to be nearly pure gold, worth some 9,000l. This they handsomely placed at the disposal of the General of their Division, and it was being beaten out for distribution among the troops, when Sir Hope Grant received intelligence of the intention, and fearing the dissatisfaction that such distribution among a portion of the army was sure to produce, and in order to make matters more equal for those whose duties prevented them from sharing in the work of spoliation, he issued orders to call in all the loot acquired by the officers, appealing to their honour as officers and gentlemen to restore faithfully all they had taken. This measure, of course, caused great grumbling on the other side among those who had put themselves to considerable trouble in the acquisition and bringing away of what they held. One officer, in particular, who had laden his horse with his treasures and trudged all the way on foot to camp some five miles, leading his steed by the bridle, became the object of many sallies of wit when the orders were published. A sale was then appointed to take place on the 11th of all the articles collected by the commission, as well as of the booty called in; but on restoring his spoil each officer had the option of redeeming it at a price fixed by the commission. When the French had finished their work of destruction in the interior of the palace, they set the Emperor's private residence on fire, and then relinquished the grounds and removed their camp to a village in front of the An-ting gate. The Seikhs and a few of the dragoons were the only privates that had found their way to the Palace, and consequently their camps, especially that of the former, were much resorted to for the purchase of silks; the price usually demanded averaging one dollar (4s. 6d.) a roll, whereas the real value of the silk might have rated at from 3*l.* to 5*l.* The store and canteen keepers who followed the camp consequently drove a large business in this article, receiving payment for stores and liquors supplied to the troops in silk at that rate. But for knicknacks and bijoux the French camp offered the greatest allurement for several days. You had only to ask the first French soldier you met if he had anything for sale, and he would soon produce gold watches, strings of jewels, jade ornaments, or furs; and numbers of British officers, who had disposable dollars, quickly found means of exchanging them for objects of greater value in the French camp. For weeks, in either camp, nothing was talked of but curiosities purloined from the Summer Palace, and what they were likely to fetch. Numbers of the French officers had acquired tolerable fortunes, and their men were rolling in dollars, which led to much disorder and serious disturbances in their camp. For days after their return from their late bivouac their soldiers were constantly to be met with in a state of intoxication, and still carrying out the acquired spirit of plunder and spoliation to the villages in their neighbourhood.

The British share of the plunder was all arranged for exhibition in the hall of the large llama temple, where the Head-quarters' Staff were quartered, and a goodly display it was: white and green jade-stone ornaments of all tints, enamel-inlaid jars of antique shape, bronzes, gold and silver figures and statuettes, &c.; fine collections of furs, many of which were of much value, such as sable, sea-otter, ermine, Astracan lamb, &c.; and court costume, among which were two or three of the Emperor's state robes of rich yellow silk, worked upon with dragons in gold thread, and beautifully woven with floss-silk embroidery on the skirts, the inside being lined with silver fur or ermine, and cuffed with glossy sable. At the end of the hall were piled immense quantities of rolls of silk and crape of various colours, with several of the beautiful imperial yellow, a kind prescribed by the Chinese law for the use of his Imperial Majesty alone.

The sale continued over three whole days, and was largely attended both by officers and men. A perfect mania of competition appeared to have seized all ranks, and the prices realized were fabulous. The most trivial article fetched two or three pounds, and one of the court robes was knocked down at the high figure of 120*l.* Had the Emperor been present he would doubtless have felt flattered at the value set by the foreigners on any object solely because it had belonged to him. Fancy the sale of an emperor's effects beneath the walls of the capital of his empire,

and this by a people he despised as weak barbarians
and talked of driving into the sea!   The proceeds of
the sale amounted to 32,000 dollars, and the amount
of treasure secured was estimated at over 61,000 dollars, making a rough total of 93,000 dollars.   Of
this, two-thirds was set apart for distribution in pro-
portionate shares to the soldiers, and one-third for
the officers, of all those engaged in active service
during the day of the capture of the palace.   Sir
Hope Grant very generously made his share over to
the men, and as a token of respect, the officers
presented him with a gold claret jug richly chased,
one of the handsomest pieces of the booty.

Several interesting documents were met with in
the Summer Palace, many of which were in the Emperor's own holograph, to which we have before made
a passing allusion.   In one San-kolinsin reports the
loss of the forts, which he attributes to the accidental
explosion of the two powder magazines, and he proceeds to tell the Emperor that he has again established himself near Tung-chow, and that there is no
occasion to be alarmed.   In a later memorial he tells
the Emperor that the barbarians are advancing; and
that, though there is little chance of their progressing
far, he would recommend him to go on a hunting
tour to Ge-hol, until matters assumed a more satisfactory appearance.   To this proposal several Ministers

in their memorials strongly object, alleging that, as for the last forty years no Emperor has been on a hunting tour, it would look in the eyes of the people, in the present crisis, very much as if his Majesty were showing the white feather. Besides, the country on the road to Ge-hol was much infested with banditti, and it would neither be safe, nor sanctioned by previous imperial custom, to undertake the recommended expedition without at least 4,000 troops, and, in the present exigent state of the capital, such a force could not be well spared. They, on the contrary, recommended him to stay in Pekin, where they might, with the reinforcements expected, manage to muster 300,000 men; and, as the barbarians had only 10,000, the Emperor would have little to fear; and that he would in so doing inspire the people with confidence. A measure they more strenuously urged was that he should go forth at the head of his troops to oppose the advance of the barbarians, and they had no doubt that his august presence would spread consternation throughout the ranks of the uncouth savages, and make them an easy prey to the brave soldiers of the imperial army. The vermilion pencil to these propositions makes rather a pusillanimous reply; it says that his Majesty will make every preparation to send his troops to the field of battle; that the people may be deceived into confidence; and

that, when the time comes for him to lead forth his
soldiers, he will quietly move off with his escort to
Ge-hol. One Minister informs the Throne that he
has heard that the greater part of the barbarian
army is composed of Cantonese recruits; and he
suggests that, as these mercenaries have engaged
their services for the sake of gain, they might be
easily won to the Chinese cause by the promise of
larger bribes; and he therefore recommends that,
instead of yielding to the barbarian claim for indemnity of 8,000,000 taels, one million of such money
might be judiciously expended in gaining over the
Cantonese portion of the barbarian army, and then
the enemy's force would be so weakened that they
would be glad to listen to any terms the Chinese
Government might choose to dictate. The majority
of the memorialists talked with comparative indifference of the invading force, and referred with much
greater alarm to the mutinous spirits within the walls
of the city, who might encourage the people to rise
and throw open the gates to the barbarians. They
seemed much to fear that some of the Chinese in the
allied camp were in league with the disaffected
citizens of the town. Many of the papers showed a
determination to resist the Allies even after the fall
of Takoo, thus confirming previous impressions that
all throughout it was the policy of the Chinese to

lure Lord Elgin on from Tien-tsin with only a small
guard, and, having got his lordship and party into
their hands, on that to base their final proceedings.

The Chinese were given to the 12th for the surrender of the An-ting gate, the one near the western
angle, and before which the French were encamped.
The authorities had already made so many excuses
that it was not to be supposed that the gate would be
ceded without some semblance of opposition. To
the left of this gate, and facing the city wall, within
200 yards, ran a wall about twenty feet high, which
girt round a large space of ground some hundred
acres in extent, in which was situated the Temple of
Earth. Behind this covering wall was considered by
our engineers a good spot to construct a battery in
which to place our siege guns for the purpose of
breaching the Pekin wall, and they at once commenced to prepare the battery, leaving the bricks
in the wall till their work was finished. The plan of
attack was to breach the city wall some fifteen feet
from the ground; and the troops, entering by the
breach, were to turn to the right, and, proceeding
along the wall, to occupy the An-ting gate. The
French to our left, and in advance of the temple
wall, soon got a trench within 100 yards of the
city wall, and they were also busily engaged preparing a battery. The Commanders-in-Chief had

threatened to commence the attack at twelve precisely, if before that time the gate was not surrendered. The day had arrived, the batteries were all prepared, and the hour was fast approaching. The Royals were already in the temple by the side of the breaching guns, and a wing of the 67th was being paraded ready for the storming. Meanwhile Mr. Parkes and Colonel Stephenson, Deputy Adjutant-General, had repaired to the An-ting gate to receive any overtures the Chinese might make. General Napier stood by the guns with a watch in his hand, counting the minutes as they lapsed. Five minutes to twelve. Every one was eager and excited, and the order to fire was almost on the lips of the gallant General, when Colonel Stephenson came galloping to the spot, and announced that the gate had been surrendered.

A party of the 67th Regiment and 8th Punjaubees were at once despatched thither. They marched a few yards into the city, driving the dense crowd before them, and then took possession of the gate, quartering themselves on the right side. The French then marched in, drums beating and colours flying, and pushing in some distance farther along the broad road, returned and established themselves on the left side of the gate-top. A rope was then stretched across the road to keep the crowd back, and sentries posted, and entrance for the time strictly forbidden.

AN TING GATE OF PEKIN

This so-called gate is a formidable-looking structure. As you approach down the road leading south
through the An-ting suburb you see in front of
you, on the top of the lofty bulging wall, an immense
square tower with four rows of loopholes one above
the other, twelve in each row : the tower is covered
with sloping tiles, and the roof ridge curls upwards
at each end in the usual style of Chinese architecture.
This tower you would naturally suppose surmounted
the gateway, but it is not so; it is built on a semicircular portion of wall projecting beyond the true
wall, on which another similarly shaped tower, without
the loopholes, but with windows and balcony instead,
stands facing the first tower. Below this second
tower stands the archway of the gate. In the approach you cross a stone bridge built over what was
perhaps once a wet fosse, but is now quite dry, and
find yourself before the first tower ; you then follow
the stoneway to the left as it sweeps round the projecting wall and enter the first gate, a massive folding
portal beneath an archway, under which you pass into
the space formed by the semicircular with the natural
wall (at the sides of which are small guard-houses
and temples), and then following the stoneway as
it bends to the left, you are led through the second
archway portal on to the broad road of the city, which
runs direct south as far as your eye can strain through

the dust and over the sea of heads that throng it. Inside of the second gate on the left a long ramp by the side of the wall carries you up to the second square tower, from which you can get a fair view of the neighbouring portion of the city on the one hand, and of the country beyond on the other. At right angles to the broad, irregular, dusty road which bends southwards from the gate, run innumerable lanes, along which are placed side by side low hovels, many of them dirty and in disrepair, much in the same style as in southern cities. Some larger and two-storied buildings, mostly temples, scattered here and there, however, relieve the eye of the flat monotony. Beyond the wall, with the exception of the few houses in the neighbourhood of the gate, open ground occurs for upwards of two miles, covered in part with trees. The natives in the town, from the way they crowded round the sentries, appeared to have little fear of the barbarians, and they soon learned to bring supplies of fowls and fruit, and to open a small market at the gate. The ramp enabled the artillery to bring up some large field-pieces on to the gate, and soon several Armstrong muzzles pointed threateningly over the city. A few guns were found on the wall, which the Chinese had pointed at our batteries; one brass one measured eleven feet in length, and was ornamented with devices and Mantchoo characters; another gun was made of wood and sheathed with copper in so able a manner as to appear to a casual observer as if wholly made of metal. The wall of Pekin is about forty feet high, and sixty-four feet broad at the top, gradually narrowing upwards from the base. It is constructed internally of earth, with a casing of bricks. Along the wall on the right, about 100 yards from the gate, our people cut a traverse through the top of the wall, and with the earth formed a battery to command the approach along the wall from the direction of the Tih-shing gate, a necessary precaution, as that gate was still in the hands of the Tartar troops.

In the afternoon of the 12th, after the surrender of the gate, eight more Seikhs and some Frenchmen were restored to the Allies, fearfully emaciated, with their arms and wrists much lacerated by the tight cords that had bound them. On the 14th, two more Seikhs were brought back, and these the Chinese declared were the last of the surviving prisoners. The poor creatures were in a fearful state of anguish, and one of them died shortly afterwards that same day.

I was out with Colonel Wolseley and a party of the cavalry on a survey of the west wall. We had just fallen in with a company of some twenty Tartar troopers, who fled before us, and we were passing the northernmost gate on that side, when we encountered a party with five carts, each cart bearing a coffin. We drew near and examined these coffins, naturally supposing that they contained the remains of our murdered countrymen. Our surmises turned out to be correct: on the head of each coffin was pasted a piece of paper, inscribed, in Chinese characters, with the name of the deceased person it contained. Chinese characters represent but poorly the sounds of foreign names, but we all agreed that the one marked " *Po-ne-pe*, died of disease on the 25th September," referred to Mr. Bowlby, the ill-fated correspondent of *The Times*. The persons in charge of the bodies told us, in answer to our questions, that the coffins had been brought from a town some forty miles north of Pekin. By the 17th, all the bodies were returned ; they were found to be in such a fearful state of decomposition that not a feature was recognizable, and it was only by the tattered garments that the doctors, who inspected the corpses, made them out to be the remains of Mr. De Norman, Attaché to H.M.'s Legation; Lieut. R. B. Anderson, of Fane's Horse ; Private John Phipps, King's Dragoon Guards ; Mr. Bowlby, *The Times'* correspondent ; and eight Seikhs. Captain Brabazon, of the Artillery, and the Abbé de Luc, alone remained unaccounted for ; but it appears from the statements of the sur-

viving prisoners, that when the party captured on
the 18th September were being conveyed to Pekin,
the Abbé and Captain Brabazon were separated from
them, and led back towards the Chinese army;
and the Russians bore out the testimony of several
Chinese citizens, who assured us that these two were
detained by the soldiers of General Paou, and when
that mandarin was mortally wounded by the French
at the Pali Bridge, in a paroxysm of rage and anguish,
the Chinese general ordered them to be decapitated.
Some time after, two headless bodies, apparently of
Europeans, were reported floating about the Yung-
leang canal. At the time they were observed, there
was no suspicion of any such murder having taken
place, and it was thought that they might have
belonged to the fairer class of Tartars. When afterwards the suspicion assumed the form of fact, a search
was made for them, but the corpses had disappeared.

From the statements of the surviving sowars, we
learned that, after the capture of their party at
Chang-chia-wan, they were led to the rear of the
Chinese troops and disarmed, but were allowed to
remain mounted on their horses, and so conducted
along the stone road towards Pekin. Before reaching
that city, they were told to dismount, and had to
spend the night all together at a wayside temple.
Next day, Captain Brabazon and the Abbé de Luc

were taken away towards Tung-chow, and the rest
of the party carried to Pekin, whence they were led
to the Summer Palace, where they were put up in
tents. About an hour after their arrival, they were
called out, one by one, thrown on their faces, and
their hands and feet tied together behind. The
sowars were tied with single cords, but the Europeans
with double ones; and not content with drawing the
cords as tight round the limbs as possible, the pitiless
captors wetted them with water, that they might shrink
firmer together. The unfortunate sufferers were then
carried into a courtyard, and exposed for three days
to the sun and the cold without either food or water.
In the daytime, the doors were left open, and the
gaping crowds admitted to stare at them in their
misery. If they spoke a word, or asked for water,
they were beaten, stamped upon, and kicked about
the head; and when they asked for food, dirt was
crammed into their mouths. At the end of the third
day, a little food was dealt out to them, and irons
were put on their necks, wrists, and ankles. On
the fourth day, they were divided into four parties,
placed in carts, and, with their limbs still bound,
driven away to four small hill fortresses, varying
twenty to forty miles from Pekin. Sir Hope Grant
writes: " Of the cause of their death, there can be
no doubt; the survivors of each party tell the same

sad tale of how they remained with their hands tightly bound with cords until mortification ensued and they died. The whole party would have doubtless shared the same fate, had not their cords been cut on the ninth day, or thereabouts."

When we learnt the sad fate of our countrymen the indignation in the camp reached a terrible pitch, and fortunate it was for the Chinese that no more encounters occurred, as they would thenceforth have found the Allies far more brutal enemies than they had hitherto proved. The indignation on the part of the Seikhs was not so easily allyed. It rankled in each individual's heart, and one striking instance occurred of the desire for retribution they showed even on guiltless individuals of the Tartar race. One evening, shortly after the restoration of the maltreated prisoners, a Chinese presented himself before the Rev. Mr. McGhee, who was out for a quiet walk, and, after sundry prostrations, signified his intention to be followed. The man led him to a house near the out-picket of Fane's Horse. A Seikh slipped out of the house and ran away, and the Chaplain, on entering, found two unfortunate Chinese villagers on their faces, tied with cords round their ankles and wrists, in precisely the same manner as our unhappy friends had been treated by the barbarous mandarins. The spirit of retalia-

21—2

tion was carried out to a nicety, for the cords were not only strained as tight round the wrists as possible, but they were even wetted. The Seikh had been, apparently, gloating over the sufferings of these unfortunate Chinese, and evidently chuckling at the chance he thus had in subjecting two of the same race to the tortures inflicted by their authorities on his captive clansman.

The Russian Minister, Count Ignatieff, who had all along lent his aid to the furtherance of the views of the Allies, and been most assiduous in procuring and communicating intelligence of the intentions of the Chinese, now came forward and offered the Russian cemetery for the interment of our much-lamented comrades; and, on the 17th, the corpses were borne to the spot on gun wagons, attended by a long procession of troops and officers, the band of the Rifles playing a slow march. The Russian cemetery is outside the city to the right of the An-ting gate, situate about a quarter of a mile off the northern wall. It is a small space of ground enclosed by a wall, with a gate on the side facing north; within this wall is another and a smaller piece of ground enclosed by another square wall. It was to the right of its gate, in the space between the two walls, that the graves had been dug. The burial service was read by the Rev. Mr.

McGhee, Chaplain to the British forces. The priest of the Russian Mission attended in his pontifical robes, holding on high the emblem of our faith. General Montauban and several French officers were present, besides the greater part of the officers of the British army and Embassy. The coffins were laid side by side, and three volleys fired over the grave. It was a bitterly cold day, and a cutting wind was driving over the heads of the attendants at the funeral; but the scene was, nevertheless, affecting, and a tear glistened down many a rough, weather-worn face in sorrow for the cruel fate of those they committed to mother earth, but not less so for the sake of the anguish that awaited the hearths of the relations and friends when, by the next mail, they would hear of the loss of their loved ones; and the boughs of the trees overhead, as they rocked to and fro, with the wind rustling through their branches, moaned aloud, and seemed to add nature's lament to the one common cause of sorrow.

The dead Seikhs were handed over to their comrades, and were by them burnt to ashes, as is their custom.

The Frenchmen had no need to accept the Russians' offer. An old Roman Catholic cemetery, constructed when the Jesuits were in the height of their power in Pekin some centuries back, lay within the west wall, and to the plot of earth within its precincts they consigned their dead.

Lord Elgin shared the general indignation at the barbarities committed on the prisoners ; but his were difficult cards to play. Sir Hope Grant had given his word that Pekin would be spared if the gate was immediately surrendered, before the murder of the victims had come to light. The cold weather was drawing on fast, and the General maintained the necessity of commencing the downward march by the 1st November. It was highly necessary that we should leave some lasting mark in the neighbourhood, of our indignation at the treachery and cruelty of the authorities, to serve as a warning in future. As, therefore, the Summer Palace was the place where the barbarous cruelties first began, and as these were committed at the Emperor's special instigation, it was forthwith determined to level his sinning Majesty's rural retreat to the ground; and, further, to insist on compensation for the bereaved friends of the murdered ones of 300,000 taels (about 100,000*l.*) In justification of the demolition of the Summer Palace, Lord Elgin writes :—" As the destruction of the Yuen-ming-yuen' is, however, an act to which exception may, with great apparent reason, be taken, it is my duty to say a few words respecting the only modes of inflicting a specific punishment for the crime in question, which, limited as were my means of action, I could have adopted as substitutes for that measure.

" I might, perhaps," have demanded a large sum of money, not as compensation for the sufferers, but as a penalty inflicted on the Chinese Government.   But, independently of the objection in principle to making high crime of this nature a mere money question, I hold on this point the opinion which is, I believe, entertained by all persons without exception who have investigated the subject, that, in the present disorganized state of the Chinese Government, to obtain large pecuniary indemnities from it is simply impossible, and that all that can be done practically in the matter is to appropriate such a portion of the customs revenue as will still leave to it a sufficient interest in that revenue to induce it to allow the natives to continue to trade with foreigners.   It is calculated that it will be necessary to take forty per cent. of the gross customs revenue of China for about four years, in order to procure payment of the indemnities already claimed by Baron Gros and me, under instructions from your lordship and the French Government.

" Or I might have required that the persons guilty of cruelty to our countrymen, or of the violation of a flag of truce, should be surrendered. But if I had made this demand in general terms, some miserable subordinates would probably have been given up, whom it would have been difficult to pardon, and impossible to punish; and if I had specified San-kolinsin, of whose guilt in violating a flag of truce evidence sufficient to cause his condemnation by a court-martial could be furnished, I should have made a demand which, it may be confidently affirmed, the Chinese Government would not have conceded, and mine could not have enforced. I must add, that throwing the responsibility for the acts of Government in this way on individuals resembles too closely the Chinese mode of conducting war to approve itself altogether to my judgment. Having, therefore, to the best of my judgment examined the question in all its bearings, I came to the conclusion that the destruction of Yuen-ming-yuen was the least objectionable of the several courses open to me, unless I could have reconciled it to my sense of duty to suffer the crime which had been committed to pass practically unavenged. I had reason, moreover, to believe that it was an act calculated to produce a greater effect in China, and on the Emperor, than persons who look on from a distance may suppose.

"It was the Emperor's favourite residence, and its destruction could not fail to be a blow to his pride as well as to his feelings. To this place, as appears from the deposition of the Seikh troopers, he brought our hapless countrymen in order that they might undergo their severest tortures within its precincts. Here have been found the horses and accoutrements of the troopers seized, the decorations torn from the breast of a gallant French officer, and other effects belonging to the prisoners. As almost all the valuables had already been taken from the Palace, the army would go there, not to pillage, but to mark by a solemn act of retribution the horror and indignation with which we were inspired by the perpetration of a great crime. The punishment was one which would fall not on people who may be comparatively innocent, but exclusively on the Emperor, whose direct personal responsibility for the crime committed is established, not only by the treatment of the prisoners at the Yuen-ming-yuen, but also by the edict in which he offers a pecuniary reward for the heads of the foreigners, adding that he is ready to expend all his treasure in the wages of assassination."

The First Division, under General Michel, was detailed for this work of destruction, and betimes on the 18th started for the Palace, where the buildings were apportioned to the different companies to destroy. The French refused to co-operate, as they condemned the measure as a piece of barbarism, forgetting that the chief mischief had been committed by themselves, not only in purloining and demolishing everything that the Palace contained in the way of art, but also in having permitted their men to incendiarise the choicest rooms of the Emperor.

Ere long a dense column of smoke rising to the sky indicated that the work had commenced, and as the day waned the column increased in magnitude, and grew denser and denser, wafting in the shape of a large cloud over Pekin, and having the semblance of a fearful thunderstorm impending. As we approached the Palace the crackling and rushing noise of fire was appalling, and the sun shining through the masses of smoke gave a sickly hue to every plant and tree, and the red flame gleaming on the faces of the troops engaged made them appear like demons glorying in the destruction of what they could not replace. The night was a warm one, and as roof after roof crashed in, smothering the fire that devoured its sustaining walls, and belching out instead large volumes of smoke, it betokened to our minds a sad portent of the fate of this antique empire, its very entrails being consumed by internecine war, how it has compelled those nations that might have been its prop to aid in its destruction, and how, beset on all sides, with nought to turn to for succour, it at last succumbs with a burst of vapour, lost in the ashes of its former self.   This seemed merely a portent, but it may not have been a truthful one, for there is time yet for China to regenerate herself, and by cultivating friendly relations with foreign empires, learn from them how in the present emergency of her case she may maintain order among her people, and keep pace with the march of progress.

The Yuen-ming-yuen, or Round and Brilliant Garden, was fast becoming a scene of confusion and desolation, but there was yet much spoil within its walls, and as they were now allowed to plunder to their hearts' content, numbers of idlers were rushing about and extending their explorations to every nook and corner.   In an outhouse two carriages, presented by Lord Macartney to the Emperor Taou-kwang, were found intact and in good order.   The Emperor appears never to have used them, preferring instead the springless native cart or the sedan.   Two howitzer guns, with equipments complete, the gift also of Lord Macartney, were likewise found; and among astronomical and various other scientific instruments, a double-barrelled English made gun in case occurred, with tins of powder and boxes of Eley's caps.   The 15th Punjaubees, who had the destruction of this most important garden, fell in with large quantities of gold, one officer alone managing to appropriate to himself as much as 9,000*l.*

A paved road leading from the left wall of the
Summer Park passes close under the wall of another
enclosed park, named the Wan-show-yuen, or Birthday Garden.   This consisted of a pleasantly wooded
hill, not many acres in extent, and covered with magnificent temples, comprising the shrines of the three
recognized superstitions of China, viz., the Confucian,
the Taouist, and Bhuddhist, with a few yellow-tiled
halls, dedicated to the Llamas of Thibet.   The temples and minarets in this ground were in excellent
repair, and many of them were fine specimens of art,
got up with much taste, and decorated with colours of
gaudy hue.   Within these temples the celestial
monarchs were wont to sacrifice and pay their homage
to the multitudinous deities and sages that the different sects of Chinese religionists suppose to over-
rule the destinies of man, on the occasion of each
birthday of the " Monarch of Endless Years," as the
ruling majesty of China is designated.   A view from
the hill-top in this garden of its palatial temples and
the country around was most perfect; you looked
down on a series of quaintly picturesque buildings,
grouped together with much taste; and beyond the
wall, towards the south-west, a large lake, with a
temple standing on its bosom, connected with the
shore by a marble bridge of arches; the flat cham-
paign stretched away south, speckled with groups of

trees and villages; a tier of hills shut in the prospect on the right, and Pekin's turrets loomed in the distance.

Continuing along the paved road, destined alone for the Emperor's use, but now blocked up at intervals with sand and stone barriers to keep passenger carts from availing themselves of it, you pass through the village of Tsing-lung-cheaow, so called from the short stone bridge it leads out on, which crosses a stream that connects the artificial waters of the park with a branch of the Peiho. The bridge past the pavement winds to the left, and finishes its graceful curve round the walls of the next garden—the Chin-ming-yuen, or Gold and Brilliant Garden. In this are two hills enclosed by a wall, the southernmost hill being surmounted by a tall stone monument, ascended internally by a winding staircase, with loopholes in each story, admitting light on small groups of josses arranged in niches inside. This column was named the Ya-tsing Pagoda, and, from its height, could be seen at a great distance, thus affording an excellent landmark. Its destruction would, consequently, have been more noticeable, but the General was struck with its simple beauty, and spared it as a work of art. The northernmost hill was crowned with a one-spired llama temple, approached by tunnels bored through the living rock, whose sides within were carved into fantastic bas-relief images and representations of Bhuddha. The temple, however, was neglected, and in ruins. The grand entrance to these gardens was by the south side, where the road widened into an outer courtyard. There were several reception halls, with thrones, within its precincts, a small lake, with a bath-house, and handsomely painted punts, tasty little minarets, triumphal arches, and some fine temples; but the whole bore the stamp of neglect, and most of the rooms appeared to have been used merely as store rooms for the reception of cast-away finery and old documents. The visits of the Emperor hitherwards must have been few and far between. It seems to have been the custom with the Chinese throughout their parks only to keep those parts in order which the imperial eyes were likely to behold. Elsewhere, bridges and other works, which cost much labour to construct, were allowed to drop to decay; and the watercourses supplying artificial basins were left choked up with dirt, and what should be a handsome piece of water to be converted into a spring was covered with rushes and dank weeds.

On the west of the garden hill stood a stately yellow-tiled llama temple, with magnificent images of a towering size. In the back rooms of this temple were discovered several large chests, containing quantities of valuable old books and pictures. From the hills of this garden

we could see, about three miles off on the side of the
tier of hills, another collection of magnificent houses
embosomed in trees, and girt round by a serpentine
wall, which ran up the face of the hills, took a circuit
over their tops, and again descended to the plain.
This was called the Heangshan, or Fragrant Hills,
and formed the fourth and last park of the Emperor.
The stone way led to its gate, but several large and
uniformly built villages, tenanted by the families of the
Mantchoo soldiers who ranged under the eight banners of the imperial army, had to be passed along the
hard, even, sandy road, before you arrived at its walls.
Close to the villages was the Mantchoo parade-ground,
a walled-in space of land, about two acres in extent,
where the bannermen practised archery, and went
through their military evolutions.   The inhabitants
of these barracks were much alarmed, thinking their
turn might come next, and consequently showed every
eagerness to conciliate us.   Women and boys stood at
the doors of their houses with teapots and cups,
tempting the troops to refresh themselves, while others
dealt round trays of cakes.   The arrangement of
these Heangshan pleasure grounds was even more
complete than that of the three before visited.   The
flights of stone steps leading from palace to palace,
with the rural summer-houses, shady bowers, delightful terraces, made the spot quite unique and of a

perfect loveliness all its own. Herds of deer bounded up the rocks, and halting on a projecting point would gaze with fixed and curious stare at the intruders. Large quantities of rare and costly enamels and bronzes were obtained here by many, with articles of value; but most of the precious things were so bulky and cumbersome, that they were obliged to be destroyed, because no one could carry them away.

The day was not sufficient to accomplish the work of demolition, so the troops had to bivouac out, and finish their work on the morrow. I was there on duty both days, and was enabled to take a cursory view of the different grounds of which I have endeavoured to give a short description above. But I confess I feel, what all must feel, how impossible it is to call to the mind's eye of the reader, by any display of words, what one glance of his own eye, however hastily snatched, would have conveyed to himself.

Before sunset of the 19th, every place had been fired, and the troops were marched back to camp. We were among the last to leave, and we passed the Summer Palace on our return; flames and smouldering ruins deterred our passage every way, and unhappily many of the peasants' houses adjoining the contagious fire had caught, and were fast being reduced to ashes. We passed the chief entrance to the Yuenming-yuen, and watched with mournful pleasure the dancing flames curling into grotesque festoons and wreaths, as they twined in their last embrace round the grand portal of the Palace, while the black column of smoke that rose straight up into the sky from the already roof-fallen reception-hall, formed a deep background to this living picture of active red flame that hissed and crackled as if glorying in the destruction it spread around. " Good for evil," is a hard moral for man to learn ; but however much we regretted the cruel destruction of those stately buildings, we yet could not help feeling a secret gratification that the blow had fallen, and the murder of our hapless countrymen revenged on the cruel and perfidious author and instigator of the crime.

22

CHAPTER XIII.

March, noble lord,
Into our city with thy banners spread.
                                    Timon of Athens.
Ay, but the case is altered.
    *   *   *   *   *
       How should you govern any kingdom
That knows not how to use ambassadors?
                              Third Part of Henry VI.

Letter of Lord Elgin to Prince Kung—Preparations for attacking Pekin—Approach of Chinese Rebels—Reconnaissance round the Walls—Signing the Convention — Tung-chow — Curious Mode of Fishing — Description of Pekin — The " Altars of Heaven and Earth "— Llamaseries — " Prayer-Machines " — Chinese Religions—Pekinese Vehicles—Chinese Dromedaries —Falconry—Resources and Produce—Cultivation—Poverty of the Inhabitants—Neglect of Education.

THE foul deeds committed on the prisoners had now, to a certain extent, been expiated by the retribution on the fair pleasure-grounds of the Emperor ; but no terms had been agreed to as regarded the payment of the compensation demanded from the Chinese on behalf of the surviving sufferers, and the friends of the murdered ones. Lord Elgin therefore gave Prince Kung to understand that " unless before 10 A.M. on the 20th, the Prince informs the undersigned in writing that the sum demanded as compensation for the British subjects who have been maltreated or murdered will be ready for payment on the 22nd, and that he will be prepared to sign the convention, and to exchange the ratifications of the Treaty of Tientsin on the 23rd, the undersigned will again call on the Commander-in-Chief to seize the Imperial Palace in Pekin, and to take such other measures to compel the Chinese Government to accede to the demands of that of Great Britain as may seem to him to be fitting. It is proper, however, that he should inform the Prince that, should the contumacy of the Chinese force him to adopt this course, he will address himself to the Commander-in-Chief of her Majesty's naval forces, as well as to the Commander-in-Chief of her Majesty's land forces. He begs to remind the Prince that the customs revenue of Canton is being collected for the profit of the Imperial Government of China, although the city is in the military occupation of the Allies; that it is the military force of the Allies which has for some time prevented Shanghai from falling into the hands of the rebels; and that the junks carrying rice and tribute to Pekin have been allowed to pass and repass unmolested, though the fleets of the Allies command both the seas and rivers.

" If peace be not at once concluded, this state of things will cease, and the undersigned will concert measures with her Majesty's naval Commander-in-

Chief, with the view of obtaining from them and other sources, indemnification for the expense which her Majesty's Government is compelled to incur by the bad faith of that of China."

Knowing the possibility of the Chinese again, at the eleventh hour, quibbling and throwing objections in the way, the General made all preparation to carry out the threat on the Palace inside Pekin. Guns were to be dragged from the gate we held to the next gate,—the *Tih-shing* (or Victory), whence they were to open fire on the city. The troops were already detailed for the attack, when a countermanding order was issued. Lord Elgin's threat had wrung the necessary reply. At 7 A.M. on the 20th, a communication was received from Prince Kung ceding everything demanded. It is said that the Russian Ambassador had had some hand in bringing about the concession, having pointed out to the Chinese the folly of holding out any longer against such powerful enemies. The two Roman Catholic priests within the capital were also said to have had their services solicited, and in return, shortly after, the Emperor honoured them with the white official button of a low sixth-class mandarin, which they wisely refused.

Before Prince Kung's answer had been received to the last ultimatum, we had heard from the Russians that the rebels were pushing on for the capital, and were now only at 100 miles distance. We took them to be at first the Taiping rebels, and wondered how they had managed to march up so expeditiously all the way from Nankin, and to be here, too, just at the nick of time; for, had the Chinese held out, the affair must, almost inevitably, have resulted in the overthrow of the dynasty. As it turned out, the rebels were only some Shense insurrectionists, who had availed themselves of the present crisis to extend their depredations. Their proximity had, however, no doubt incited the Chinese to precipitate the settlement of their difficulties with us, in order better to turn their attention to the quelling of what promised to assume an equally formidable trouble; and now San-kolinsin was reported to be making preparations to stop their further advance on the capital.

Had the Chinese held out, an unforeseen difficulty appeared on our side, which would have tended considerably to have baulked the keeping of our word as to the attack on the Palace in default of the concession to the demands being made. It appears the French had fixed the period of their ultimatum for the 23rd, and they gave out that they could not cooperate in any attack on the city until the expiry of that term. Fortunately, however, the concession was made, and all further difficulty obviated.

Winter was fast drawing on, and the sylvan scenery day by day throwing off its livery of already-seared foliage; each morning was ushered in by a hard frost, with its coverlet of snow daintily spread on the tops of the semicircular range of hills; and though the sun continued to rise and walk his course each day through a clear, unsullied sky, yet his beams brought little glow of warmth in their rays, and the chilling air began to affect the health of the natives from the sunny south and of that of the Indian horses. It was, therefore, with no small delight that we hailed the prospect of peace and a speedy termination to the privations of a camp life.

Though the concessions had unconditionally been made, confidence had by no means been restored in our camp in favour of the honest intentions of the Chinese. The Russians had warned us to be careful that no further tricks were played on us, as they suspected treachery; and, in proof of this, we were informed that San-kolinsin was at no great distance from our camp to aid in the confusion, if the attempt were successful. With all our inquiries we had not succeeded in discovering where the Tartars had fled to, and their reported proximity, therefore, the more astonished us. They were said to be near the west wall of the city. Accordingly, on the 22nd, Probyn and Fane with their troopers were despatched along

the face of that wall, to try and ascertain more particulars about their encampment. The Seikhs turned
the west angle of the wall, and passed the first gate,
when they came upon a Tartar picket, who scampered away; and as our troopers advanced two and
two through a long lane, they suddenly found themselves in the Tartar camp. The Tartars all rushed
together and formed line, but did not attempt any
violence, as our irregulars, somewhat startled at the
suddenness of the rencontre, produced a white flag.
The Tartar officer came forward and asked them
what they wanted; he said that these were merely
the garrison of the city, who had lately received
orders to encamp outside the wall, and that San-
kolinsin was not in the camp. The encampment
covered a good space of ground, and seemed to contain a very large force. The officer was desired to
accompany the Seikhs back to the British camp,
which he did without much reluctance, a body of
Tartar cavalry also following for some part of the
road back. Prince Kung, it appears, was close to
this camp on his return to the city; but, on hearing
of the approach of the enemy's cavalry, he fled to a
spot five miles farther off. This unexpected discovery of the enemy's force so near our own took us
all by surprise, and led us to suspect the sincerity
of the desire for peace professed in Prince Kung's

letter ; but, as it was generally understood that matters were approaching a satisfactory issue, it would not have become the Allies to resume the quarrel on a mere suspicion. It had, however, the effect of making the General more circumspect, and prompted him to take every precaution within the compass of his thought to elude the possibility of success in any attempt at treachery on the enemy's part.

With regard to the indemnity, the Prince was true to his word. The whole amount demanded was paid on the appointed 23rd. The French had fixed on that date for the signature of their treaty, but, some of the requisite papers not being quite prepared, they postponed the event.

The ratification of the British treaty and signature of the convention were appointed for the 24th, and the hall selected for the ceremony was that pertaining to the Board of Ceremonies, one of the six Imperial Boards. Messrs. Parkes and Wade were entrusted with the arrangement of the room for the reception of the commissioners, and with the settlement of points of etiquette thereanent ; and, as some whispers passed round of the probability of the place being mined, Colonel Wolseley and some other officers accompanied the civilians to have a careful look round at the precincts of the chosen spot.

At 3 P.M. on the appointed day, the procession
attending Lord Elgin to the Hall of Ceremonies
entered the An-ting gate. A detachment of cavalry
led the way, followed by detachments of the various
infantry regiments, with two regimental bands, who
continued playing alternately the whole way. Then
came sundry officers on foot, and then the mounted
officers (those being chosen in preference who could
muster full uniforms); then the General and Staff;
Lord Elgin in his green sedan-chair, carried by
sixteen coolies in scarlet livery, his Staff on horseback on either side, and the rear brought up by more
infantry and cavalry. As the procession entered the
gate, the French guard on the left side turned out
and saluted, striking up "God Save the Queen."
The main street on either side was lined with British
infantry, amounting to 2,000 men, who followed up
the procession as it passed, forming altogether a
force of 8,000 men marching through the capital. A
raised mud causeway, about twenty feet broad, runs
through the centre of the road. On either side of
this the Chinese had mustered in large numbers, and
in the crowd near the gate we saw some of the
members of the Russian Mission, mounted on their
small ponies. The road was full of ruts, and only
in parts watered from the drinking-troughs that
occurred here and there; consequently large clouds

of dust darkened the air and confined the prospect
to within a few yards of the person. We followed
this road almost due south for some three miles, till
we approached the south or Chinese wall, when a
sharp turn was made to the right, and, passing close
along the yellow-topped wall that girts the Emperor's
palace, another turn brought us before the dilapidated gate that commands the entrance to the Hall
of Ceremonies. Over this gate was written, in conspicuous letters, " Board of Ceremonies." This gate
led into a large courtyard, where the procession filed
off to the right and left, leaving an avenue for the
passage of Lord Elgin's chair. The left side of the
courtyard was occupied by Chinese menials and
animals, and the right side by those of the British.
Prince Kung and numberless mandarins were already
in waiting in the open hall which stood at the other
end of the courtyard. As his lordship advanced up
the avenue, the troops presented arms and the band
saluted him with the national air. The Earl
walked to the farther end of the hall and took the
seat of honour prepared for him, at the same time
motioning the Prince to take the lower seat on the
right, about fifteen feet off. A table, covered with
tawdry red cloth, stood before each. Sir Hope Grant
sat on Lord Elgin's left; and ranged behind a row
of tables down the hall, on the left, sat and stood

the other officers that were present at the ceremony.
Behind similar tables on the right were ranged
native princes and mandarins of every button.   The
attachés and interpreters of the Embassy stood
between the High Commissioners, at a central table,
whereon were placed despatch-boxes, paper, and other
official apparatus; and the Prince had standing by
him Hangke and two other mandarins.

After the exhibition of the respective full powers
of the Commissioners, the convention was signed.
Two articles had been admitted which was not proposed in the previous convention drawn out at Tien-
tsin; the one legalizing coolie emigration, and the
other ceding to her Majesty's Government the peninsula of Kowloon, opposite Hong Kong, which had
previously been rented from the Governor-General of
Canton, as alluded to in the first chapter.   After the
signature of the convention followed the exchange
of the ratifications of the Treaty of Tien-tsin.   A
minute, recording the proceedings which had taken
place in connection with the exchange of ratifications,
was then drawn up in duplicate, and, being signed
and sealed by the Plenipotentiaries, one copy was
given to Lord Elgin and the other to Prince Kung.

The scene was interesting, but there was little
appearance of that Oriental magnificence which one
would be led to expect on such an occasion in the

capital of a vast Eastern empire, in an assembly of
her princes and nobles.   The old hall bore the stamp
of neglect and decay of the thousand and one other
public buildings in Pekin, and the tapestry that hung
from the unceiled roof was of cheap stuff and faded ;
the Chinese grandees themselves were dirty and badly
dressed.   These last, however, probably looked worse
than they actually were, as the overwhelming dust of
the roads through which they had passed may have
diminished the gloss of their multi-coloured apparel.
It certainly had not tended to improve the appearance
of our people.   The Prince, a cadaverous-looking
young man of twenty-three, with a long, pale, smooth-
shaven face, bore a timid, sulky demeanour throughout the ceremony, and answered snappishly to the
questions put by the interpreters.   He was dressed
in a long, purple, damasked silk, with a round,
dragon-flowered patch on each shoulder, breast, and
back ; and on his head he wore the winter official
cap, but with a button of twisted red silk instead of
the various mineral buttons that decorate mandarins.
A necklace of carved beads hung round his neck.
His nether garments were yellow and his boots embroidered.   An attempt to photograph the scene, on
the part of Signor Beato, was a signal failure.   The
Prince had proposed to give a banquet after the
ceremony, but this was declined, as it was still feared

that the treachery of the Chinese might find vent in poisoning the food. So soon as the business was concluded, Lord Elgin took his leave, accompanied by the procession, as before, and the guns on the An-ting gate announced to the world that peace had been concluded between Great Britain and China.

The French exchanged ratifications on the following day, on which occasion Prince Kung was reported to have been in much better spirits. The French accepted a banquet after the ceremony, and their day passed more pleasantly than had ours.

On the day after the signing of our treaty, Lord Elgin took up his quarters inside the Tartar town in the large walled-in collection of small houses, known as the Palace of Prince E, not far from the north-east gate, the Royal Regiment accompanying him as body-guard.

That same day, I was ordered to proceed to Tung-chow to assist Captain Dew in engaging boats for the conveyance of the heavy baggage to Tien-tsin; and I availed myself of the company of M. Zill and a French officer who were also bound for the same place. The beaten track by which the baggagers travelled to and fro was about fourteen miles. The depôt was established near half way, and afforded a good resting-place. It was a well-chosen spot, surrounded and sheltered by luxuriant groves of

fine timber.   The French had a small station or
" poste " near Tung-chow, at the Pa-le bridge.

Tung-chow is a large walled town comprising the
old and new cities, one thick wall some thirty-five feet
in height encircling the whole. A narrow stream from
the Peiho runs through the town, and is bridged over
in several places; but there is nothing in the town
inviting a second visit: the houses are small, dirty,
and squalid, and the temples second-rate. The marines
were quartered in the suburb beyond its north wall,
on the banks of the narrow stream that branches
from the Peiho.   The banks of this stream presented
a busy and interesting scene. Hundreds of large
flat barges were ranged side by side in the water,
all numbered and marked; some were being laden
with heavy baggage from the front, which was fast
arriving in military train waggons, while others were
discharging to reload the waggons.   The blue-jackets
were in charge of this water transport, under Captain
Dew, and very ably they performed it. A well-
supplied market was also established on this strand.
Behind the suburb lay the canal in calm repose
between its rush-fringed banks, its waters winding
past the north wall, on which stood the finest sight
at Tung-chow—a lofty minaret of twelve stories,
some 150 feet high.   The great nuisance of this
suburb were the beggars, who, covered with all

manner of loathsome diseases, swarmed the lanes, and lay about the doorsteps half naked. Colonel Travers showed me much kindness while a guest at the hospitable board of the marines, and I was happy, by the use of my tongue, in some measure to requite his kind attentions. The magistrate of the city brought a complaint against certain soldiers unknown, who had entered the town by a southern gate, and broken into a house for plunder, killing one man and wounding several others. The Colonel knew this could be none of his men, as they were well looked after, and on inquiry, the Chinese affirmed them to be soldiers with red trowsers and caps. The matter was therefore carried before the French commandant in charge of the station, and the marauders proved to be some of the French troops on their way from Ho-see-woo to the *poste* at Pa-le-cheaou.

Before returning to the capital, I took a ride with Captain Dew over the small bridge above Tung-chow, and along the opposite bank of the river to the junction canal some two miles up. In one part of the shallow river some fishermen were engaged drawing the stream for fish, and as the operation seemed an ingenious one, I will briefly describe it. A wicker barrier was stretched across the river in a zigzag line, converging into two angles with open vortices, to each of which was applied a large basket, with mouths

shaped like those of baskets used at home for catching lobsters. The fishermen then stripped, and
stretching a large weighted sieve-net across the river
some distance higher up, dragged the river with the
net towards the barrier; the men holding the two
ends of the net meeting as they approached the
wicker angles. Several of the larger fish leapt over
the net, but the majority that escaped its meshes took
refuge in the baskets at the angles.

Below Tung-chow a double ferry was established
across the two branches of the river, and the con-
course of people that went to and fro showed a large
traffic with the town. As we approached they seemed
much alarmed, scuttling away with cattle, horses, and
goats, as if afraid that we should take forcible possession of them. After a few words exchanged to establish
good feeling, we returned, and shortly after 5 o'clock
I accompanied Captain Dew to the camp at Pekin.

Colonel Wolseley and Lieutenant Harrison were
ordered down to Tung-chow to superintend the trans-
missal of baggage, unfortunately before they had
completed their survey of the capital; so our department was broken up.

The city was now open, and officers were allowed
to stroll wherever they had a fancy within its walls,
except in the precincts of the imperial grounds. As
a precaution, however, at first, orders were issued

GRAND ENTRANCE OF THE WINTER PALACE, PEKIN

that people visiting the city should not go in less numbers than three at a time, and then well armed.

The ancient city of Pekin, capital of the district of Shun-teen, and metropolis of China, has been so often and so ably described by the Jesuits and others, that it would only be tiring the patience of our readers to enter into too minute details. We will, therefore, only record a few of the scenes within its walls to which ourselves were witness. Five centuries ago, the famous Venetian traveller, Marco Polo, visited this wondrously antiquated city, which he calls Kamballi, during the reign of the great Mongolian monarch, Kublai Khan, and it is wonderful how touchingly true are many of his descriptions of places within the city which have lasted throughout this vast lapse of time. His description of Kublai's palace would serve equally as well for the residence of the present monarch, at least, so far as a glimpse within its wall convinced us. He tells us truly, that " the roof is externally painted with red, blue, green, and other colours, and is so varnished that it shines like crystal, and is seen to a great distance around." The buildings, however, show marks of neglect and dilapidation, and the " magnificent lake" Marco talks of, is now naught but a dried bed of dank grass. The grand entrance facing south, with its pavement of marble, and marble lions and columns, is stained

23

by the browning hand of time, and moss-grown. The artificial hill in the imperial gardens, constructed by Kublai, still stands conspicuous, with the pagoda on its top, and at once attracts the eye of the stranger who casts a glance over the flat row of houses in the city. As you ride along the broad road from the Kefa Gate, on the east side, past Prince E's palace (the temporary residence of Lord Elgin), and through the eight triumphal arches, towards the main road from the An-ting Gate, your eye rests with pleasure on this round wood-covered hill rising picturesquely from the midst of the glittering roofs and umbrageous trees within the palace walls. Hear Marco speak of this hill:—" Towards the north, about a bowshot from the palace, Kublai has constructed a mound, full a hundred paces high, and a mile in circuit, all covered with evergreen trees, which never shed their leaves. When he hears of a beautiful tree, he causes it to be dug up, with all the roots and the earth around it, and to be conveyed to him on the backs of elephants, whence the eminence has been made verdant all over, and is called the Green Mountain. On the top is a palace, also covered with verdure; it and the trees are so lovely that all who look upon them feel delight and joy."

Pekin, as all are aware, consists mainly of two

portions: the northern, or Tartar city, girt in by a lofty and massive rectangular wall, with immense imposing square corner towers and nine double gates; and a large southern suburb, tacked on at later date by an extension of the surrounding wall, and known as the Chinese City. The southern wall of the old city, with its three gates, still divides the two portions. The suburbs outside the walls are small and confined chiefly to the immediate neighbourhood of the gates, and the country round about is sparsely populated. The main streets of the two divisions are broad, and run, for the most part, either directly north and south, or east and west; but the intermediate streets are narrow and often very tortuous. All are uneven, full of ruts, in dry weather unpleasantly dusty, and in wet weather fearfully muddy. In the heart of the Tartar city, a rectangular space is walled in, and apportioned to the residences of nobles and grandees, and within this another wall encloses the grounds of the imperial master. The Tartar city in olden times was appropriated by the Tartars alone, but now little distinction is made between the races. It is divided into quarters, or parishes, assigned to the Mongolians, Mantchoorians, Chinese, or Mahommedans; each division having its police, who are responsible for the order of their several parishes, and, on occasions of mandarins passing on duty, have to appear with whips to command order among the populace. Most of the houses in the Tartar quarter are private residences, but the main streets are lined with shops.

The busy portion of the city, however, is the Chinese part, and to that the officers crowded for the purchase of curiosities. On the right of the central gate leading to the Chinese city, in a small street, several fine curiosity-shops occurred, and the crowds that thronged that street made it insufferable. All the army was desirous to purchase some memento of the great city of Cathay, and the six or seven shops which were well supplied with every kind of *article de luxe* that the great empire produces, drove a flourishing trade during the period of our stay. The Chinese were very well-disposed towards us, and often said that they much regretted " our majesties " were so soon about to leave; they had hoped that now we were masters of the city we would hold possession of it. In front of the central southern gate was the grand entrance to the imperial palace, from which a paved road ran under the gate and down the broad central road that divides the Chinese city. Both sides of this road were lined with shops and stalls, and crowds of natives pressed backwards and forwards, engaged on their various errands.

As we rode south about a mile and a half from the

gate, no more houses or shops occurred, and the busy throng of men were with them left behind. The road still continued, but on either hand was waste land, and we passed on in comparative solitude, with the few ragged boys at our heels who followed to hold our horses for a trifling gratuity. The central south gate of the Chinese wall now appeared in sight, with a large walled-in enclosure on either side of the road, the left enclosing the Altar of Heaven, or Tien-tan, the right the Altar of Earth, or Te-tan. These sacred spots are never trodden by aught save the Emperor and his high mandarins; to all others the right of entrance is denied. Even the victorious allies found some difficulty at first in gaining admittance; but a firm insistance on the right soon over-ruled, and thenceforth all that presented themselves were admitted. We entered through a side door into the large waste park in the first enclosure of Heaven's Altar. The grass was all dried up and the trees, for the most part, leafless, so the place presented a barren appearance. The gateway and the walls were roofed with glistening green tiles. The roadway led under some cedar-trees to a small enclosure, in which were several buildings—the refreshment-hall among others —and in the centre a somewhat conically-shaped structure, covered with purple tiles, and surmounted by a golden knob. This turret was situated on a broad circular terrace of marble, which dropped to two other narrower terraces, and then to the ground, by means of steps. The central series of steps facing the south had each flight divided by a large tablet, carved either with dragons or phœnixes on its face. Up this the Spirit of Heaven ascends into the temple. The series of steps on the right is consecrated to the Emperor's celestial footsteps alone, and the series on the left to the mandarins that ascend with him. In like manner there were three entrances to the temple —one large central portal for the Spirit to enter, and two side ones for the Emperor and his mandarins. The floor of the temple was paved with black marble, and facing the central doorway a raised platform of white marble, with steps leading down. At the back of this was placed a black throne, whereon the Spirit of Heaven is supposed to sit in majesty. A table, with an incense-burner, stood in front of it, and a large offering-stand in front of that again. On the right side, within the temple, were four thrones, and on the left four, all with incense-burners before them. These were dedicated to the eight canonized monarchs of the ruling dynasty.

On New Year's Day, his Imperial Majesty, seated in his yellow sedan, with sixteen bearers, a select cortège following, proceeds in great pomp along the paved road leading from his palace to this temple, the people, while the procession passes, meekly falling on their knees, with eyes cast down. His Majesty enters the temple by the right flight of steps through the right door. The two other doors are thrown open for the admission of Heaven and the favoured sons of earth. Incense rises in clouds from each altar; a slaughtered bullock is placed on the stand as the pledge offering; and the Son of Heaven, retiring backwards from the incense he has placed on the altar, descends the steps, prostrates himself on the floor, and, with nine kow-tows, acknowledges, for once throughout the rolling year, that there is a being superior to himself. The thanksgiving over, the bullock is taken outside and burnt over an iron-grated dry well, which receives the ashes. The choice assembly then retire to the banquet-hall, where refreshments are laid out ready to satiate the imperial appetite and cheer the imperial heart. The banquet over, the procession returns with all the pomp it came.

We found the place much neglected; weeds covered the marbled terraces, and dust the heavenly temple; but our guide took the trouble to assure us that all things were put into order before the advent of each new year.

We then crossed the road, and by another side-door entered the enclosure of the Altar of Earth.

Here there was again a large waste park, speckled with trees, and on the left a smaller walled enclosure with buildings, many of which were in sad disrepair. About the centre of the place stood a square terrace of marble, raised some five feet above the level of the ground, with steps on each side. In front of this was the land turned year after year by the imperial plough. On the right, among some trees, was raised another marble terrace, with incense-burners; and in the rear the halls of refreshment. It is during the feast of Tsing-ming, in the third moon, that the Emperor favours this spot with his august presence. Incense is burnt on the altar, and he proceeds with his imperial hand " to guide the well-used plough, to lend his shoulder, and commence the toil." This feat is proclaimed to the world by the blowing of trumpets and great cheering. He is said to break the soil for the third of a " mow " (Chinese acre); he then ascends the central terrace, and, on a throne brought there for the purpose, contemplates the attempts of his princes, as they work each one his " mow's " breadth. At the conclusion of this rustic farce, the banquet hall is cheered by the celestial smile, and leave taken as before. " Then through the field the sower stalks, and liberal throws the grain into the faithful bosom of the soil. The harrow follows harsh and shuts the scene." Wheat and Indian corn are usually sown on these occasions, and the produce of the small plots stored in the imperial garner.

The Temple of Confucius is worthy of mention as a fine two-storied building, but in style it resembles all others dedicated to the tablet-worshiping fraternity found in southern cities.

We must not pass over the old Roman Catholic cathedral of the Jesuits, near the third gate of the Chinese wall. This building had long been deserted, as the celebration of Catholic services was forbidden within its walls, and the cross had disappeared off its top. The two priests residing, disguised in Chinese garb in the capital, gained the influence of the French in reinstating the establishment, and erecting a fresh cross on its summit. When the place was put into thorough repair, the officers of the allied army were invited to attend the first service, and once more the *Te Deum* was chanted within its long-neglected walls, in grateful homage to the Almighty Maker.

The population of Pekin has been rated at 3,000,000, but, judging from the broad streets, the scattered houses, and large waste places within both Tartar and Chinese towns, we should venture the statement that the actual population does certainly not exceed *one* million.

The Russian Mission is established in a small house in the Tartar city, near the wall which divides the two cities; and a Cossack sentry, in his long grey coat and fur cap, stands posted at the entrance.

About two miles beyond the north and east walls, a long mound, thirty feet high, runs parallel with the wall, with occasional breaks to let the main roads run through. This earthwork is now grass-grown, and looks, at first sight, like a freak of nature, but tradition marks it as the boundary of an encampment held centuries ago by a conqueress of the Chinese race against the Mongol Tartars. The north road from the city is said to lead to the Great Wall, which is put down about forty miles distant, but none of us proceeded sufficiently far to get a view of it.

Outside the city wall on the north face between the two gates is the grand Tartar parade-ground, occupying about two square miles of irregular space. Beyond this are arranged side by side a row of splendid llama monasteries, their yellow-tiled roofs glittering conspicuously between and almost hidden by the large-limbed trees among which they are ensconced. One of these San-kolinsin had lately occupied, but it now had the honour of being the head-quarters of the French Embassy. The temple adjoining was the largest and most beautifully got up, with large gaudily painted images, and shrines covered with old specimens of porcelain jars and beautiful ornaments of inlaid enamel. On our first arrival the General thought proper to place a guard over this temple to save its costly treasures from being plundered, but afterwards, when it was assigned as quarters to the Military Train, the guard was removed and every article worth the taking carried away. This temple was built under the patronage of the Emperor for the Teshu Llama, the spiritual ruler of Greater Tibet; and in one of the court-yards a splendid monument of pure white marble some thirty feet high, with a gilt top, and highly wrought all over with bas-relief carvings, is dedicated to this spiritual chief under the name of the Ka-tang, or Pan-ching-fay. It is truly a splendid piece of workmanship, and much credit is due to the Commander-in-Chief for having maintained throughout a guard at its base to save it from the fate that all else in its neighbourhood shared. In a gallery above this court-yard was a row of blue and green coloured images, the male figures with hideous hydra heads, celebrating the loves of the great male and female principles of nature. These uncouth and indelicate josses found their votaries among the barren women who came periodically to beseech these deities to grant them issue. In another part of the temple were the private rooms set apart for the accommodation of the envoy delegated by the Teshu Llama to the court of his imperial master. The next temple was smaller, and consecrated to the reception of the legate of the Dalai Llama, the spiritual chief of Little Tibet; and in this all the priests were still remaining. Most of them were Tibetans, and could scarce speak a word of Chinese. Their costume was a yellow robe, with a red girdle, and their head-dress a cap with a fur-covered rim, yellow on the crown, with a red knob of twisted silk. Their polls were shaven, and they possessed a strong, unpleasant odour, not unlike that of *sheep*, which the Chinese attributed to the quantity of mutton they daily consumed. This second temple was also ornamented with huge ugly josses, and painted cloths hanging from the roofs covered with bad representations of skulls and skins of flayed human victims. But what struck us most was the large prayer-boxes placed about the room, called by them Ma-me, filled with scrolls of Tibetan writings, carefully rolled and put inside, the box spinning round on a pivot. We had read before of these boxes in the travels of the Abbé Huc through Tartary. The votary gives the box a spin, repeating an incantation to each turn, and at each revolution is supposed to have offered all the prayers that the box contains. Small boxes similarly crammed with prayers, and made to revolve on pivots lengthened into handles, are served out to the believers. The box is written round with the incantation, and from its side, attached by a piece of string, depends a weight, which gives a measured force to the revolutions. The incantation, as given me by the priests, may be thus syllabled : " Oom-ma-nay-put-mear-hoom," or, " Oong-pang-sara-pa-nay-hoom-put," which is intended for an invocation to the deities that preside over " heaven, earth, man, wounds, fire, and misery."

I was told that all the images had similar prayers inserted in their composition, and we found such to be the case in certain small josses which we examined. Within the metal plate on which they stood were inserted small rolled up slips of pith written over with Tibetan characters; each slip being rolled separately by itself and tied round with red silk, and the whole carefully covered with a scented piece of yellow silk.

The majority of the llama temples were situated outside the wall, and most of them were on a magnificent scale, indeed much finer than any of those dedicated to China's three adopted religions. It seems to have been the policy of the Chinese emperors to have extended a most munificent patronage to the religion of the llamas, and to have allowed them to build large and splendid temples in the neighbourhood of the capital, in order to exercise the better hold over the countries of Tibet, where this sect of Bhuddha incarnate finds its nursery.

Mahommedanism has also a firm root in the capital, and the number of its votaries is no despicable one. Their mosques occur, though not so numerously as the llamaseries, and there are a few of them even within the city walls. I mentioned before the fellowship that existed between the celestial followers of the Prophet and the Mussulman Seikhs. By way of recognition between them, it was a common practice to thrust forward the right hand, and as speedily to close it, leaving the thumb standing up conspicuous. But a similar sign was made by any native who wished to show the sincerity of his heart. He would point to the sky and to the earth, then to his heart, and would finish the demonstration by holding up his thumb; thus meaning that he called upon heaven and earth to witness the integrity of his heart. The officers declared that these signs of mutual trust and sincerity were proof positive that freemasonry had long been known and established in China.

The mass of loyal subjects of the empire who feel in duty bound to acknowledge one of the three established religions in China — to wit, Confucianism, Taouism, and Bhuddhism—may all get suited in the numerous temples dedicated to each of these within and without the metropolitan walls; but, as far as my experience leads me to infer, a very confused idea is entertained by the material Chinese masses of the relative differences of the three. The majority pay like homage to all. You will often see a literary character who feels bound to be a staunch upholder of Confucian doctrines, burn incense and bow before the dull images of wood and stone worshiped by Bhuddhists; and again, a farmer or sailor who daily and nightly chants prayers to the presiding deity of his class bodied in hideous material form and be-daubed with gaudy hues, will turn with reverence to a Confucian tablet, thinking it must bear a sacred character, because wiser and more lettered heads than his pay to it homage.

Sedan chairs are of rare occurrence in Pekin, the chief conveyance being the small springless cart we have before described. In these the highest classes of mandarins ride, jolting over the uneven roads. The private turn-outs are cushioned inside, and cur-tained in front, and Prince Kung himself paid visits in one of his own. We often met mandarins dressed in full costume riding past, sitting cross-legged within, and peering out through a convenient hole cut in the curtain. No retinue with gongs and bellowing executioners attend them on these occasions, as in the south. The imperial despot is alone to receive

honour within his chief city, and the highest functionary goes about, in consequence, attended by the
driver of the cart and a follower or two on horseback.   The poorest classes, however, patronise the
wheelbarrow.   This is guided by the two hands of
a man, as in ordinary barrows in use at home, but the
load is more thrown on the wheel by the latter being
larger and removed into a central position.   The
wheel is higher than the sides, and being caged over
forms a convenient back to the seats on either side.
This ingenious contrivance is well adapted either to
convey passengers seated back to back, or to carry
packages.   The Pekinese are more addicted to riding
than their more timid southern fellow-countrymen, and
you often meet men mounted on fine strapping mules ;
but their horses are small, and not much to boast of.

A stranger cannot help being struck by the long
strings of dromedaries he meets, especially in the
Chinese town, stalking along, jingling the bells
attached to their necks.   They all carry pack-saddles
fitting round their double hump, and held on by a
double girth, and are led by ropes fastened to a
ring through the nose.   The foremost beast is led
by a man, and the file that follows are tacked
each by a string to the tail of the one in advance.
They are very docile, and seldom show themselves
unruly, though it was not considered safe for a

stranger to go too near their heads. When alarmed, or in a passion, the brutes emit a cry somewhat between a loud shriek and a sneeze. They are wonderfully hardy animals, bearing equally well the violent heat of the Pekin summer and the cramping cold of its winter; in the former season their skins becoming almost bare, and at the latter acquiring a thick rough coat. The Chinese prize them much for the small quantity of food they consume as compared with the heavy burdens they carry with ease; and I should say that they would form an acceptable addition to the beasts of burden at home, where in flat portions of the country they might be usefully and economically employed.

Falconry, mentioned by Marco Polo as one of the pastimes of the great monarch Kublai Khan, still continues to have its votaries among the Pekinese; but it is now chiefly confined to the poorer classes as a means of support, the effete nobility and gentry generally preferring the luxurious life of indoor indolence and ease to the health-giving sports of the field. Men were frequently seen with hooded falcons on their hands. The red-legged falcon and the merlin are the species chiefly employed in hawking, but a large species of buzzard is also trained for hares and the larger feathered game; the small falcons being mostly flown after quail, which abound in the large tracts of

24

autumnal stubble. The birds are reclaimed with a tufted hood of much the same form as those used in Holland, and are at first flown with a long string attached to the wrist of the master after quail, who timidly cower when the hawk hovers over to pounce on them. The hawk seizes the bird, and is hauled up to the master's wrist again, where he is rewarded with a piece of the captured quarry. This teaches him to return to the wrist so soon as he has pounced on the bird; and after continued training the string is removed, and he is cast at much longer flights. The buzzard is, I suspect, what Marco talks of as Kublai's trained *eagles*. Hares are especially abundant and tame, and therefore offer an easy quarry for this larger hawk. So tame are they that in winter, when they come down from the hills in large numbers, they are easily knocked over with sticks, and supplied at cheap prices in the market. The excessive cold benumbs all kinds of game to comparative tameness, and the fowlers, by means of their matchlocks and nets, have therefore little trouble in keeping the market constantly supplied with large quantities of wild-fowl and palatable birds.

The country produces articles of food in great abundance. Flesh is more largely consumed here than in the south, and you see fine healthy-looking mutton hanging up in the butcher's shops, and sold at $2\frac{1}{2}d$. a pound. An old tradition prohibits the slaughter of the ox, which toils for man, within the prefecture of Shun-teen, but no such law obtains in the neighbouring districts, and therefore the poor beast is led into the adjacent country to be butchered, and its flesh brought to Pekin for sale, where the price of beef rules at $2d$. the pound. Water in the capital is mostly procured from wells along the roads, near which drinking troughs are provided for passengers' cattle; and for every animal that drinks at the trough, the owner throws in one cash (tenth of a halfpenny) into the water, by way of remuneration to the man who stands by to draw from the well and feed the troughs.

Coal is procured in the San-kia-teen hills, some thirty miles distant to the west, and brought to the capital on the backs of dromedaries. It is of the description known as anthracite, and realises 16s. per ton. It is ground to dust and rolled with clay into round balls, which are used for heating stoves, and have the advantage of yielding a glowing heat with but little smoke.

Bricks used for building, tiling, and flooring, are made in large quantities in the neighbouring kilns. They are fashioned out of the clay of the pits and arranged round the inside of the kiln, where they are burnt for three days. The fire is then extinguished

24—2

by application of water, and the bricks removed as they cool.

Blown glass for windows, and glass-ware generally, is imported from Canton. The use of this material for windows is commoner than in southern cities, but it is chiefly confined to the residences of the wealthier classes.

Pine-wood or deal is the timber mostly used in house-building, and is procured from the forests at no great distance, where charcoal is also manufactured in large quantities. The finer woods for furniture are imported viâ Tien-tsin from south China and the Straits.

The land is laid out in open fields, marked occasionally with boundary ditches surrounding particular plots of ground; and as the alluvial soil is very rich and productive, it is seldom allowed to lie fallow long. The chief produce of the country is the *Kaouleang*, or Barbadoes millet (*Sorghum*), which, besides being largely used in the distilleries for making spirits, gives food to man and beast. Its seed-time is March, when the rigours of the winter have scarce abated. The ground is then covered with ashes as manure, which is ploughed into the soil preparatory to sowing; and the harvest is looked for in September. The stalks, some eight or ten feet high, are then cut down, leaving from two to three feet of stem still standing, which dry and harden into stiff pegs all over the face of the country. Cotton and small beans are frequently sown in April between the rows of millet, and not coming to maturity till later in the year, yield a crop after the millet has been cleared away.

Three other descriptions of millet are also grown for food.

Yellow maize is sown in March, white maize in May, both yielding a harvest in September.

Jute of large growth is sown in March and gathered in October; its berries are ground into flour, and its bark twisted into cordage.

Coxcomb has the same periods as the last; its seeds are used for cakes.

Tobacco is planted in March, and attaining a moderate height by June, the large leaves as they show symptoms of decay are plucked, rolled up, and strung on strings to dry. When thoroughly dry, they are considered ready for use.

The castor-oil (*Ricinus officinalis*) is planted in March; the berries begin to ripen in July. An oil is extracted from them, and used for lubricating purposes; its medicinal properties being unknown.

Wheat, a bearded variety, is cultivated in spring in fields of low level, and irrigated in the manner of rice. Another variety is sown in October, undergoes the frostbites of the severe winter, and yields a crop in May or June. But very little wheat is comparatively grown, large quantities being imported from Shan-tung and elsewhere.

Sweet potatoes (*Batatas edulis*), brinjalls, groundnuts, and buckwheat, are other crops which engage the attention of the husbandman, as well as other plants used for oil, or forming into besoms, whose Chinese names I am alone acquainted with.

Human manure is used for the cultivation of vegetables, but in the field-crops ashes supersede it. Much care is bestowed on the cultivation of vegetables, and many kinds, together with apples, pears, and grapes, are preserved the winter through in covered pits, the air in fine weather being admitted through loopholes, which are carefully closed in very cold or damp weather.

The people are comparatively poorer and dress more shabbily than those in the south. The villages and towns are less densely populated, and the inhabitants, notwithstanding their antipathy to water, seem to enjoy fair health from the salubrity of the climate. The diseases most prevalent are fevers and bowel complaints, which our military doctors asserted to be of an obstinate and persistent character in regard to the British troops. Occasional cases of cholera and small-pox occur.

Education is much neglected; and I think I may safely affirm that scarce one man in twenty, of the country people at least, is capable of writing more than his own name and the name of his village.

CHAPTER XIV.

Till now myself, and such
As slept within the shadow of your power,
Have wandered with our traversed arms, and breathed
Our sufferance vainly. Now the time is flush
When crouching marrow, in the bearer strong,
Cries of itself—" No more ! "

Timon of Athens.

Declaration of Peace.—Marauding Parties.—Death of Dr. Thompson—Proclamations.—Canton Coolies.—The downward March of the Second Division.—H. M.'s Legation.—Disordered State of the Country.—The Cold Season.—Departure of the remaining Force. — Embarkation of the Troops. — Increase of Cold. — Résumé.—Overweening Confidence of the Chinese.—Rapid Communication of News.—Our future Policy towards China. The present Condition of the Country.—Conclusion.

On the 1st November, the French started on their march to Tien-tsin, leaving their ambassador, Baron Gros, and his guard, still at Pekin; and the British army removed the same day from the village before the Tih-shing gate to the An-ting Mount, where the French had before been quartered. Peace had now been declared, and, consequently, no more foraging-parties were allowed. But a habit that the followers of an army have acquired by permission, requires time and severe admonitions before it can be thoroughly uprooted. Extreme vigilance was demanded on the part of the provost-marshal; and it must be said in praise of that gallant officer, that both he and his sergeants were constantly about the country on the look-out for plundering-parties. The natives themselves were also on the alert, roving about the fields in gangs. Six unfortunate riflemen disappeared about this time in a somewhat mysterious manner. They left the camp unarmed one morning with the intention of raking up the neighbourhood of the Summer Palace for valuables, and were in all probability murdered; but as they had ostensibly set out for plunder, notwithstanding the strict injunctions that had been issued against looting, no inquiries were made after them. The mandarins had posted up proclamations, ordering all the villagers who had spoiled property from the imperial pleasure-grounds to restore what they had taken on pain of death. This many failed to do; and on strict search being instituted throughout the villages, and imperial effects being found in private houses, the possessors were forthwith dragged out and decapitated, and their carcases left rotting in the highways. These headless trunks we frequently saw in our rides being torn and dragged by crows and dogs. The owners of the houses in the An-ting suburb now began to return, and some of them clamoured before Prince Kung to have their premises restored to them. So, on representation to the General, a few of the houses had to be given up, and the men quartered in them to be lodged under canvas.

On the 4th November, poor Dr. Thompson, the P. M. O. of the Second Division, breathed his last, lamented by all who knew him. He had for some weeks past complained of an affection of the liver. His remains were interred with due honour in the Russian Cemetery, side by side with the four unfortunate sufferers whose untimely end was brought about by the cruelty of the Chinese.

The imperial edict confirming all that Prince Kung had signed was duly received, and large proclamations on the 6th were posted up all over the city, making the terms of peace patent to all the Celestials. This last performance of the great act was considered so important that the army interpreters were deputed to accompany the mandarins commissioned for the purpose of having the same placarded in all conspicuous parts of the great city; and parcels of proclamations were made up ready for posting at important places on the downward march. Much cordiality now existed between Lord Elgin and Prince Kung, and visits were frequently exchanged. The Prince threw off the nervous restraint and show of bad humour that marked his first interview. He sat with pleasure for his photograph before the camera of Signor Beato, and we are thus enabled to give a view of his far from comely visage to our readers. He is said to bear a strong resemblance to the Emperor ; and, indeed, a carefully executed portrait of his Celestial Majesty, which was secured by an officer from the Summer Palace, called so forcibly to our mind the physiognomy of the Prince that we declared it could be no other, until, from the Chinese inscription on the top, it was deciphered to represent the Emperor.

The Chinese authorities bore a lasting grudge towards the Cantonese coolies in pay of the army, and took every opportunity of picking off any of them that straggled. They had a particular objection to these men entering the city, and even went so far as to make it a condition, when the gate was surrendered, that admission within its walls should be denied them. The promise was given, but it was simply impossible to perform, as the sentries could seldom distinguish between the coolies and the natives of the place. But many of the Cantonese, who did stray far into the city, contrary to the prohibition, had reason to repent of the act. On one occasion we had the opportunity of preserving one of these mercenary children of the south from the rigours of the law. As we were riding through the streets, in the suite of the General, we heard loud plaintive cries of " Ingke-le-coolie," and, looking round, beheld one dirty, emaciated Chinese being led in chains by another. The General drew up to see what was the matter, and found that the individual whose shouts had attracted our notice was a Cantonese coolie, who had been imprisoned for some ten days by the Chinese authorities, and was now being led by an officer, with a despatch addressed to the Board of Punishments bearing his death-warrant. The General ordered both parties to be conveyed to the camp, and, as the coolie turned out to be in French employ, the case was handed over to Baron Gros.

The Second Division, under General Napier, left on the 7th, on the downward march, and the rest of the army was to have followed on the morrow, but Mr. Bruce's arrival deferred their departure till the 9th. Lord Elgin, as a closing measure, thought it necessary to introduce H. M.'s Minister to Prince Kung before his own departure. There had been as yet no time to provide a suitable residence for the Legation at Pekin, and, as it would have been un-dignified for H.M.'s representative to make shift in any quarters the Chinese should choose to apportion to him, it was determined, after an introduction and a short exchange of courtesies, that the plenipotentiary should retire and pass the winter at Tien-tsin, with the intention of returning in the ensuing spring and taking up his permanent abode in the capital. It was, however, necessary that some one should remain after the removal of the army to superintend the preparation of a suitable establishment for the Legation, and also to act as a pledge for the good faith of the Chinese, and for their future behaviour towards the residents at Pekin. Mr. Adkins was chosen for this purpose, and left unattended, except by a few Chinese domestics, to the tender mercies of the Pekinese.

The country was in a sad state of disorder, and the neighbourhood of our suburb infested with gangs of ragamuffins, who brought fruit and other articles for sale, but whose real purpose was to catch up whatever valuables chanced to fall in their way.

The weather now grew colder and colder, the thermometer ranging at 29° in the mornings, with continued hard frost the whole day through, and we began to realize the misery of a life at such a temperature in the dirty paper-windowed hovels we were compelled to live in. We had exhausted the novelties of the city, and seen all the sights that its dirty, uneven, and poorly populated streets afforded, and began to feel the dulness of our condition. It was, therefore, with no small delight that we hailed the advent of the morning of the 9th. At that date the troops now remaining—comprising the Rifles, 15th Punjaubees, Probyn's and Fane's Horse, and Barry's Battery—commenced their march to Tien-tsin. The baggage was ordered to collect at the Temple of the Earth outside the city at 8 A.M., and thence make a fair start; by this means the baggagers were enabled to get well away before the column marched a couple of hours later. Lord Elgin and party, accompanied by the 99th Regiment, 75th Seikh Horse, 25th Punjaubees, and two Armstrongs of Barry's Battery, issued out at the Tungche gate of the city, and marched along the stone causeway direct to Tungchow, whence his Lordship proceeded by water to Tien-tsin. The French, at the same time, took their leave of the city, and the only representative of the Allies remaining was Mr. Adkins, whose solitude was by no means enviable, though he had the members of the Russian Mission to sympathize with him.

From the depôt we picked up the detachment of Rifles quartered there, and thence proceeding, crossed the Eight Le bridge, and encamped on the other side for the night. However chilling and uncomfortable we found living in the native houses, a night passed under canvas in such cold weather was infinitely more disagreeable. Next morning our marching column was increased by Lord Elgin's guard and the marines from Tung-chow, and as we passed Chang-chia-wan we were joined by the party of Fane's Horse stationed there. We spent the night at Matow, whence the Commander-in-Chief hastened on to Tien-tsin by boat. The next day's march brought us to Ho-see-woo, where the 31st Regiment was still in possession. The 15th Punjaubees, Fane's Horse, and Barry's Battery had to remain at this place a few days, until the larger part of the troops that thronged Tien-tsin should be shipped off. The rest of the retiring column marched on, and in two and a half more days reached Tien-tsin in safety, where the Quartermaster-General's department was hard at work shipping off the Army; and in less than a fortnight the whole of the troops destined for embarkation were shipped off without accident. The Rifles, 67th Regiment, and Fane's Horse were left to garrison Tien-tsin and the Takoo forts, under Brigadier Staveley. Of the interpreters borrowed from the Consular Service, Mr. Mongan alone was retained as interpreter to the garrison, and Mr. Davenport to the naval squadron, which had received orders to winter at the Miaou-taou islands, off Chefoo. The rest of us were taken off the list of Military and Naval Service, and we were directed to report ourselves to her Majesty's Minister.

The cold increased daily in intensity, and the thermometer for several days stood at 15°. Ice soon formed over the river, and the last gunboat that attempted to force its way failed in the attempt, and, narrowly escaping being jammed in, had to steam down again. I was, therefore, not sorry when I received my orders to leave for my post in the south. The Head-quarters' Staff had completed their duties at Tien-tsin and had already started on the march to Takoo. The General was about to leave on the 29th; and tendering my services to him as interpreter, I was glad to gain permission to follow in his suite.

We spent the first night at Kih-koo, and the forenoon of the second day saw us at Ta-koo, where, on presenting a letter from Mr. Bruce to the Admiral, I was ordered a passage to Hong Kong in the steamer *Lightning*. It was a bitterly cold morning, clothed in a moist fog, when we left Kih-koo to follow the orchard-lined road to the forts; the face of nature displayed a lovely phenomenon, which has been aptly and brilliantly described in the following lines of Ambrose Phillips:—

> " Soon as the silent shades of night withdrew,
> The ruddy morn disclosed at once to view
> The face of nature in a rich disguise,
> And brightened every object to my eyes:
> For every shrub and every blade of grass,
> And every pointed thorn, seemed wrought in glass;
> In pearls and rubies rich the hawthorns show,
> While through the ice the crimson berries glow.

The thick sprung reeds, which watery marshes yield,
Seemed polished lances in a hostile field.
The spreading oak, the beech, and towering pine,
Glazed over, in the freezing ether shine :
The frighted birds the rattling branches shun,
Which wave and glitter in the distant sun."

The campaign is now over. Its short-lived career
has indeed been a glorious one, though mournful on
account of the one black deed that stains its fair
face. The object sought by the costly undertaking
has been signally won. We had too long been blind
to our own interests in allowing ourselves to be
trampled under foot and branded as barbarians by
an effete government, who well appreciated the value
of our trade, but whose jealous and niggardly policy,—
ever fearing that the ingress of western civilisation
would lead to an encroachment on that territory,
which had been usurped by the present incumbents
through treachery and low cunning,—long prescribed
to western nations, within very narrow limits, the
right of trade with a people eminently notorious for
their love of gain and commercial enterprise. And
where such trade was allowed, no opportunity was
lost of humbling its promoters before the eyes of the
Chinese populace. Thanks to the expedition, a new
era has now opened in foreign relations with China.
The unapproachable and impregnable city of the

25

native idea has entirely succumbed, without a blow, before the approach of the Allies, and such terms and privileges have been wrung from the wily Emperor that any nation may well be proud of.

So sure were the Southern Chinese that we would be defeated in the north, that the Cotton Guild at Canton offered to bet 50,000 dollars against the capture of the forts, and this money they agreed to lodge in the Oriental Bank at Hong Kong on the risk; but, strange enough, the British merchants lacked confidence in our authorities to take up the wager. A few American merchants only came forward to back the side of the Allies, but then refused to stake more than 10,000 dollars, which the Guild declined, saying that they would only bet at the figure they had first stated. The Cantonese took a great interest in the northern struggle, both politically and with a mercantile view, and one large firm in particular was always well advised on the progress of the Allied arms. The chief of this firm had a brother at a town near Tien-tsin, who communicated to him the events that transpired in his neighbourhood. The news was always in possession of this firm within twelve days of any occurrence in the north, the letters containing it being carried by relays of couriers over some 1,300 miles' extent of country in this wondrously short space of time. Thus many of the Chinese were advised of the various actions long before intelligence reached Hong Kong by steam. Mr. Pedder, interpreter at the British Consulate, Canton, ingratiated himself into favour with this particular firm, and was regularly supplied by them with the earliest intelligence, which he was thus enabled to forward to the Foreign Office and to Mr. Bruce, through the Consul at Canton, long before it could reach them from any other source. Many people at first smiled at the possibility of the news arriving at Canton with this almost electric speed, but in nearly every instance the facts conveyed by this means were confirmed by the subsequent arrival of the steamer from Shanghai. The gathering of the ships off Pehtang was first reported, the correspondent giving their number, and expressing surprise at the presence of some Americans among them.

Then came the landing of the troops and the concentrating of the Allied forces at Pehtang; their first skirmish while on reconnaissance, which was, of course, magnified into a defeat. The engagements at Sinho, Tangkoo, and, finally, the capture of the north fort; the explosion in which latter was mentioned, the writer adding that he was not sure whether it was that of a magazine or a mine fired purposely by the besieged. He spoke of the loss being heavy on both sides, but considerably more so on that of the Chinese. Several Cantonese coolies in the engagement were killed. The other forts appeared to have surrendered without a struggle, why, he could not say. He then talked of the advance of the Allies on Tien-tsin, which city it was not the intention of the Chinese to defend.; as if the Allies could take the forts, their force, which would be chiefly naval, would find little difficulty in capturing Tien-tsin, whither access by water was easy. San-kolinsin had withdrawn to take up a position nearer Pekin, where ample time was being allowed him to establish himself, as the mandarins, by making excuses, were detaining the Allies from advancing. That the Allies would eventually be induced to march towards Pekin in small numbers, under the impression that peace was made; and as then they would not be able to carry their big guns or supplies with them, for want of further water communication, they would fall an easy prey to the Tartar host.

All these and later particulars of the campaign were supplied to the Canton firm by their constituents in the north with wonderful exactitude; and had we at the time known what reliance might have been placed on their reports, much trouble and loss of time might have been saved to the Allies. As it is, they afford one testimony more to the deeply-laid treachery of the Chinese authorities towards the

Allies, and show that no secret even was made of the matter to their own people.   The Chinese little doubted the success of their schemes, as they imagined the barbarians they had to deal with were merely strong on the seas, but in the field infinitely inferior to their own brave Tartar troops.

It remains with our civil authorities now mildly to insist on the performance of what our arms have so ably won.   To the few ports we before had permission to resort to, we now have an accession of several others, which in the course of a few years are likely to prove vastly greater emporiums of trade ; and while additional wealth is wafted thence to the shores of Great Britain, we trust, in return, that Christianity, with her civilising influences may gradually flow in, and, taking firm hold on China's millions, lead them to bless the scourge of war that for a few short months ravaged their lands, and, in spite of their preconceived hostility to foreign opinions, insisted on right of access being granted to foreign nations.   The opening of Neuchwang lays patent to our mart free competition with encroaching Russia.   Tang-chow and Tien-tsin put us in possession of the high roads of commerce to the capital. Swatow throws open a fine river bordering the provinces of Canton and Fuhkeen ; and promising fields are offered to us in the large and little-

known islands of Hainan and Formosa. The much-
desired admission to the heart of China is also now
secured by the ports opened to our commerce on its
shores, whence access is procured to the vast lands
where the best teas and silks are manufactured. The
great obstacle there, however, is the devastating inroads of the rebels, who, to the disappointment of all
interested in their movements, have lately well proved
that plunder is their object and luxury their god.
But they have very properly been taught by the late
repulse they received at Shanghai, from the hands
of the Allies, that their existence depends on the
good conduct they show towards the promotion of
trade. Rebellion, such as this, which amounts to
little else than brigandism, is an event always to be
dreaded in whatever country; but it is not for me to
point out the course that should be pursued, whether
of strict neutrality or of interference on the im-
perialist side. It is true that the energy of China
is at present much shaken; but, as in former years
she has ridden through simllar storms, if her history speak true, it is not improbable she may yet
regain strength, and in one mighty effort quench
this glowing spark that has for years been slowly
consuming her vitals. The field is now open for
us, and it is our course to " go in and win." By
upholding firmly the character and honour of our

country, and at once resenting any show of enmity, we may long continue to maintain friendly relations on a satisfactory footing, and gradually develop the vast resources of this country. The footing we have now gained is mainly due to the success of the late expedition, which, thanks to the exertions of all the departments concerned, was enabled to supply, notwithstanding the vast distance travelled, the most complete army, perfect in all its branches, that has ever yet taken the field; and though every Englishman naturally grumbles at the expense incurred, yet he cannot help feeling gratification at its signal success, more especially when he surveys the large tract of country it has thrown open to our enterprise, and from which great advantages are likely to be derived.

THE END.

LONDON :
PRINTED BY SMITH, ELDER AND CO.,
LITTLE GREEN ARBOUR COURT, OLD BAILEY, E.C.

65, *Cornhill, London,*
October, 1861.

NEW AND STANDARD WORKS

PUBLISHED BY

SMITH, ELDER AND CO.

NEW WORKS FORTHCOMING.

History of the Four Conquests of England:
Roman, Anglo-Saxon, Danish, and Norman.
By James Augustus St. John, Esq.
Two Vols. 8vo.

The Correspondence of Leigh Hunt.
Edited by his Eldest Son.
Two Vols. Post 8vo, with Portrait.

Narrative of the North China Campaign of 1860.
By Robert Swinhoe,
Staff Interpreter to Sir Hope Grant. 8vo, with Illustrations. [*Now ready.*

Selections from the Writings of J. Ruskin, M.A.
One Volume. Post 8vo, with a Portrait.

The Lady's Guide
To the Ordering of Her Household, and the Economy of the
Dinner Table.
By a Lady. Post 8vo.

The Wonderful Adventures of Tuflongbo and
his Elfin Companions in their Journey through the
Enchanted Forest, with Little Content.
By Holme Lee.
Author of " Legends from Fairy Land," &c.
With Illustrations. Small post 8vo.

Household Education.
By Harriet Martineau. A New Edition. Post 8vo.

—◇—

The Early Italian Poets.
Translated by **D. G. Rossetti.**
Part I.—Poets chiefly before Dante.   Part II.—Dante and his Circle.
Post 8vo.

—◇—

Astronomical Observations
Made at the Sidney Observatory in the year 1859.
By W. Scott, M.A.   8vo.   6s.

—◇—

Experiences of an English Sister of Charity.
Small Post 8vo.

—◇—

The Four Georges:
Sketches of Manners, Morals, Court and Town Life.
By W. M. Thackeray.
Crown 8vo.

—◇—

Lovel the Widower.
By W. M. Thackeray.
Post 8vo.

—◇—

CHEAP EDITIONS.

Framley Parsonage.
By Anthony Trollope.
One Vol.   Crown 8vo.

—◇—

Lavinia.
By the Author of "Doctor Antonio," "Lorenzo Benoni," &c.
Small Post 8vo.

—◇—

NEW NOVELS.

The Cotton Lord.
Two Vols.

—◇—

Warp and Woof.
By Holme Lee.
Author of "Sylvan Holt's Daughter," "Against Wind and Tide," &c.
Three Vols.

—◇—

Said and Done.
In One Vol.

HISTORY AND BIOGRAPHY.

History of the Venetian Republic:

Her Rise, her Greatness, and her Civilization.
By W. Carew Hazlitt.
Complete in 4 vols. 8vo, with Illustrations, price 2*l.* 16*s.*, cloth.

** Volumes III. and IV. may be had separately.

The Life and Letters of Captain John Brown,

Who was Executed at Charlestown, Virginia, December 2, 1859, for an armed Attack upon American Slavery : with Notices of some of his Confederates.
Edited by Richard D. Webb.
With Photographic Portrait. Small post 8vo. Price 4*s.* 6*d.* cloth.

Life of Schleiermacher,

As unfolded in his Autobiography and Letters.
Translated by Frederica Rowan.
Two vols. post 8vo, with Portrait. Price One Guinea, cloth.

The Life of Charlotte Brontë (Currer Bell).

By Mrs. Gaskell.
Fourth Edition, revised, one vol., with a Portrait of Miss Brontë and a View of Haworth Parsonage. Price 7*s.* 6*d.* ; morocco elegant, 14*s.*

Life of Edmond Malone,

With Selections from his MS. Anecdotes.
By Sir James Prior,
Author of the "Life of Edmund Burke," "Life of Oliver Goldsmith." Demy 8vo, with Portrait, price 14*s.* cloth.

The Autobiography of Leigh Hunt.

One vol., post 8vo, with Portrait. Price 7*s.* 6*d.* cloth.

Life of Lord Metcalfe.

By John William Kaye.
New Edition, in Two Vols., post 8vo, with Portrait. Price 12*s.* cloth.

Life of Sir John Malcolm, G.C.B.

By John William Kaye.
Two Vols. 8vo, with Portrait. Price 36*s.* cloth.

The Autobiography of Lutfullah.

A Mohamedan Gentleman ; with an Account of his Visit to England.
Edited by E. B. Eastwick, Esq.
Third Edition, small post 8vo. Price 5*s.* cloth.

The Life of Mahomet.

With Introductory Chapters on the Original Sources for the Biography of Mahomet, and on the Pre-Islamite History of Arabia.
By W. Muir, Esq., Bengal C.S.
Complete in Four Vols. Demy 8vo. Price 2*l.* 2*s.* cloth.

** Vols. III. and IV. may be had separately, price 21*s.*

Robert Owen and his Social Philosophy.

By William Lucas Sargant,
Author of "Social Innovators and their Schemes."
1 vol., post 8vo. 10*s.* 6*d.* cloth.

Shelley Memorials.

Edited by Lady Shelley.
Second Edition. In one vol., post 8vo. Price 7*s.* 6*d.* cloth.

VOYAGES AND TRAVELS.

Scripture Lands

in connection with their History:

With an Appendix · and Extracts from a Journal kept during an Eastern Tour in 1856-7.

By the Rev. G. S. Drew,

Author of "Scripture Studies," &c.

Post 8vo, with a Map, 10s. 6d. cloth.

A Visit to the Philippine Isles in 1858–59.

By Sir John Bowring,

Governor of Hong Kong, and H.M.'s Plenipotentiary in China.

Demy 8vo, with numerous Illustrations, price 18s. cloth.

Heathen and Holy Lands;

Or, Sunny Days on the Salween, Nile, and Jordan.

By Captain J. P. Briggs, Bengal Army.

Post 8vo, price 12s. cloth.

Narrative of the Mission to Ava.

By Captain Henry Yule, Bengal Engineers.

Imperial 8vo, with Twenty-four Plates (Twelve coloured), Fifty Woodcuts, and Four Maps. Elegantly bound in cloth, with gilt edges, price 2l. 12s. 6d.

Egypt in its Biblical Relations.

By the Rev. J. Foulkes Jones.

Post 8vo, price 7s. 6d. cloth.

Japan, the Amoor, and the Pacific.

A Voyage of Circumnavigation in the Imperial Russian Corvette "Rynda," in 1858-59-60.

By Henry Arthur Tilley.

8vo, with illustrations, 16s. cloth.

Through Norway with a Knapsack.

By W. M. Williams.

With Six Coloured Views. Third Edition, post 8vo, price 12s. cloth.

Turkish Life and Character.

By Walter Thornbury.

Author of "Life in Spain," &c. &c.

Two Vols., with Eight Tinted Illustrations, price 21s. cloth.

Voyage to Japan,

Kamtschatka, Siberia, Tartary, and the Coast of China, in H.M.S. *Barracouta.*

By J. M. Tronson, R.N.

8vo, with Charts and Views. 18s. cloth.

To Cuba and Back.

By R. H. Dana,

Author of "Two Years before the Mast," &c.

Post 8vo, price 7s. cloth.

Life and Liberty in America.

By Dr. C. Mackay.

Second Edition, 2 vols., post 8vo, with Ten Tinted Illustrations, price 21s.

WORKS OF MR. RUSKIN.

—◆—

Modern Painters.

Now complete in five vols., Imperial 8vo, with 84 Engravings on Steel, and 216 on Wood, chiefly from Drawings by the Author. With Index to the whole Work.   Price 8*l.* 6*s.* 6*d.*, in cloth.

EACH VOLUME MAY BE HAD SEPARATELY.

Vol. I.,   6th Edition.   OF GENERAL PRINCIPLES AND OF TRUTH. Price 18*s.* cloth.

Vol. II., 4th Edition.   OF THE IMAGINATIVE AND THEORETIC FACULTIES.   Price 10*s.* 6*d.* cloth.

Vol. III. OF MANY THINGS. With Eighteen Illustrations drawn by the Author, and engraved on Steel.   Price 38*s.* cloth.

Vol. IV. ON MOUNTAIN BEAUTY.   With Thirty-five Illustrations engraved on Steel, and 116 Woodcuts, drawn by the Author. Price 2*l.* 10*s.* cloth.

Vol. V.   OF LEAF BEAUTY; OF CLOUD BEAUTY; OF IDEAS OF RELATION. With Thirty-six Engravings on Steel, and 100 on Wood.   Price 2*l.* 10*s.*   With Index to the five volumes.

—◆—

The Stones of Venice.

Complete in Three Volumes, Imperial 8vo, with Fifty-three Plates and numerous Woodcuts, drawn by the Author.   Price 5*l.* 15*s.* 6*d.* cloth.

EACH VOLUME MAY BE HAD SEPARATELY.

Vol. I. The FOUNDATIONS, with 21 Plates. Price 2*l.* 2*s.*   2nd Edition.

Vol. II. THE SEA STORIES, with 20 Plates. Price 2*l.* 2*s.*

Vol. III. THE FALL, with 12 Plates.   Price 1*l.* 11*s.* 6*d.*

—◆—

The Seven Lamps of Architecture.

Second Edition, with Fourteen Plates drawn by the Author.   Imp. 8vo. Price 1*l.* 1*s.* cloth.

—◆—

Lectures on Architecture and Painting.

With Fourteen Cuts, drawn by the Author.   Second Edition, crown 8vo. Price 8*s.* 6*d.* cloth.

The Two Paths:

Being Lectures on Art, and its relation to Manufactures and Decoration.

One vol., crown 8vo, with Two Steel Engravings.   Price 7*s.* 6*d.* cloth.

—◆—

The Elements of Drawing.

Sixth Thousand, crown 8vo, with Illustrations drawn by the Author.   Price 7*s.* 6*d.* cloth.

—◆—

The Elements of Perspective.

With 80 Diagrams, crown 8vo.   Price 3*s.* 6*d.* cloth.

—◆—

The Political Economy of Art.

Price 2*s.* 6*d.* cloth.

RELIGIOUS.

Sermons:

By the late Rev. Fred. W. Robertson, Incumbent of Trinity Chapel, Brighton.

FIRST SERIES.—Eighth Edition, post 8vo. Price 9s. cloth.
SECOND SERIES. — Seventh Edition. Price 9s. cloth.
THIRD SERIES.—Sixth Edition, post 8vo, with Portrait. Price 9s. cloth.

Expositions of St. Paul's Epistles to the Corinthians.

By the late Rev. Fred. W. Robertson.

Second Edition. One thick Volume, post 8vo. Price 10s. 6d. cloth.

Lectures and Addresses.

By the late Rev. Fred. W. Robertson.

Post 8vo. Price 7s. 6d. cloth.

Sermons:

Preached at Lincoln's Inn Chapel.

By the Rev. F. D. Maurice, M.A.

FIRST SERIES, 2 vols., post 8vo, price 21s. cloth.
SECOND SERIES, 2 vols., post 8vo, price 21s. cloth.
THIRD SERIES, 2 vols., post 8vo, price 21s. cloth.

The Province of Reason;

A Reply to Mr. Mansell's Bampton Lecture.

By John Young, LL.D., Edin.,

Author of "The Mystery; or, Evil and God." Post 8vo. Price 6s. cloth.

"Is it not Written?"

Being the Testimony of Scripture against the Errors of Romanism.

By the Rev. Edward S. Pryce.

Post 8vo. Price 6s. cloth.

Historic Notes

On the Old and New Testament.

By Samuel Sharpe.

3rd and Revised Edition. 8vo. 7s. cl.

Tauler's Life and Sermons.

Translated by Miss Susanna Winkworth.

With Preface by Rev. C. KINGSLEY. Small 4to, printed on Tinted Paper, and bound in Antique Style, with red edges, suitable for a Present. Price 7s. 6d.

Quakerism, Past and Present:

Being an Inquiry into the Causes of its Decline.

By John S. Rowntree.

Post 8vo. Price 5s. cloth.

** This Essay gained the First Prize of One Hundred Guineas offered for the best Essay on the subject.

Women of Christianity

Exemplary for Piety and Charity.

By Julia Kavanagh.

Post 8vo, with Portraits. Price 5s. in embossed cloth.

MISCELLANEOUS.

Ragged London.
By John Hollingshead.
Post 8vo, 7s. 6d. cloth.

Philo-Socrates.
Parts I. & II. " Among the Boys."
By William Ellis.   Price 1s. each.

Social Innovators and their Schemes.
By William Lucas Sargant.
Post 8vo.   Price 10s. 6d. cloth.

Ethica ;
Or, Characteristics of Men, Manners, and Books.
By Arthur Lloyd Windsor.
Demy 8vo.   Price 12s. cloth.

Slavery Doomed ;
Or, the Contest between Free and Slave Labour in the United States.
By Frederick Milns Edge.
Post 8vo.   Price 6s. cloth.

The Conduct of Life.
By Ralph Waldo Emerson,
Author of " Essays," " Representative Men," &c.   Post 8vo, price 6s. cloth.

*** Also a Cheap Edition, 1s. cloth.

Bermuda :
Its History, Geology, Climate, Products, Agriculture, &c. &c.
By Theodore L. Godet, M.D.
Post 8vo, price 9s. cloth.

Tea Planting in the Himalaya.
By A. T. McGowan.
8vo, with Frontispiece, price 5s. cloth.

Man and his Dwelling Place.
An Essay towards the Interpretation of Nature.
Second Edition.   With a Preface.
Crown 8vo, 6s. cloth.

Annals of British Legislation :
A Classified Summary of Parliamentary Papers.
Edited by Leone Levi.
The yearly issue consists of 1,000 pages, super-royal 8vo, and the Subscription is Two Guineas, payable in advance. The Forty-ninth Part is just issued, completing the Fourth Year's Issue. Vols. I. to VIII. may now be had. Price 8l. 8s. cloth.

A Handbook of Average.
With a Chapter on Arbitration.
By Manley Hopkins.
Second Edition, Revised and brought down to the present time.
8vo.   Price 15s. cloth ; 17s. 6d. halfbound law calf.

Manual of the Mercantile Law
Of Great Britain and Ireland.
By Leone Levi, Esq.
8vo.   Price 12s. cloth.

Gunnery in 1858 :
A Treatise on Rifles, Cannon, and Sporting Arms.
By William Greener,
Author of " The Gun."
Demy 8vo, with Illustrations.
Price 14s. cloth.

Sea Officer's Manual.
By Captain Alfred Parish.
Second Edition.   Small post 8vo.
Price 5s. cloth.

Victoria,
And the Australian Gold Mines in 1857.
By William Westgarth.
Post 8vo, with Maps.   10s. 6d. cloth.

New Zealand and its Colonization.
By William Swainson, Esq.
Demy 8vo.   Price 14s. cloth.

The Education of the Human Race.
Now first Translated from the German of Lessing.
Fcap. 8vo, antique cloth.   Price 4s.

Germany and the Tyrol.
By Sir John Forbes.
Post 8vo, with Map and View.
Price 10s. 6d. cloth.

Life in Spain.
By Walter Thornbury.
Two Vols. post 8vo, with Eight Tinted Illustrations, price 21s.

Life in Tuscany.
By Mabel Sharman Crawford.
With Two Views, post 8vo.
Price 10s. 6d. cloth.

Captivity of Russian Princesses in the Caucasus.
Translated from the Russian by H. S. Edwards.
With an authentic Portrait of Shamil, a Plan of his House, and a Map.
Post 8vo, price 10s. 6d. cloth.

On the Strength of Nations.
By Andrew Bisset, M.A.
Post 8vo.   Price 9s. cloth.

Results of Astronomical Observations
Made at the Cape of Good Hope.
By Sir John Herschel.
4to, with Plates.   Price 4l. 4s. cloth.

On the Treatment of the Insane.
By John Conolly, M.D.
Demy 8vo.   Price 14s. cloth.

Visit to Salt Lake.
Being a Journey across the Plains to the Mormon Settlements at Utah.
By William Chandless.
Post 8vo, with a Map.   2s. 6d. cloth.

The Red River Settlement.
By Alexander Ross.
One vol. post 8vo.   Price 5s. cloth.

Fur Hunters of the West.
By Alexander Ross.
Two vols. post 8vo, with Map and Plate.   Price 10s. 6d. cloth.

The Columbia River.
By Alexander Ross.
Post 8vo.   Price 2s. 6d. cloth.

Hints for Investing Money.
By Francis Playford.
Second Edition, post 8vo.   2s. 6d. cloth.

Men, Women, and Books.
By Leigh Hunt.
Two vols.   Price 10s. cloth.

True Law of Population.
By Thomas Doubleday.
Third Edition, 8vo.   Price 6*s.* cloth.

England and her Soldiers.
By Harriet Martineau.
With Three Plates of Illustrative Diagrams. 1 vol. crown 8vo, price 9*s.* cloth.

Grammar and Dictionary of the Malay Language.
By John Crawfurd, Esq.
Two vols. 8vo.   Price 36*s.* cloth.

Turkish Campaign in Asia.
By Charles Duncan, Esq.
Post 8vo.   Price 2*s.* 6*d.* cloth.

Poetics:
An Essay on Poetry.
By E. S. Dallas.
Post 8vo.   Price 2*s.* 6*d.* cloth.

Juvenile Delinquency.
The Prize Essays.
By M. Hill and C. F. Cornwallis.
Post 8vo.   Price 6*s.* cloth.

The Militiaman.
With Two Etchings, by JOHN LEECH.
Post 8vo.   Price 9*s.* cloth.

The Endowed Schools of Ireland.
By Harriet Martineau.
8vo.   Price 3*s.* 6*d.* cloth boards.

European Revolutions of 1848.
By E. S. Cayley, Esq.
Crown 8vo.   Price 6*s.* cloth.

Woman in France.
By Julia Kavanagh.
Two vols. post 8vo, with Portraits.
Price 12*s.* cloth.

Table Talk.   *By Leigh Hunt.*
Price 3*s.* 6*d.* cloth.

The Court of Henry VIII.:
Being a Selection of the Despatches of Sebastian Giustinian, Venetian Ambassador, 1515-1519.
Translated by Rawdon Brown.
Two vols. crown 8vo.   Price 21*s.* cloth.

Traits and Stories of Anglo-Indian Life.
By Captain Addison.
With Eight Illustrations. 2*s.* 6*d.* cloth.

Commercial Law of the World.
By Leone Levi.
Two vols. royal 4to.   Price 6*l.* cloth.

Indian Exchange Tables.
By J. H. Roberts.
8vo.   Second Edition, enlarged.
Price 10*s.* 6*d.* cloth.

The Turkish Interpreter:
A Grammar of the Turkish Language.
By Major Boyd.
8vo.   Price 12*s.*

Russo-Turkish Campaigns of 1828–9.
By Colonel Chesney,
R.A., D.C.L., F.R.S.
Third Edition.   Post 8vo, with Maps.
Price 12*s.* cloth.

Military Forces and Institutions of Great Britain.
By H. Byerly Thompson.
8vo.   Price 5*s.* cloth.

Wit and Humour.
By Leigh Hunt.
Price 5*s.* cloth.

Jar of Honey from Hybla.
By Leigh Hunt.
Price 5s. cloth.

Manual of Therapeutics.
By E. J. Waring, M.D.
Fcap 8vo. Price 12s. 6d. cloth.

Zoology of South Africa.
By Dr. Andrew Smith.
Royal 4to, cloth, with Coloured Plates.

MAMMALIA	£8
AVES	7
REPTILIA	5
PISCES	2
INVERTEBRATÆ	1

Memorandums in Ireland.
By Sir John Forbes.
Two vols. post 8vo. Price 1l. 1s. cloth.

Life of Sir Robert Peel.
By Thomas Doubleday.
Two vols. 8vo. Price 18s. cloth.

The Argentine Provinces.
By William McCann, Esq.
Two vols. post 8vo, with Illustrations.
Price 24s. cloth.

Education in Oxford:
Its Method, its Aids, and its Rewards.
By James E. Thorold Rogers, M.A.
Post 8vo, price 6s. cloth.

Shakspere and his Birthplace.
By John R. Wise.
With 22 Illustrations by W. J. Linton.
Crown 8vo. Printed on Toned Paper,
and handsomely bound in ornamental
cloth, gilt edges, price 7s. 6d.
*** Also a cheap edition, 2s. 6d. cloth.

National Songs and Legends of Roumania.
Translated by E. C. Grenville Murray, Esq.
With Music, crown 8vo. Price 2s. 6d.

The Novitiate;
Or, the Jesuit in Training.
By Andrew Steinmetz.
Third Edition, post 8vo. 2s. 6d. cloth.

Signs of the Times;
Or, The Dangers to Religious Liberty
in the Present Day.
By Chevalier Bunsen.
Translated by Miss S. WINKWORTH.
One vol. 8vo. Price 5s. cloth.

Principles of Agriculture;
Especially Tropical.
By B. Lovell Phillips, M.D.
Demy 8vo. Price 7s. 6d. cloth.

William Burke the Author of Junius.
By Jelinger C. Symons.
Square. Price 3s. 6d. cloth.

In-door Plants, and How to Grow Them.
By E. A. Maling.
Fcap 8vo, with Coloured Frontispiece.
Price 2s. 6d. cloth.

Household Medicine;
Describing Diseases, their Nature,
Causes, and Symptoms, with the
most approved Methods of Treatment, and the Properties and Uses
of Remedies.
By John Gardner, M.D.
8vo, with numerous Illustrations.
Price 10s. 6d. cloth.

The Book of Good Counsels:
Being an Abridged Translation
of the Sanscrit Classic, the
"Hitopadesa."
By Edwin Arnold, M.A., Oxon.
Author of "Education in India," &c.
With Illustrations by Harrison Weir.
Crown 8vo, 5s. cloth.

WORKS ON INDIA AND THE EAST.

Caste:
Considered under its Moral, Social, and Religious Aspects.
By Arthur J. Patterson, B.A., of Trinity College.
Post 8vo.   Price 4s. 6d. cloth.

The Sanitary Condition of Indian Jails.
By Joseph Ewart, M.D.,
Bengal Medical Service.
With Plans, 8vo.   Price 16s. cloth.

District Duties during the Revolt
In the North-West Provinces of India.
By H. Dundas Robertson,
Bengal Civil Service.
Post 8vo, with a Map.   Price 9s. cloth.

Campaigning Experiences
In Rajpootana and Central India during the Mutiny in 1857-8.
By Mrs. Henry Duberly.
Post 8vo, with Map.   Price 10s. 6d. cloth.

Narrative of the Mutinies in Oude.
By Captain G. Hutchinson,
Military Secretary, Oude.
Post 8vo.   Price 10s. cloth.

A Lady's Escape from Gwalior
During the Mutinies of 1857.
By Mrs. Coopland.
Post 8vo.   Price 10s. 6d.

The Crisis in the Punjab.
By Frederick H. Cooper, Esq., C.S., Umritsir.
Post 8vo, with Map.   Price 7s. 6d. cloth.

Views and Opinions of Gen. Jacob, C.B.
Edited by Captain Lewis Pelly.
Demy 8vo.   Price 12s. cloth.

The Theory of Caste,
By B. A. Irving.
8vo. 5s. cloth.

Papers of the late Lord Metcalfe.
By John William Kaye.
Demy 8vo.   Price 16s. cloth.

British Rule in India.
By Harriet Martineau.
Sixth Thousand.   Price 2s. 6d. cloth.

The English in India.
By Philip Anderson, A.M.
Second Edition, 8vo.   Price 14s. cloth.

Life in Ancient India.
By Mrs. Spier.
With Sixty Illustrations by G. SCHARF.
8vo.   Price 15s., elegantly bound in cloth, gilt edges.

Christianity in India.
By John William Kaye.
8vo.   Price 16s. cloth.

The Parsees:

Their History, Religion, Manners, and Customs.

By Dosabhoy Framjee.

Post 8vo. Price 10s. cloth.

Tiger Shooting in India.

By Lieutenant William Rice,
25th Bombay N.I.

Super-royal 8vo. With Twelve Plates in Chromo-lithography. 10s. 6d. cloth.

The Vital Statistics

Of the European and Native Armies in India.

By Joseph Ewart, M.D.

Demy 8vo. Price 9s. cloth.

The Bhilsa Topes;

Or, Buddhist Monuments of Central India.

By Major Cunningham.

One vol. 8vo, with Thirty-three Plates. Price 30s. cloth.

The Chinese and their Rebellions.

By Thomas Taylor Meadows.

One thick volume, 8vo, with Maps. Price 18s. cloth.

Hong Kong to Manilla.

By Henry T. Ellis, R.N.

Post 8vo, with Fourteen Illustrations. Price 12s. cloth.

THE

Botany of the Himalaya.

By Dr. Forbes Royle.

Two vols. roy. 4to, cloth, with Coloured Plates. Reduced to 5l. 5s.

Travels in Assam.

By Major John Butler.

One vol. 8vo, with Plates. 12s. cloth.

Infanticide in India.

By Dr. John Wilson.

Demy 8vo. Price 12s.

The Defence of Lucknow.

By Captain Thomas F. Wilson.

Sixth Thousand. With Plan. Small post 8vo. Price 2s. 6d.

Eight Months' Campaign

Against the Bengal Sepoys during the Mutiny, 1857.

By Colonel George Bourchier, C.B.

With Plans. Post 8vo. 7s. 6d. cloth.

The Commerce of India with Europe.

By B. A. Irving, Esq.

Post 8vo. Price 7s. 6d. cloth.

Moohummudan Law of Sale.

By N. B. E. Baillie, Esq.

8vo. Price 14s. cloth.

Moohummudan Law of Inheritance.

By N. B. E. Baillie, Esq.

8vo. Price 8s. cloth.

The Cauvery, Kistnah, and Godavery:

Being a Report on the Works constructed on those Rivers, for the Irrigation of Provinces in the Presidency of Madras.

By Col. R. Baird Smith, F.G.S.

Demy 8vo, with 19 Plans. 28s. cloth.

Land Tax of India.

According to the Moohummudan Law.

By N. B. E. Baillie, Esq.

8vo. Price 6s. cloth.

FICTION.

Miss Gwynne of Woodford.
Two Vols.

Hills and Plains.
Two Vols.

Who Breaks—Pays.
In Two Vols.
By the Author of " Cousin Stella."

Agnes Tremorne.
By I. Blagden. Two Vols.

Lavinia.
By the Author of " Doctor Antonio," "Lorenzo Benoni," &c.
Three Vols.

The Wortlebank Diary:
With Stories from Kathie Brande's Portfolio.
By Holme Lee. Three Vols.

Over the Cliffs.
By Mrs. Chanter,
Author of " Ferny Combes." 2 vols.

Scarsdale;
Or, Life on the Lancashire and Yorkshire Border Thirty Years ago. 3 vols.

Esmond.
By W. M. Thackeray.
A New Edition, being the third, in 1 vol. crown 8vo. Price 6s. cloth.

Herbert Chauncey:
A Man more Sinned against than Sinning.
By Sir Arthur Hallam Elton, Bart.
In 3 vols.

Transformation;
Or, the Romance of Monte Beni.
By Nathaniel Hawthorne. 3 vols.

The Firstborn.
By the Author of " My Lady."
Three volumes.

The Tragedy of Life.
By John H. Brenten. Two Vols.

Framley Parsonage.
By Anthony Trollope,
Author of "Barchester Towers," &c.
Illustrated by J. E. Millais, R.A.
Three Vols. Post 8vo, 21s. cloth.

Netley Hall;
or, the Wife's Sister.
Foolscap 8vo. 6s. cloth.

Confidences.
By the Author of " Rita."

Cousin Stella;
Or, Conflict.
By the Author of " Violet Bank."
Three volumes.

Phantastes:
A Faerie Romance for Men and Women.
By George Macdonald.
Post 8vo. Price 10s. 6d. cloth.

The Fool of Quality.
By Henry Brooke.
New and Revised Edition, with Biographical Preface by the Rev. CHAS. KINGSLEY, Rector of Eversley.
Two vols., post 8vo, with Portrait of the Author, price 21s.

CHEAP SERIES OF POPULAR WORKS.

Sylvan Holt's Daughter.
By Holme Lee.
Price 2s. 6d. cloth.

The Autobiography of Leigh Hunt.
Price 2s. 6d. cloth.

WORKS OF THE BRONTE SISTERS.
Price 2s. 6d. each vol.

By Currer Bell.
The Professor.
To which are added the POEMS of Currer, Ellis, and Acton Bell. Now first collected.
Jane Eyre.
Shirley.
Villette.

Wuthering Heights and Agnes Grey.
By Ellis and Acton Bell.
With Memoir by CURRER BELL.

The Tenant of Wildfell Hall.
By Acton Bell.

Life of Charlotte Brontë
(Currer Bell).
By Mrs. Gaskell.

Lectures on the English Humourists
Of the Eighteenth Century.
By W. M. Thackeray,
Author of "Vanity Fair," "Esmond," "The Virginians," &c.
Price 2s. 6d. cloth.

The Town.
By Leigh Hunt.
With Forty-five Engravings.
Price 2s. 6d. cloth.

Transformation.
By Nathaniel Hawthorne.
Price 2s. 6d. cloth.

Kathie Brande:
The Fireside History of a Quiet Life.
By Holme Lee. Price 2s. 6d. cloth.

Below the Surface.
By Sir A. H. Elton, Bart., M.P.
Price 2s. 6d. cloth.

British India.
By Harriet Martineau. 2s. 6d. cloth.

Italian Campaigns of General Bonaparte.
By George Hooper.
With a Map. Price 2s. 6d. cloth.

Deerbrook.
By Harriet Martineau. 2s. 6d. cloth.

Tales of the Colonies.
By Charles Rowcroft. 2s. 6d. cloth.

A Lost Love.
By Ashford Owen. 2s. cloth.

Romantic Tales
(Including "Avillion").
By the Author of "John Halifax, Gentleman." 2s. 6d. cloth.

Domestic Stories.
By the same Author. 2s. 6d. cloth.

After Dark.
By Wilkie Collins. 2s. 6d. cloth.

School for Fathers.
By Talbot Gwynne. 2s. cloth.

Paul Ferroll.
Fourth Edition. Price 2s. cloth.

JUVENILE AND EDUCATIONAL.

The Parents' Cabinet

Of Amusement and Instruction for Young Persons.

New Edition, revised, in Twelve Shilling Volumes, with numerous Illustrations.

*** The work is now complete in 4 vols. extra cloth, gilt edges, at 3s. 6d. each; or in 6 vols. extra cloth, gilt edges, at 2s. 6d. each.

Every volume is complete in itself, and sold separately.

By the Author of "Round the Fire," &c.

I.

Round the Fire:

Six Stories for Young Readers.
Square 16mo, with Four Illustrations. Price 2s. 6d. cloth.

II.

Unica:

A Story for a Sunday Afternoon.
With Four Illustrations. 2s. 6d. cloth.

III.

Old Gingerbread and the Schoolboys.

With Four Coloured Plates. 2s. 6d. cl.

IV.

Willie's Birthday:

Showing how a Little Boy did what he Liked, and how he Enjoyed it.
With Four Illustrations. 2s. cloth.

V.

Willie's Rest:

A Sunday Story.
With Four Illustrations. 2s. cloth.

VI.

Uncle Jack, the Fault Killer.

With Four Illustrations. 2s. 6d. cloth.

Legends from Fairy Land.

By Holme Lee,

Author of "Kathie Brande," "Sylvan Holt's Daughter," &c.
With Eight Illustrations. 3s. 6d. cloth.

The King of the Golden River;

Or, the Black Brothers.

By John Ruskin, M.A.

Third Edition, with 22 Illustrations by Richard Doyle. Price 2s. 6d.

Elementary Works on Social Economy.

By William Ellis.

Uniform in foolscap 8vo, half-bound.

I.—OUTLINES OF SOCIAL ECONOMY. 1s.6d.
II.—PROGRESSIVE LESSONS IN SOCIAL SCIENCE.
III.—INTRODUCTION TO THE SOCIAL SCIENCES. 2s.
IV.—OUTLINES OF THE UNDERSTANDING. 2s.
V.—WHAT AM I? WHERE AM I? WHAT OUGHT I TO DO? &c. 1s. sewed.

Religion in Common Life.

By William Ellis.

Post 8vo. Price 7s. 6d. cloth.

Books for the Blind.

Printed in raised Roman letters, at the Glasgow Asylum.

Rhymes for Little Ones.

With 16 Illustrations. 1s. 6d. cloth.

Stories from the Parlour Printing Press.

By the Authors of the "Parent's Cabinet."

Fcap 8vo. Price 2s. cloth.

Juvenile Miscellany.

Six Engravings. Price 2s. 6d. cloth.

RECENT POETRY.

Poems.
By the Rev. George E. Maunsell.
Fcap 8vo.   Price 5s. cloth.

Prometheus' Daughter:
A Poem.
By Col. James Abbott.
Crown 8vo.   Price 7s. 6d. cloth.

Christ's Company, and
other Poems.
By Richard Watson Dixon, M.A.
Fcap 8vo, price 5s. cloth.

Sybil, and other Poems.
By John Lyttelton.
Fcap 8vo, price 4s. cloth.

Memories of Merton.
By John Bruce Norton.
Fcap 8vo.   Price 5s. cloth.

Hannibal; a Drama.
Fcap 8vo.   Price 5s. cloth.

A Man's Heart: a Poem.
By Dr. Charles Mackay.
Post 8vo.   Price 5s. cloth.

Edwin and Ethelburga:
A Drama.
By Frederick W. Wyon.
Fcap 8vo.   Price 4s. cloth.

Shelley; and other Poems.
By John Alfred Langford.
Fcap 8vo.   Price 5s. cloth.

Magdalene: a Poem.
Fcap 8vo.   Price 1s.

Homely Ballads
For the Working Man's Fireside.
By Mary Sewell.
Ninth Thousand. Post 8vo. Cloth, 1s.

Stories in Verse for the
Street and Lane:
By Mrs. Sewell.
Post 8vo.   Cloth, price 1s.

THE CORNHILL MAGAZINE.

Edited by W. M. Thackeray.

Price One Shilling Monthly, with Illustrations.

MR. THACKERAY'S NEW STORY, "PHILIP,"

Commenced in January, and a series of

"BIRD'S-EYE VIEWS OF SOCIETY," BY RICHARD DOYLE,

Commenced in April.

VOLUMES I., II., and III., each containing 768 pages of Letterpress, with 12 Illustrations, and numerous Vignettes and Diagrams, are published, handsomely bound in Embossed Cloth.   Price 7s. 6d. each.

For the convenience of Subscribers, the Embossed CLOTH COVERS for each Volume are sold separately, price One Shilling.

READING COVERS for separate Numbers have also been prepared, price Sixpence in plain Cloth, or One Shilling and Sixpence in French Morocco.

London : Printed by SMITH, ELDER and Co., Little Green Arbour Court, Old Bailey, E.C.

CPSIA information can be obtained
at www.ICGtesting.com
Printed in the USA
LVHW091516260520
656574LV00002B/663